SECOND *edition*

Seasons
COME TO PASS

A POETRY ANTHOLOGY
for southern African students

edited by

Helen Moffett
Es'kia Mphahlele

OXFORD
UNIVERSITY PRESS
SOUTHERN AFRICA

OXFORD
UNIVERSITY PRESS

Southern Africa

Oxford University Press Southern Africa (Pty) Ltd

Vasco Boulevard, Goodwood, Cape Town, Republic of South Africa
PO Box 12119, N1 City, 7463, Cape Town, Republic of South Africa

Oxford University Press Southern Africa (Pty) Ltd is a subsidiary of
Oxford University Press, Great Clarendon Street, Oxford OX2 6DP.

The Press, a department of the University of Oxford, furthers the Univeristy's objective of
excellence in research, scholarship, and education in publishing worldwide in

Oxford New York

Auckland Cape Town Dar es Salaam Hong Kong Karachi
Kuala Lumpur Madrid Melbourne Mexico City Nairobi
New Delhi Shanghai Taipei Toronto

With offices in

Argentinia Austria Brazil Chile Czech Republic France Greece
Guatemala Hungary Italy Japan Poland Portugal Singapore South Korea
Switzerland Turkey Ukraine Vietnam

Oxford is a registered trademark of Oxford University Press
in the UK and in certain other countries

Published in South Africa
by Oxford University Press Southern Africa (Pty) Ltd, Cape Town

Seasons come to pass: a poetry anthology for southern African students
ISBN 978 0 19 578 757 3

This selection © Helen Moffett and Es'kia Mphahlele 2002
Addition material © Helen Moffett 2002

© Oxford University Press Southern Africa (Pty) Ltd 2006

First published 2004
Second edition 2002
Sixteenth impression 2012

Commissioning Editor: Arthur Attwell
Editor: Emily Bowles
Designer: Christopher Davis
Indexer: Helen Laurenson
Proofreader: Norton Tennille

Set in Adobe Caslon Regular and Universe 47 Condensed Light by Shuttle Publishing and Design
Printed and bound by ABC Press, Cape Town
117594

'... *indeed, it is a dry white season*
but seasons come to pass.'
– MONGANE WALLY SEROTE

'*poetry*
survives
against all odds'
– PABLO NERUDA, from *Odes to Opposites*

This anthology remains dedicated to all our
students, who have taught us more than
they can ever know.

In loving memory of Es'kia Mphahlele (1919 – 2008),
co-compiler of this anthology,
trailblazer, literary giant, teacher and mentor.
Thanks are inadequate for all you did,
all you were.
Tsamaea hantle, ntate.

Contents

viii

[More poems and Notes for Teachers can be found
on the Internet at www.oup.com/za/seasons.]

How to use this book

We suggest that you read the Introductory notes carefully, and discuss these either in tutorials or with friends who are doing the same course as you. These notes are divided into two parts; the first section is designed to give you a very brief overview of the historical backdrop against which the English language and its literature evolved. This is not intended as a list of facts you need to study and digest in order to come to grips with poetry; rather, it will hopefully give you a broad time-frame into which you can fit the poems you will study. It will give you a sense of how poems from various periods in history fit together, as well as sketching how scientific, religious, philosophical, geographical, political, and cultural shifts over time affected the development of literature. A very rough outline of how English assumed its present shape will also shed some light on both the infuriating inconsistencies and rewarding richness of the English language.

The second part of the introduction gives some very basic indications, with examples, of how to go about 'analysing' a poem. Treat these as guidelines, and refer back to them at regular intervals, as you become more practised and confident in your dealings with poetry. Bear in mind that in learning to read and analyse poetry, you are acquiring a skill, not learning a syllabus. Developing sensitivity to the language used around you, and evolving a set of personal critical skills, will stand you in good stead in your future studies, work and recreation, and can add to your self-confidence and communication skills. It is important not to gloss over this section, even if it seems strange at first. Giving written instructions on how to approach poetry is never quite satisfactory, as it needs to be practically demonstrated; it is rather like trying to teach someone to swim by writing them a letter! This is why you will need to go back to this section once you have become immersed in the poems themselves, and to discuss the suggestions given with other students and your teachers.

You will find that some of the poems are accompanied by suggestions for discussion, in the form of 'Talking points.' You and your teacher may decide to use these in the classroom; you also have the option of working through them in a study group, informally (by just chatting with a friend), or alone. Your teacher might also like to set some of these as written exercises. You could also draw up your own workshops, using some of ours as examples.

In our 'Talking points', we have also suggested that you compare certain poems with others. This is because while we believe that it is necessary to present poems in chronological order to prevent historical confusion, one of the most exciting ways of reading poetry is to look at how poems interact with each other, and add to our understanding of specific themes and issues. Poems that look very different might communicate the same basic message or emotion; or poems on similar topics might provide very different viewpoints – which can spark interesting classroom debates.

As explained in the Introductory notes, it is vital that you have the necessary contextual information in order to gain the maximum enjoyment from a poem. We have provided brief biographies of the poets at the bottom of the page, as well as additional helpful material on individual poems. You will also notice that certain words have been marked with an asterisk (*). This indicates that a short definition of that term can be found in the Glossary at the back of the book. However, you might also like to look for further information, either about the context of a poem, or a literary concept, in a library. In this case, it can be a bit daunting to leaf through books crammed with detailed information, or you might struggle to find specific books. A good starting place is the reference section of a library, with an encyclopaedia or companion to literature in English. By looking up the name of a specific poet, or a type of poem (sonnet, ballad, and so forth), or a historical period (the Renaissance, for example), you should be able to find well-written, reliable and short pieces that should explain the facts in a clear and accessible manner. If you have Internet access, you could also try searching the web. This can be a lot of fun, and especially handy if you are looking up a modern poet. However, be aware that material found this way isn't necessarily always reliable; and if you try to research a very broad and well-known topic, you will be overwhelmed. The one advantage a library has over the Internet is that while browsing through shelves, you can find things you didn't know you were looking for!

Poetry can be an adventure; we hope you enjoy it.

Introductory notes

English History and Literature: A Contextual Time-frame

Few small islands have been as repeatedly invaded, pillaged, ransacked, and finally settled as a colonial territory, as the damp and green British Isles off the west coast of Europe. At a time when the pyramids of Egypt had been standing guard over the tombs of the Pharaohs for over 2 000 years, four centuries after the armies of the young Greek general Alexander the Great had reached as far as India, and about 100 years after the birth of Jesus, the first conquerors established their outposts on British soil.

These were the Romans, whose military power overwhelmed the British peoples. However, there was no notion of British identity or nationhood at this early stage; the inhabitants of the British Isles were made up of isolated and often warring groups, who were fiercely tribal. They were also deeply superstitious and shared a rich folklore.

Roman conquest

The languages they spoke bore no resemblance whatsoever to the English that is spoken today; they were drawn from a language pool broadly identified as Celtic. Few Celtic languages have survived till the present day, although various forms still persist in Ireland, Wales, and the remoter parts of Scotland. Traces of the Celtic languages are hard to find in English today, although some words and sounds can still be found. For example, the Scottish word for lake, 'loch', has the last two letters pronounced as a soft 'g' (a gentler version of the way the letter 'g' is pronounced by Afrikaans and German speakers). This derives from Celtic origins, and is a sound that has fallen away in modern English usage. Speakers of Celtic languages stress the beauty and musical qualities of these ancient dialects, and they are associated with poetry, story-telling, the singing of songs, and prayer. The attempts to keep these languages alive in present-day Britain are linked with nationalist movements, particularly in Ireland, which has a longer history of colonization by the British than any other territory in the world. (Northern Ireland is still regarded by some as a region under British occupation.)

It is not surprising that Celtic languages persist only in the western and northern corners of the British Isles, when we consider that most invasion and settlement came from the south and the east. The clans that resisted the conquerors retreated to the more inaccessible and mountainous parts of the country. Even trained Roman troops could not penetrate into what is present-day Scotland, and, in fact, they experienced so much harassment from local tribes that they built a defensive wall across the northern boundary of the conquered territory. (See Auden's 'Roman Wall Blues', p. 136.)

The Roman conquest meant that Latin became the language of education, law, commerce, and administration. Over a period of time, many Roman settlers blended their culture with that of their new home. Nevertheless, Britain was not considered a particularly useful or strategic colony, and with the final collapse of the Roman Empire the occupying militia returned home, leaving behind the legacy of their language, architecture, and engineering. Those who stayed behind were absorbed into the local population. However, the westward migration of Germanic tribes whose aggression had contributed to the downfall of the power of Rome, now threatened the inhabitants of the British Isles as well.

Dating from about the fourth century CE, Britain's eastern shores were battered by wave after wave of invading Angles and Saxons, tribes from what is today central Germany.

Angles, Saxons, and Vikings

Further north, the eastern shores of Scotland were also under attack from Norse or Viking tribes from the Scandinavian regions of northern Europe (see 'The Viking Terror', p. 3). Many of these Germanic tribes had developed superior seafaring skills to their neighbours, and were therefore easily able to mount raids on the unfortunate British. It is tempting to wonder whether the xenophobia (fear or hatred of foreigners) with which the British are often charged perhaps dates from these bitter times, when the sight of alien sails on the horizon usually meant that the local men could expect to be killed or enslaved, the women raped, their dwellings burned or wrecked, their livestock slaughtered, and their crops stolen. Still deeply fragmented along tribal lines, the British could put up no sustained resistance to the invaders, and by the seventh century Britain was almost entirely subject to Anglo-Saxon rule. As centuries passed, the settlers became increasingly identified with their new home, and their languages took their turn in further submerging the already Latinized Celtic languages.

Within a few centuries Britain was relatively stable, with original inhabitants and descendants of settlers well integrated. No matter how brutal their invasion practices were, the Germanic tribes had no interest in ruling a conquered land as a dominion (as the Romans did), but preferred to make it their new home, both assimilating the native inhabitants and themselves being assimilated. The country was fragmented, however, as the earlier arrivals, the Anglo-Saxons, found themselves wrestling with the later Danish invaders for control of the island. Meanwhile, both groups of settlers were to come under threat from a different quarter.

The ruler of the province of Normandy in France laid claim to the throne of Britain, and in 1066 his Norman troops invaded England, defeated the Saxon king, and laid down their own system of administration, law, customs, and leadership, as well as yet another language: Norman French. The English, already a highly mixed nation, were once again subject to alien rule, and once again the invaders slowly became assimilated into the melting pot of English culture. To further complicate matters, medieval Latin was introduced as an official language in order to cope with the difficulties of administering a multilingual nation. So the forceful, heavy, and sombre language of the Anglo-Saxons met and married with the graceful, colourful, and musical French of the Normans, with a good dash of the formality of Latin stirred in.

Norman conquest

It is only once we understand this history that we can appreciate both the richness and the inconsistencies of the English language. The many languages that have fed into it have created an almost bewildering array of synonyms – different words with the same meaning – and this gives English literature its complex texture and extraordinary powers of description. On the other hand, there is an equally bewildering range of differing pronunciations, spellings, idiomatic expressions, and grammatical quirks that are all exceptions to the rules of the language.

The centuries that elapsed after the Norman conquest eventually led to the development of a literature, during the later Middle Ages (1300–1450 CE), which is accessible to modern English speakers. English was slowly shaping into the form in which we know it today. Medieval English (known as Middle English by scholars, to distinguish it from Modern English) usually seems foreign to the first-time reader – but it can be recognized and read. Of course, there was no official adoption of a national language; the English spoken throughout the Middle Ages was made up of a range of broadly similar, but regionally influenced dialects, which differed in some important respects. The English spoken today is the descendant of the south-eastern dialect used by Chaucer (see p. 4), and it came into predominance partly because it centred on the capital city, London, and the River Thames (along which international and local shipping and commerce flowed) and partly because of the invention of the printing press. The first books to be printed were written in the south-eastern dialect, and thus entrenched its status.

Medieval era

Printing made books and written material available to ordinary people for the first time. Up till then, books could only be copied by hand, a slow and expensive process. Printing was to have a profound impact on literacy, which gradually moved beyond the grasp of the church and a few aristocrats. Literature of this time still relied heavily on oral roots, however; poems and stories were largely passed on by reading or reciting aloud. Chaucer's *Canterbury Tales* (see p. 4), for example, are cast as the stories told for entertainment in a pub by a rowdy band of pilgrims travelling towards Canterbury; and many medieval lyrics were songs that were learnt by heart and passed on, with the names of their original creators left behind and lost.

The literature of medieval England speaks of a rural, agricultural nation, superstitious in spite of the hold the Catholic church exercised over every aspect of life, deeply rooted in and dependent on the cycle of nature. Society was organized along feudal lines, with the land-owning classes believed to have a God-given nobility and authority to rule over the 'common' people. It was only the gradual rise of a wealthy and urban middle class, which had access to education, that finally weakened the hierarchical structure of society.

People were down to earth and did not share modern taboos about birth, sex, and death; these were part of everyday experience in a society in which privacy was a rare luxury. For example, a dead body would have been a common sight: people died at home, and members of the community would gather to lay out the body. Women were openly second-class citizens, considered the property of either male relatives or their husbands. They had no legal rights, and little or no say in who they married. Most marriages were arranged for economic or political reasons, rather than romantic ones, and a wife was valued for her ability to work hard and her fertility.

Blatant and open anti-Semitism was considered normal and acceptable, and attacks on Jewish communities were among the uglier aspects of medieval life. This was also the time of the Crusades; these were pilgrimages by European Christians to the Holy Land (present-day Israel), many of which involved waging war on the Arab people (considered 'infidels' or 'heathens') who lived in these sacred territories.

This contact with Arab culture was to benefit Europeans. Many of the great libraries of the Islamic empire (which spread from the Middle East through North Africa) held the writings of the ancient Greek scholars, whose work had been largely lost to Europe during the Dark Ages that followed the barbarian invasions. The system of numbering we follow today is called 'Arabic', and comes from the principles of mathematics developed by Arab scholars.

Two central shifts in European cultural and religious life brought the Middle Ages to a close, and led to the transformation of the colourful, cyclical, simple, and sometimes violent way of life of most medieval folk living in Britain. These were the Renaissance – a flowering of new scientific and literary knowledge that began in Italy and spread through Western Europe – and the Reformation, which split the Christian church down the middle, with complex political and social results that were to echo for centuries.

Renaissance

The Renaissance had its roots in, among other things, the rediscovery of the scientific, literary, and philosophical writings of the ancient Greeks and Romans by several brilliant Italian scholars. This coincided with a rise in status of vernacular (indigenous) languages and with the development of national literatures. New forms of writing were being experimented with, and new scientific, geographical, and astronomical discoveries were being made that banished the beliefs of the medieval world for good. A new emphasis and value was placed on education and culture, with secular scholars moving into what had for centuries been the domain of the church.

The Renaissance came to Britain a little late, but there it enjoyed a particularly rich flowering, sometimes called the 'Golden Age'. After nearly a century of devastating civil war between different contenders for the throne of England (known as the Wars of the Roses) during the 1400s, the Tudor dynasty was securely established, with first Henry VIII and then Elizabeth I on the throne. The preceding century had been a barren period in literary terms, apart from the first comprehensive effort to weave the many legends of King Arthur and his knights into one major work, and the development of the lyric poem (see p. 9). Now, however, literature and the arts flourished, and rapidly reached new heights.

Dramatists such as Jonson, Marlowe, and Shakespeare were producing plays of astonishing wit, wisdom, and impact; in their hands, as well as in those of many other gifted poets, such as Spenser and Sidney, language was being used with new flair. There were new innovations in poetry, at first tentatively borrowed from classical Latin writings, then developed with growing confidence and vigour. (You might want to look at some Renaissance sonnets as an example of the kind of poetic innovations of these times; see pp. 15, 18, 23–25.) Meanwhile, sailors such as Sir Francis Drake and Sir Walter Raleigh were sailing round the globe, establishing Britain's seafaring power for the first time. Many exploratory voyages were little more than glorified raiding parties, but these nevertheless brought great prestige to the monarchy of England.

This apparently golden age was nonetheless a bloody one, largely because of the Reformation referred to above. In 1517, a German monk named Martin Luther made public his objections to the practice of selling indulgences (crudely put, the forgiving of sins and guaranteed admission into heaven in exchange for money – see the notes to Chaucer's 'The Pardoner's Prologue', p. 5, for more details), and began a process of rebellion against the Catholic church that was to change the face of Western Europe. At the time, Catholicism was the only form of the Christian religion. What began as an attempt to reform the church and purge it of its excesses led to a split or schism. The various Protestant groupings (so named because of their protest against the various failings of the Catholic church) broke away and formed new religious denominations of their own. The results were sometimes tragic, as communities were divided against each other, political allegiances shifted, and civil wars broke out. For several centuries, Catholic and Protestant monarchies in various countries battled each other for power. The succession of a Protestant monarch often meant persecution for Catholics, and vice versa. Rebellions were often planned on religious grounds, with invariably violent results. (See p. 21 for an example of a poem by a young man condemned to death for his part in a Catholic plot against the Protestant queen Elizabeth I.)

Reformation

The Tudor king Henry VIII began the process of the English Reformation by announcing himself to be the head of both Church and State in England, establishing new bishops (who promptly gave him permission to divorce his first wife and marry his mistress), breaking up the monasteries, and distributing the lands and wealth of the church among his nobles. After his death, his daughter Elizabeth embarked on her long and successful reign, which established the sway of the new Protestant Church of England. The great writers mentioned above (Spenser, Sidney, Shakespeare, and Marlowe) are mostly associated with her reign, which was a period of exploration, cultural development, and glamour. Elizabeth herself was a noted scholar, whose work included poetry and translations. She died childless, and was succeeded by her cousin James, already King of Scotland.

James's successor, Charles I, was to run into trouble. During the seventeenth century, a new movement began among those who wished to extend the power of parliament. (This was not the same as a modern, democratically elected parliament, as members inherited their seats rather than being voted in. Nevertheless, laws were debated and voted on; this obviously had the potential to restrict the authority of the king.) Many parliamentarians, fuelled by a desire to carry the Reformation to further and stricter extremes, wished to limit the privileges and powers of the monarchy, and legislate their own brand of religious Puritanism, a strict type of Calvinism that frowned on secular* pleasures. (The first settler colonies in North America were established during this period by Puritans who wished to be free to practise their religion without interference.)

The growing tension between the two factions led inevitably to civil war between supporters of the monarchy (the Cavaliers) and the parliamentary forces (the Roundheads). This ended with the defeat and execution of Charles I, and the establishment of parliamentary rule under Oliver Cromwell. Culturally, this was a repressive time; dress, entertainment, and so forth were governed by strict rules. One of the first steps taken by the Puritans was to close the theatres; after a century and a half of brilliance, the golden age of English drama went into eclipse. However, after eleven years, popular pressure led to the restoration of the monarchy with the return of Charles II from exile.

Civil war

Against the backdrop of this political and religious upheaval, and in spite of the blow to drama with the banning of plays, this was a fruitful period in English literature, especially for poetry. The great poets of this era were ranged on all sides of the political spectrum; Carew, Vaughan, and Herrick were supporters of the monarchy (and are still referred to as Cavalier poets); Anne Bradstreet was a Puritan who sailed to the new colony of America to practise her religion in freedom; Milton and Marvell supported parliamentary rule and used their talents in government service. Nevertheless, these poets are not necessarily remembered for their political allegiances, but for the brilliance of their wit and for their contributions, together with Donne and Herbert, to the original and intellectually challenging school of what was later termed Metaphysical poetry. (See p. 41 for further discussion of this type of poetry.)

Compared with the passion of the preceding centuries, the eighteenth century may seem a little tame. Sometimes called the age of enlightenment, or the age of reason, this was an era in which extreme religious and political beliefs gave way to a more questioning and rational way of thinking. New scientific discoveries by scientists such as Isaac Newton gave rise to a belief in an organized and ordered universe, and writings by philosophers such as Descartes and Voltaire preached tolerance and the importance of rational thought. This was very much a time of 'the head rather than the heart'.

The Enlightenment

In literary terms, the first half of the eighteenth century was to see the rise of the novel, with writers like Henry Fielding and Samuel Richardson paving the way for the skilled novels that Jane Austen was writing by the end of the century. This was also the great age of satire; poets such as Pope ridiculed the foolish behaviour and excesses of their contemporaries in long and technically skilful works. Satire was also used to comment on social and political matters; such as irresponsible behaviour on the part of the land-owning upper classes; see, for example, Samuel Johnson's 'A Short Song of Congratulation' (p. 46). Johnson also compiled the first dictionary of the English language, with typical eighteenth-century enthusiasm for classifying and ordering information. This played a vital role in finally stabilizing and standardizing English.

The emphasis by thinkers such as the French philosopher Rousseau on the rights and dignity of humankind was to plant one of the fundamental seeds of the Romantic movement, which was also an inevitable reaction against the detachment of much Enlightenment thinking. Romanticism, which in England bridged the late eighteenth

The Industrial Revolution and Romanticism

and early nineteenth centuries, emphasized the importance of emotion, and preached a return to Nature as a source of moral and creative guidance. Beauty was especially valued for its ability to instruct, comfort, and inspire. With the beginnings of the Industrial Revolution, with its immense and often destructive physical impact on the English landscape, the recognition that natural loveliness was under threat was combined with a growing movement towards democracy. This blended with growing indignation at the conditions in which the new urban labouring classes worked. Most of the early Romantic poets, most notably Wordsworth and Coleridge (see pp. 54–59 for further details) were initially supporters of the French Revolution, with its rallying cry 'liberty, equality and brotherhood'.

The rise of Romanticism meant a completely new direction for poetry. Although some Romantic poems, with their passionate and unselfconscious pouring forth of emotion in response to beauty, may sometimes seem alien to modern readers, we are all post-Romantics to some degree; the Romantic vision of poetry as a vessel for passing on beauty and truth has left an indelible mark on the way we read literature. Another interesting shift was in the perception of the role of the poet; the Romantics saw themselves as visionaries, with a mission to search for higher truths, and a responsibility to challenge orthodoxy. The later Romantic poets especially considered it their moral duty to rebel against society's norms. (See the biographical information on Byron and Shelley on pp. 60 and 62.)

Romanticism blended into the Victorian age in 1830, when Victoria ascended the throne of Britain and began a long and relatively stable reign. This was the great age of empire; European nations were staking their claims to territorial ownership all over the globe, and Britain led the race. This was partly because of the need for raw materials for the factories of England, now in full swing. Legislation scrambled to keep up with the social impact and ensuing problems of industrialization and urbanization. Social reform and scientific progress rubbed shoulders with extreme poverty and often appalling working conditions. Slavery was finally abolished (see p. 48 for an example of an anti-slavery poem), but child labour went a fair way towards taking its place.

Victorian era

This era marked the growth of an educated middle class with leisure and money to spend on books, entertainment, and consumer goods. Fundamental issues were being brought into question: Karl Marx's economic theories and Darwin's theories of evolution (which contradicted the biblical creation myth) cast doubts on previously unchallenged assumptions. One of the results was considerable nostalgia for a mythical and less complex past. Victorian artists and writers turned to legends, myths, an idealistic vision of rural life, and the distant past for more comforting sources of inspiration.

The nineteenth century also marked the beginnings of the struggle for legal and political representation by women. This was met by a flurry of writing advocating the home and domesticity as women's natural and ordained sphere. Nevertheless, women's activities in and contributions to all spheres of life increased; Florence Nightingale established nursing as a respectable profession for women; charity work by middle-class women and governessing by their less wealthy sisters slowly developed into social work and teaching; and female writers flourished as never before. In general, this was a period of considerable richness in literature: poets such as Lord Tennyson, Matthew Arnold, Elizabeth Barrett Browning, and Robert Browning provided a feast of lyrical, narrative, epic, and reflective poetry. Likewise, novelists such as Charles Dickens, the Brontë sisters, George Eliot (the pseudonym of Mary Ann Evans), and others were at the height of their powers.

The latter half of the nineteenth century saw the rise of the pre-Raphaelite movement, a reaction against the middle-class values of the bourgeoisie, and a rather unrealistic attempt to return to medieval values. It produced not only a colourful and sometimes sentimental school of painting, but also poets such as Christina Rossetti. Their emphasis on the value of nostalgic beauty and mysticism was to influence the aesthetic principles of both artists and writers well into the twentieth century.

It was also during the Victorian age that the literature of the colonies and of North America became more widely known. American philosophers such as Thoreau and writers such as Longfellow, Hawthorne, and Poe were popular on both sides of the Atlantic. The waning of the century saw an increase in 'empire' literature, with the works of colonial officials and travellers such as Rudyard Kipling becoming part of the body of English literature. In South Africa, the writings of Olive Schreiner and Pauline Smith were admired.

The First World War and Modernism

At the time of Queen Victoria's death, the British empire ('on which the sun never set') was at its height of power. However, there were rumblings of discontent. The Anglo-Boer War, now more correctly known as the South African War, fought at the turn of the century over the establishment of Boer republics where gold had been discovered, led to eventual victory but considerable loss of prestige for the British. (See pp. 90 and 94 for poems and more information on this topic.) However, what finally destroyed all remnants of the Victorian way of life and 'blew a hole in the face of civilization' was the First World War, or the Great War (1914–1918). Most of Europe and its colonies were involved in this long and bloody war, which cost the lives of millions, and which was to sow the seeds of the next world war. (For more details, and some examples of poets of the Great War, see pp. 110 and 122.)

It is hard to draw a dividing line between the late Victorians and the early Modernists in literature. The poetry of Hopkins, for example, who falls into the Victorian period, is strikingly modern in its style and effect; while the work of several great twentieth-century poets (such as Yeats and, even later, Dylan Thomas) draws heavily on the traditions of nineteenth-century poetry.

Modernism refers among other things, to the breakdown of 'realism' in art. This meant that, for example, a painter no longer necessarily represented subjects as they would appear to the naked eye. Writers, musicians, and artists reinvented the rules, developing sometimes astonishing and provocative new techniques. The notion that art could shock, disturb, and challenge as well as entertain, educate, and inspire became explicit for the first time. With the rise of the Freudian and Jungian schools of psychoanalysis, and the recognition of the subconscious and unconscious components of the mind, it was inevitable that creators would begin to explore their inner as well as their outer worlds. Poetry especially moved into the realm of association rather than explanation, with words being used for their evocative effect, rather than as explicit means of communication. (See, for example, the poems by T.S. Eliot, pp. 113–16.)

Second World War

The issues of censorship and political alignment of literature were especially vital in the decades after the First World War, which saw the rise of fascism in Europe. Many intellectuals and activists had to flee their native countries, Germany in particular, where the rise of Nazism under Hitler was eventually to precipitate the Second World War (1939–1945). This war was to introduce two new horrors that have haunted human consciousness since. The first was the Holocaust, the systematic murder of six million Jewish people in an insane attempt to establish 'racial purity'. The second was the dropping of the first atomic bomb on the Japanese city of Hiroshima, which inflicted devastation, death, and long-term radioactive poisoning on a scale that had previously been unimaginable.

The Age of '-isms'

After the war, the countries of the northern hemisphere settled into the 'Cold War' – the state of hostility between what was then the Soviet empire, and the Western democracies. Meanwhile, independence movements were growing throughout the southern hemisphere, with various colonies demanding and achieving independence from their former colonial 'masters'. This process was often bumpy and sometimes even chaotic. However, in terms of literary output, there was tremendous growth in what came to be known as post-colonial* literature and culture in various newly independent countries, particularly in Asia, Latin America, the Caribbean, the Pacific, and Africa.

The latter half of the twentieth century has been noteworthy for the richness and complexity of critical debates that have sprung up around literature. Different theories of literary criticism have been fiercely contested, and Marxist, feminist, and post-colonial ideologies have all been brought to bear on the way we read literature and the questions we ask of it.

In particular, there was a hotly debated and defended shift from the principles of so-called 'new criticism' to those of post-structuralism. 'New criticism' followed a system of closely scrutinizing works of literature in order to identify their moral and aesthetic values (the word 'aesthetic' implies qualities of beauty that give pleasure and inspiration). It therefore assumed a universal set of standards by which art could be assessed. Post-structuralist theories, however, are broadly concerned with revealing the way language is structured into hierarchically ranked binary oppositions (male/female, white/black, urban/rural, society/nature, sun/moon), and the power dynamics that are exposed in texts as a result (a form of analysis known as deconstruction). New theories concerning the retrieval of history, as well as input from various ideologies have also led to a more sophisticated approach to the social and historical context of literature. Post-colonial and feminist critiques in particular have placed burning questions of race, gender, class, sexuality, and culture at the centre of literary and other forms of analysis. Certainly the myth of objective and detached criticism is now a thing of the past. Possibly the most obvious effect of these debates is that literary criticism, of whatever kind, is now considerably more self-conscious and aware of the complexities of the global community. As twenty-first-century readers, we try to bear in mind how our identity, assumptions, and social values determine and shape our responses to art and entertainment.

Analysing poetry

The difference between poetry and prose

Before we can begin to analyse poetry, it is necessary to grasp what it is that makes poetry different from other forms of literature. In particular, how does it differ from prose (the everyday form of writing that we find in novels, newspapers, business letters, and so forth)?

To begin with, poetry is a particularly dense and concentrated form of expression. Every single word is chosen for effect, and then combined with others and shaped with a specific end in mind. Poetic language goes much further than conveying factual information; its aim is to generate strong responses, to vividly recreate a specific scene or mood. Imagery, or vivid use of language, is at the heart of poetry. It must be remembered that words are not always restricted to their specific dictionary meaning or factual content. Many words in the English language have acquired layers of meaning, and it is these implied meanings – associations or connotations – that poetry thrives on.

There are two essential hallmarks that distinguish poetry from prose. These are sound and shape.

If we consider sound first, we find that unlike most other forms of literature, most poetry must be read aloud to be properly appreciated. Poems are designed to be heard with the ear as well as seen by the eye. Words are chosen by poets not only for their meaning and associations, but for their musical and sensuous qualities.

Rhythm and rhyme, in particular, are components that set poetry off from other forms of writing. Although modern poets have experimented freely with rhythm and rhyme, these features are often governed by complex rules similar to those found in musical composition; in certain types of poem, there will be a set number of 'beats' or stresses per line, just as a phrase of song can be broken up into bars and beats. It is not always necessary to know the technical terms used to describe these principles, but it is important to be able to identify the rhythm and rhyme scheme of a poem. For example, the rhythm can be quick, slow, smooth, monotonous, faltering, and so forth – the possibilities are endless.

The next important distinguishing feature of poetry is its shape. This refers to the distinctive appearance of poetry on the page; a poem is immediately recognizable because it is laid out in lines. This lends special emphasis to the words of a poem, as we have to consider their arrangement and layout. Just as prose might be compared to flowers growing at random in the veld, the art of poetry might be likened to the careful arrangement of flowers in a vase. Placing words in a line sets them apart, and creates a little pause before the next line begins. We can see the effect that arranging words into lines has if we look at

these extracts from 'The Abandoned Old Woman' by Stephen Watson
(from *Return of the Moon*):

> Our mother, old, unable to walk,
> lay there, incapable,
> alone in her old grass and reed hut.
> . . . .
> It was none of our fault;
> we were all of us starving.
> No-one could help it,
> that we had to leave her behind.

The meaning of these lines would not change if we wrote them out as
prose sentences: 'Our mother, old, unable to walk, lay there, incapable,
alone in her old grass and reed hut.... It was none of our fault; we were
all of us starving. No-one could help it, that we had to leave her
behind.' However, the emotional impact of these words is greatly
lessened if they are presented this way. Their message becomes more
matter-of-fact, and less poignant, when the words are run together
over the full width of the page. Look at the contrast between the two
ways of writing out these sentences, and note how the shaping of
sentences into lines gives extra emphasis to the words at the beginning
and end of lines.

It is worth checking the words chosen by the poet to start and end
lines; these are often significant. The ordering of the poem into lines
also sometimes creates what are called 'run-on' lines, when the flow of
the words travels across a line break without a pause; for example,
Delius's 'Deaf-and-Dumb School' (p. 146), begins: 'On a black tarmac
playground dark / Nuns, ...'. Here the end of the line comes before we
see what word the adjective 'dark' is describing. In this case, the run-
on line breaks up the phrase, so that we are forced to pause and
consider the implications of the words used. In other instances, this
device can be used to quicken the pace of these lines, or to subtly alter
or emphasize the meaning of the words concerned.

So the arrangement of words into lines in poetry is never arbitrary.
Just as rhyme and rhythm contribute to the effect that poetry has on
the ear, the shaping of words into lines gives poetry its visual impact.
The following poem by Lionel Abrahams, on the difference between
poetry and prose, might help make these distinctions clear:

Note in Prosy Verse

Prose on the page
fills the space from margin to margin.
Like water or unmoulded clay it has no shape
of its own. Prose words are bodiless symbols
combining in messages which only the mind can translate,
and only then their infinite meaning begins.
Verse is shaped in its own shape
visible even before the reading begins.
The lines end where they mean to end
and the form they compose does not lie
passive on the paper but strives

to lift off, to fly free like a moth,
or rather a breath. It remembers
that once it was speech or even was song.
Poetry possibly favours verse because
a poem begins as an impassioned thought,
a felt idea so strong it has to
tell itself and end with being felt again.
The poem thus needs embodiment:
each word must ring its sound, each line its tune.
The shapes on the paper are never the poem
but only the signs that a poem has been made.
Embodied, audible, palpable,
the whole made thing is made to make
the meaning felt, not merely known.

Having identified some of the features that differentiate poetry from prose, we come a little closer to engaging with poetry itself. We have also established some useful areas to investigate when we move on to analysis.

Getting to grips with a poem: preparatory work

The next question is, how do we approach a poem? A great deal of ground needs to be covered before the actual analysis of a poem can begin. The importance of this preliminary work cannot be stressed strongly enough. Thorough preparation is crucial if we are to complete a successful analysis of a chosen poem. Obviously we cannot leap in with a detailed discussion of an image used in the first line if we have not established what kind of poem we are dealing with, know little or nothing about its context or history, or are still not certain of the meaning in some parts.

These initial stages in the process of getting to grips with a poem can be enjoyable as well as fruitful, and are best done in your tutorial or study group. Even friends and family can be drawn into the discussion.

One suggested outline for this preparatory process could be the following:

1 Discussion
2 Dictionary
3 Context
4 Connections
5 Paraphrase.

Discussion

It is extremely helpful to discuss the poem with others in an informal context. Here you will be asking questions such as 'What is the poem about?' 'What does it mean?' 'What sort of poem is it?' 'What does it remind me of?' 'What is its basic message?' 'Does it communicate this effectively? How?' At this stage, you are sorting out your initial responses to the poem, as well as familiarizing yourself with its outline and overall meaning. You will find the questions asked will shift from the general to the specific; from 'What's it about?' to 'I don't understand what the last two lines mean – does anyone have any ideas?'

Next, you will find it worthwhile to identify and look up the meaning of all unfamiliar words. Every word in a poem counts, so it is essential to establish exactly what each one means. This is the point at which you will need to use a dictionary. It is worth double-checking words that you are fairly sure you understand; dictionaries often alert the reader to the more obscure meanings of words, and this can sometimes enrich the understanding of the poem.

Dictionary

However, looking up unknown words in a dictionary is not always enough to answer all the questions that arise about the meaning of a poem. This leads us to the question of context. Here you must decide what background information you need to fully understand and enjoy a particular poem. This is one of the more important areas to investigate before beginning an analysis; many poems from past centuries may seem rather pointless, or even slightly ridiculous if you don't know their historical and political context. Blake's 'And Did Those Feet' (see the website) is an example of a poem that seems at best eccentric and at worst incomprehensible unless its specific background is understood. And some poems by the Romantic poets can seem alien and exaggerated unless you have some understanding of the poetic creed or beliefs they represent.

Context

If you have contact with other students, here it is helpful if everyone pools their knowledge. Some of you may already have done some research; or your lecturer may be able to fill in background details. The poem itself might have explanatory footnotes. If you still feel that there are gaps in your understanding of the poem and its context, you will find an encyclopaedia or a guide (sometimes called a companion) to English literature a welcome resource. These can be found in the reference section of your local or university library. Use them to look up poets, literary periods, or genres, which will be listed alphabetically. You can also use the Internet to search for particular topics. However, you might find yourself overwhelmed with material if you enter a word such as 'Shakespeare', so perhaps keep this as a backup system for finding out more about unusual or obscure topics.

A rewarding way of discussing context further is to work out whether there are any connections between the history and circumstances of the poem, and your own present-day situation. For example, Elizabeth Barrett Browning's indictment of her country's political complacency and lack of compassion (see 'A Curse for a Nation', p. 67) has an extremely contemporary feel to it – the poem's criticisms apply as much to many modern democracies as they once did to nineteenth-century England. Likewise, many women married within traditional or conservative communities today will be able to identify with Lady Mary Chudleigh's seventeenth-century poem 'To the Ladies' (p. 42). And in the case of many poems by South African or African writers, any discussion of their work would be pointless without some understanding of the histories of colonialism and apartheid. This background will have powerfully affected the day-to-day lives of many readers of this anthology.

Connections

A note of caution here: establishing the parallels between your own situation and that of a long-dead poet can be extremely exciting, but it is not a substitute for analysis. Unless you are specifically asked to do so in an assignment, do not use a poem as a launching pad for telling your own personal or political history. Nevertheless, establishing links across centuries or cultures (or both) is a valuable part of the preparation for analysis.

To consolidate the ground covered in your discussion and research, it often helps to paraphrase the poem. This means retelling it in your own words. It is worth stressing that this is an extremely helpful exercise if done before attempting an analysis, but it cannot take the place of analysis itself – a common mistake made by students.

Paraphrase

One way of illustrating the difference between the two procedures is to imagine two different ways of looking at a painting. An initial approach might be to list the different components found in this imaginary painting; noting, for example, that it contains the colours green and blue with small amounts of yellow, and that it shows tall trees, a cloudless sky, and a winding road. The second response, by comparison, would go further by describing how these components work together to suggest a certain mood. It might read: 'The use of the cool blue and green colours conveys a calm and natural atmosphere, which is given a hint of warmth by the slight touches of yellow that brighten the landscape. The height of the trees gives a sense of upward movement to the composition; the cloudless sky suggests unbroken tranquillity (there are literally no clouds on the horizon); and the winding curves of the road enhance the sense of natural harmony. No harsh colours or jagged lines disrupt the peaceful mood of this painting. This is a beautiful and idealized rural scene.'

The first approach is similar to paraphrase, the stage in which the 'ingredients' of the poem (or this case, a painting) are listed, sorted, and clarified. However, it is the second process, which reflects on the *effect* of these components combined, that constitutes analysis.

Another way of demonstrating the difference between the two processes is to look at the following accounts (adapted from actual essays) of the first two lines of Christina Rossetti's 'A Birthday': 'My heart is like a singing bird / Whose nest is in a watered shoot.'

'The speaker's organ of circulation is like a small melodious feathered creature that has made a place of rest in a plant which has a plentiful water supply.'

'By beginning with the word "my", the speaker makes the description of her joy personal. She uses the image of a singing bird to convey a sense of natural and spontaneous delight. The fact that the bird has a nest adds a sense of security; the word "nest" has connotations of safety and warmth. The "watered shoot" also suggests something that is growing and flourishing in a fertile environment. One conclusion might be that the speaker has secure emotional grounds for her happiness. Perhaps a new relationship is developing; the word "shoot" (which suggests new or fresh growth) might refer to this.'

The first extract is clearly an exaggerated illustration of paraphrase, while the second is an example of close analysis. (Although it is not necessarily an ideal example of analysis, the contrast between this approach and that of paraphrase should clearly illustrate the differences.)

This suggested programme of preparatory work on a poem need not be followed in the order described. For example, you might like to do research on the context of the poem and look up new words in the dictionary before the class discussion takes place. Or the discussion itself might centre on the connections the poem suggests to you and your fellow students. Your teacher might also suggest that you paraphrase the poem as a written exercise, either before the tutorial or as an initial stage before moving on to an essay analysing the poem.

Critical analysis: a definition

By now, you have no doubt formed an impression of the process of analysis, which has been repeatedly referred to above. However, a fuller definition is necessary, as is some discussion of the more problematic aspects of this process. Critical analysis (sometimes referred to as practical criticism or close reading) is a contested, but nevertheless valuable tool when beginning critical reading, and a rewarding skill that can be applied in a variety of different situations. It involves reading something (in this case, a poem) very carefully and closely, word by word and line by line (usually in chronological order) in order to identify the parts that make it up and evaluate their effectiveness. The next step is to describe the mood and tone (or resonance) created by this particular blend of words, images, visual shapes, and sound effects. (This is one of the features that distinguishes critical analysis from paraphrasing; see the examples given above.) Finally, depending on the theoretical tools being used, critical analysis sometimes ends with an assessment of the 'value' of the poem or its message, or comments on what it reveals about social dynamics.

Critical analysis has inherent limitations. It stems from a school of mid-twentieth century literary criticism that has come under fire for its assumption that all readers have access to a set of absolute and universal values or criteria that can be used as yardsticks to measure a piece of art (see p. xxi above). This is clearly not the case. For example, many Westerners might find the symphonies of Beethoven or Mozart exquisitely beautiful, and claim that such beauty is universal; yet to a Tibetan monk, whose chants are sung according to an entirely different tonal scale, they might sound like the most hideous and confusing noise.

Furthermore, many have pointed out that it is not always appropriate or even possible to judge whether art is 'good' or not, as this raises the thorny questions of what constitutes 'good' or 'bad' art, and who gets to define and decide on these standards. Recent trends in literary criticism have focused instead on what art reveals about society, what power relations it describes, the ideological and political shifts and stances represented in cultural expression, and the extent to which a literary or artistic work can act to question or undermine the status quo.

However, it is unrealistic to try to entirely avoid making value judgements in assessing any piece of art, including a poem. A glance at the film reviews in any newspaper will reveal the extent to which we rank culture and entertainment according to a graded scale of values – a 'five-star' film is generally one with an excellent script and performances, one with 'three stars' is considered to be fairly entertaining, and a 'one-star' film is a piece of trash to be avoided. So to a degree, the tendency to evaluate art and entertainment according to a broad set of 'standards' is embedded in most of our cultures. Perhaps the important thing to bear in mind is that the question 'Is this a good poem?' is not the only one to ask; there are other important questions that might reveal rewarding insights.

Nevertheless, in spite of its limitations, critical analysis remains a valuable 'first stage' in acquiring critical skills. Many students find it useful in their everyday work and study; its principles can be applied when reading newspapers, magazines, advertisements, and business letters; when watching films, television, or plays; even when listening to the radio or to music. It can be of practical use when querying material you suspect of being less than honest or straightforward; propaganda, for example, or simply the small print in a document you are asked to sign. If you are interested in alternative theoretical or ideological approaches to literature, you will find that close reading remains a useful tool to have in your stock of critical skills. The ability to critically analyse poetry also remains an important part of most English poetry courses at tertiary educational institutions, and it is a skill that you are likely be required to demonstrate in your poetry essays and exams.

Guidelines for analysing a poem

Once you have completed the preliminary stages, you have reached the point of plunging into the poem itself. The following steps are very basic and flexible guidelines for carrying out an analysis. As you gain more confidence, you will be able to refine this list, add pointers of your own, and shuffle the order around to suit your approach.

First of all (bearing in mind the distinguishing aspects of poetry discussed above), familiarize yourself with the sound and shape of the poem. Remember that poetry is created to be heard and seen, not just understood. If you have not already done so, begin by reading the poem aloud, or asking someone else to read it to you. Listen as if it were a piece of music. This will alert you to various important aspects of the poem: its rhyme scheme, pace and rhythm, the specific sounds of its words. Does the poem sound lulling and soothing? Brisk and quick? Harsh and jarring? Racy and breathless? Or do contrasting sounds follow one another to change the effect on the ear? Hearing the poem also gives an initial impression of those poetic devices that are used to create specific sound effects, such as alliteration or onomatopoeia (see below for definitions and examples).

Next, look at the overall shape and structure of the poem. Note whether it is divided into stanzas, and where these breaks fall. It is also worth counting the number of lines, especially in shorter poems: this is often the easiest way to spot a sonnet (which always has fourteen lines). The shape will often help you to identify the type of poem; repeating choruses, for example, usually point to a song or ballad. Check for lines that are repeated, or that stand alone (these are usually significant).

At this stage, you should have enough material to draft brief introductory notes, if you are planning to turn your analysis into an essay. By now you know what kind of poem you are dealing with, understand its general meaning, and have some sense of its context and atmosphere. You might want to leave your introductory paragraph till later, when you have finished working your way through the poem; on the other hand, jotting down your overall sense of the poem at this stage might help you to deal with the most intimidating stage: getting started.

What follows forms the 'meat' of the analysis; the examination of the poem line by line and word by word. It is best to proceed chronologically, and work your way through from beginning to end without skipping sections or backtracking.

Begin with the title, if the poem has one. (Poems without titles are usually identified by their first line, which is used as a heading under which the poem stands.) Some titles simply state the topic, but more often they contain essential additional information that illuminates the poem that follows. They can also establish an aura or atmosphere before the poem itself starts; the French title of Keats' 'La Belle Dame sans Merci' (p. 65) helps to create a mysterious and exotic mood even if we are not certain what it means. Bear in mind that even short, simple titles can make a profound contribution to the poem as a whole; the title of Wilfred Owen's poem 'Futility' (p. 122) expresses the speaker's opinion of war with a bitterness that is largely absent from the poem itself.

Now examine the poem line by line, keeping an eye open for any words or phrases you find striking. As you proceed, bear the following checklist in mind. The pointers and questions it suggests are not meant to be prescriptive, and should not be followed rigidly, as each poem will present slightly different challenges. Nevertheless, it will provide you with options for making your analysis as thorough and rewarding as possible.

Identify significant words, and note where they are placed in the structure of the poem. Do they fall at the beginning of lines or stanzas? Do they stand alone? Are they repeated? Is our attention drawn to them because they 'jar' or 'jump out' of an otherwise smoothly flowing line? Is there anything else unusual about where they are placed?

Look more carefully at any *repeated words or lines*. What effect does the repetition have? Does it lend special emphasis? Does it act as a chorus? Is the effect that of a lullaby or song? If a line or phrase is repeated at intervals throughout the poem, check whether the impact of the words remains the same. If any changes are made to a repeated line, what effect does this have?

Check punctuation, which becomes particularly expressive in poetry. Dashes, colons, semi-colons, exclamation and question marks will have obvious effects on the meaning of the poem; also investigate the placing of commas and full stops. Do any of these fall in unusual places? How do they contribute to the pace of the poem; do they hurry it along, or break it up? (See Tennyson's *In Memoriam* poems [pp. 72–75] for examples of how punctuation can underline the message contained in words.)

If you are really stuck, you could break the poem down into its *grammatical components*. This can be surprisingly revealing. A poem crammed with verbs will be punchy, full of action, brisk, and swift; one that uses many adjectives and adverbs is more likely to be descriptive, flowery, and slow-paced. It is also often rewarding to look at the pronouns used; the third-person pronoun 'one' is associated with a style that is formal, detached, and even cold; the second-person pronoun ('you') is much more immediate and informal in its effect, but still indicates a degree of distance; and the first-person pronoun ('I', 'we') is intimate, personal, and confessional. The use of 'I' can also indicate power, as the speaker then 'owns' the words spoken, and has control over any description that follows.

Pay attention to *word-music*. This draws on the earlier stage of listening to the poem to gauge its sound effects. Two common poetic devices or techniques that specifically affect how poetry sounds are onomatopoeia and alliteration. Knowing how to spell these terms is not as important as being able to recognize them! Onomatopoeia involves using words that sound like the action or object described; some examples are 'the <u>hissing</u> of waves on sand'; 'the <u>clip-clop</u> of hooves'; 'the <u>clashing</u> cymbals'. Alliteration is the repetition of the same letter or sound in several successive words; for example, '<u>green</u> and <u>golden grows</u> the <u>grass</u>.' (The first stanza of 'Binsey Poplars' by Hopkins [p. xxxv below] features alliteration in almost every line; read it for further examples.) Sometimes both alliteration and onomatopoeia can appear together in the same phrase: 'the mournful moan of doves'. It should be clear that these are often very evocative or sensuous aspects of a poem, which can add colour and texture.

Rhythm and rhyme scheme have been mentioned above. Now is the time to note where and how the rhythm of a poem changes, and to ask why that specific change takes place. (Marvell's 'To His Coy Mistress' on p. 40 is an excellent example of how changes in rhythm reinforce the argument of the poem.) Also consider the rhyme scheme; how many rhyming sounds are there, and in what pattern do they occur? What do these sounds suggest to you? The rhyme scheme is often important in that it contributes control and structure to the poem. A poem governed by a strict sense of rhyme and rhythm will often come across as complex and carefully crafted, while a poem in free verse (no rhyme scheme) tends to be loose and informal.

Also consider how the rhythmic and rhyming features of a poem contribute to or amplify its meaning. Usually, they intensify the message of the words (see, for example, Wyatt's 'My Lute, Awake!' [p. 13] and Tichborne's 'Elegy' [p. 21]). However, there is sometimes a deliberate contrast between the argument of the poem and its rhythm and rhyme scheme; see Millay's 'I, Being Born a Woman and Distressed' (p. 118) for an example of sharp contrast between the elegant formality of the strict rhythm and rhyme scheme (and equally elegant vocabulary), and the humorous, cynical, and bawdy message of the poem.

One of the more important (and enjoyable) parts of analysis is the examination and assessment of the *images, or 'word-pictures'*, that appear in the poem. Broadly speaking, images refer to anything described in particularly vivid and picturesque language. However, most imagery involves a comparison (either explicit or implicit) of some kind. Comparisons involve a transfer of associations between two different things that nevertheless share a specific quality or have some features in common. In other words, if we wish to suggest that someone is brave, we can either say so directly, or we could describe them as a 'lion'. This does not mean that they have literally changed species; instead, everything we associate with the word 'lion' (courage, majesty, power and so forth) is transferred momentarily to that person. The power of comparisons to illuminate and illustrate should be obvious; it is far more dramatic to greet a courageous friend with the words 'You are a lion!' than to state 'You are brave'.

Comparisons can be found in two forms in literature: as metaphors and as similes. In the case of a simile, the comparison is made explicit by the linking words 'as' or 'like'; for example, 'she is as brave as a lion' or 'he sings like an angel'. Metaphors collapse the comparison into a single image; for example, 'She is a lion'; 'His song is angelic'. Metaphors and similes are often found in everyday speech ('politicians should get off the gravy train'; 'the price of petrol is daylight robbery'; 'it's like taking sweets from a baby' and so forth), and can be quite commonplace. Your task is not simply to identify the metaphors and similes in the poem, but to judge their effectiveness. Are they ordinary? Vivid? Unusual? You will also need to 'unpack' the associations involved; to return to our 'lion' example, it is obviously not enough to say in your analysis: 'In this metaphor, the person is compared with a lion.' You would need to list the qualities suggested by the image of a 'lion', and to link these associations with the person being described.

In a poem, imagery can be used in an accumulative way. One image often builds on another, weaving different associations together into a united whole. This means that you should not study the images in the poem in isolation. Check to see if they are linked to one another, or whether you can trace any development between them. (The suggestions for discussion on Mtshali's poem 'Men in Chains' [p. 198] provide practical questions on metaphor and simile.)

It is essential to bear *mood or tone* in mind. These are very difficult qualities to define or pin down. One way of clarifying mood and tone might be to refer to the emotional resonance of the poem: what feelings does it evoke? If you struggle to express these, the following questions might help (use them to identify your responses, not as part of a formal analysis): what flavour does the poem have? If you had to illustrate it, what colours would you choose? Would they be bright, warm, murky, or cool? If you had to choose music to match the poem, what kind of music and instruments would you pick? Ominous drums, laid-back jazz saxophones, energetic rap, a romantic waltz?

It is also important to track the shifts in tone; do you notice any abrupt changes? Are there parts where it is more intense? One way of monitoring these often subtle changes is to ask what effect is being created at various stages in the poem. At this point, these guidelines may seem frustratingly vague – it might help to turn back to the examples of paraphrase and analysis above. Here you will see that one of the features that distinguishes the written samples of analysis from those of paraphrase is that analysis includes descriptions of mood and tone. As you read and analyse more poetry, you will develop your own 'mood thermometer', but this aspect of analysis takes practice at first.

Finally, it is extremely important to keep asking the questions 'How?' and 'Why?' *How* was this effect achieved, and *why*? (Analysis demands endless curiosity.) These questions are essential to prevent your analysis from reverting to a catalogue of parts. It is all too easy to reduce your findings to a mechanical list, which might run something like this: 'this poem features a metaphor in line 4, alliteration in line 5, use of the first person throughout, three semi-colons, and the repetition of the last line of each stanza'. At all costs, you must engage with each poem that you analyse and remain alert to the shifts and transformations within the tiny landscape it seeks to create; repeated questioning will aid you in this task. The 'how' question also acts as a reminder that in written analysis it is vital to quote from the poem to support our arguments.

Once you have worked your way through the poem armed with this checklist, you are likely to see new connections and relationships between the different parts. As the poem is put back together again, a message may emerge that was not clear before. If the analysis has been successful, you will find that you have gained a new appreciation of the poem, or developed a more sophisticated critique of it. You might like to use these discoveries as the basis for concluding remarks, if you are planning to turn your analysis into an essay. This is also the stage at which you might find it interesting to swop findings with fellow students, noting the differences and similarities between your efforts.

Above all, remember that the task of analysis is an individual process. This is because our response to poetry is extremely personal. Each reader will interact with the text in a different way; individual taste, differing value systems, cultural heritages and so forth will all determine our responses to some degree. Life would be very boring if we all liked identical clothing, food and music, and indeed the value of diversity has become a catch-phrase for South Africa in recent years. This principle is a valuable one in the development of critical skills; you should be encouraged to make personal choices and express preferences when engaging with poetry. (A revealing exercise would be for you and several classmates each to list your favourite five or ten poems from this anthology, and state your reasons for choosing them. You will find the wide range of choices that is bound to result most enlightening.) However, remember that you will seldom be examined on whether or not you like a poem and why!

It must also be stressed that there are no right or wrong answers when analysing a poem, although there might be weak and strong answers. Strong answers are those that reflect a sensitivity towards the language and intention of the poem, and that provide evidence from the poem for each conclusion drawn. Remember that two different interpretations of the same poem might be equally valid, even if they contradict each other. If both arguments are clear, logical, and well supported, both should be equally worthy of praise.

Writing a draft essay

If you are asked to write a critical analysis of a poem, then to some extent the shape of that poem will determine the shape of your essay. Begin with some broad introductory statements; these should arise out of your pre-analysis preparations (described above). If there is vital contextual information that shapes your reading of the poem, now is the time to set it out. Next, collate the notes you have made on the poem itself (following the guidelines for analysis suggested above), and organize them so that the individual points are clear as you write, and the line of discussion flows easily. Remember to proceed chronologically through the poem; do not hop from discussing line 11 to line 22 and then back to something you have noticed in line 17. However, if the poet is developing a particular image that is subtly changing, then refer back to the points you have already established, but without repeating yourself. (For example: 'The description of the house, which was presented as a warm, cosy environment in the second stanza, has become increasingly eerie and threatening by the time we reach stanza four.')

It is extremely important to support your opinions by quoting from the text, even if only a few words are used. Turn back to the hypothetical analysis of a painting on p. xxvi, and imagine that it reads 'This painting has a cool, calm and natural feel, with touches of warmth. It has a sense of height and upward movement, and conveys a tranquil atmosphere of harmony.' This leaves us with a description of the onlooker's personal feelings and responses rather than an analysis. Yet these claims become perfectly valid if they are supported with evidence. Vague statements (such as 'this poem has a good feeling') are not much use, so ensure that your responses to the poem are firmly grounded in the text. It is a good idea to quote those words or images that trigger a specific response.

Finish by drawing some kind of conclusion, or by summarizing your findings: this is a good place to restate your basic interpretation of the poem. At the end of an analysis of an anti-war poem, for example, you might write something along the lines of:

'This bitter catalogue of the brutality and destructive power of warfare spells out the message that war is both immoral and futile.'

Or, at the end of a poem about township life, you might conclude:

'This poem combines a celebration of the liveliness and resourcefulness of township dwellers with a stinging indictment of the apartheid policies (in particular, the Group Areas Act) that led to the creation of these settlements.'

This is probably the best point at which to include your own personal response to the poem, but be careful to focus on summing up the essence of the poem itself, rather than ending with a mini-essay on your own beliefs and views.

If you are asked a specific question that also involves a close reading of the poem, the process may become a little more complicated, but the essential procedure remains the same. In these cases, you are analysing the poem in search of specific evidence. For example, if you are asked to write an essay on the use of irony in a poem, you will need to tease out all aspects of the poem that contribute to this feature. Try to establish exactly what is expected of you. Begin by 'analysing' the question; break it down into its component parts, and ensure that you understand what these mean; use a dictionary if necessary. Later, when you have finished the rough draft of your essay, go back to the question, and check that every aspect of it has been covered.

Close critical analysis is extremely useful if you are asked to compare two or more poems in an essay. The closer the scrutiny of each poem, the richer the level of contrasts and parallels between them.

Bear in mind that it is vital to write all your essays in draft form before beginning the final copy. You should now edit your draft with a critical eye. (A hint: if you read it aloud to yourself, you will find yourself automatically picking up and correcting errors.) By all means ask friends and fellow students for their comments. This is quite different from asking them to do the work for you; at this stage, get as much feedback as possible. Your lecturer might also be willing to comment on your draft before you submit your final essay. Your writing can only benefit from reworking and polishing.

How much should you rely on critical works when planning and writing a critical analysis? We feel that during the initial stages of learning this skill, you should not rely too much on the works of commentators and critics. Rather read up more about the background of the poem, or read further poems by that poet. It is easy to be intimidated by critics who are experts in their field, and to submit your opinions to theirs. There is also a tendency to feel that because their assessment of a poem or poet is in print, it must necessarily be correct and of more value than anything you can offer. This means that you run the risk of turning your analysis into a patchwork of other people's ideas and interpretations. It also detracts from the pleasure and sense of exploration of establishing your own personal response to a poem. Bear in mind that your goal is to develop your own critical skills, not to defer to the opinions of others.

To provide some practical help with the process of moving from analysing a poem to writing a formal essay on it, we have given some examples of poems ('Binsey Poplars' by Gerard Manley Hopkins and 'For Albert Luthuli (21.7.67)' by Jennifer Davids), which have rough notes scribbled all over them. It helps a lot to begin by jotting down your analysis all over the poem itself; this process of 'dissection' makes the poem less daunting, and means that you are less likely to leave out important points. We have also provided some samples of written analysis, to demonstrate how your rough notes can be transformed into a formal essay, or at least the first draft of one.

Below are two possible beginnings for a written critical analysis of this poem, based on the notes made on the poem. Both are equally valid interpretations. Although you might find one or the other more convincing, both support their conclusions with evidence drawn from the poem itself.

Essay 1:

This poem is one of mourning for the loss of a group of trees that were an integral part of a beautiful country scene. The title resembles the headstone of a grave, with the date and manner of death ('Felled 1879') written below the name. This immediately strikes us as unusual, as it suggests that these trees are being commemorated in the same way that we mourn loved ones who have died.

This provides evidence that the poplar trees are extremely important to the speaker, who speaks of them as if they were humans he loved very much. This is confirmed by the first

Binsey Poplars

FELLED 1879

newspaper headline?
date of 'death' – gravestone?

1st person pronoun
personal, possessive

loving

My aspens dear, whose airy cages quelled,
Quelled or quenched in leaves the leaping sun,
All felled, felled, are all felled;
Of a fresh and following folded rank

alliteration –
rustling leaves?
death knell
of soldiers?

no mercy

Not spared, not one
That dandled a sandalled
Shadow that swam or sank
On meadow and river and wind-wandering
weed-winding bank.

lazy, relaxed images

words suggest shape of river: slow, curving

shift: from description of trees to 'sermon' on the environment

O if we but knew what we do
When we delve or hew –
Hack and rack the growing green!
Since country is so tender
To touch, her being so slender,
That, like the sleek and seeing ball
But a prick will make no eye at all,
Where we, even where we mean
To mend her we end her,
When we hew or delve:
After-comers cannot guess the beauty been.
Ten or twelve, only ten or twelve
Strokes of havoc únselve
The sweet especial scene,
Rural scene, a rural scene,
Sweet especial rural scene.

1–4: move from aimless words to language of torture

delicacy, nature is feminized

image of extreme vulnerability: ouch!

words look similar, but have opposite meanings

Most NB point of poem. Irony: the beauty lost has been recreated in the poem

repetition: emphasis on how little it takes to create devastation

repetition: chanting, mourning

harsh, extreme word

words of the poem: 'My aspens dear'. The use of endearments and the first person implies that he had a personal relationship with the trees, and strengthens the impression that this poem is an elegy. The first two lines reveal both the speaker's love for the trees and their beauty. The words 'airy cages' give a strong visual impression of the shape of the trees, with the branches and leaves forming the bars of the 'cage'. This image looks like an apparent contradiction (or paradox); the sense of freedom and light conveyed by the word 'airy' dissolves the sense of enclosure that 'cage' gives. The music of the words 'quelled, / Quelled or quenched in leaves the leaping sun' tries to imitate the sound of rustling leaves, as we find repetition of both words ('quelled, / Quelled') and sounds ('que' and 'lea'). The images also suggest the constant interplay of light and shade caused by the movement of branches and trees.

Essay 2:

This poem traces the intense emotional involvement of the speaker with a specific place of natural beauty, and charts his passionate response to the destruction both of this particular spot and the rural environment in general.

The title makes one think of an obituary column in a newspaper, with the name of the deceased and the date of their death laid out as a headline. In this case, the 'dead' are the poplar trees near Binsey (a village outside Oxford, where Hopkins studied). Obituaries are often written by someone close to the person who has died, and in this case the speaker feels personally involved.

We know this because the first word of the poem is the first-person possessive pronoun 'My'. This suggests that the speaker 'owns' the aspens, or feels extremely possessive of them. The use of the first person tells us that the speaker is no detached onlooker; he is personally affected, and feels he has the right to describe and define both the beauty of the trees and the extent of his bereavement.

The sheer loveliness of the trees (described in the first and second lines) makes way for the death knell in the third line: 'All felled, felled, all are felled.' Here the swift, light rhythm of the first two lines, which suggests the rapid and graceful movements of poplar leaves in the wind, is displaced by a slow and repetitive beat, like the tolling of a bell to announce a death. The word 'felled' both looks and sounds like the word 'knell'.

'For Albert Luthuli' is a good example of a poem that needs a fair amount of contextual background filled in before any analysis can begin. As this was written on the occasion of Albert Luthuli's death, it is important to know who he was and something about his life. At the very least, you need to know that he was one of the great leaders of the ANC during the 1950s and 60s, a chief, and a Nobel Prize winner. He was constantly harassed by the apartheid regime, and eventually placed under a banning order. This restricted his movements, forbade political involvement, and attempted to isolate him. Luthuli is perhaps best remembered for a speech in which he spoke of 'knocking on a door', a metaphor for his life's engagement in the struggle against apartheid. He died in a train accident, on the date mentioned in the title of the poem. This information sheds light on several of the references in the poem.

Here we have provided some examples of how imagery might be analysed. (Note that this is not a complete essay; there is no introduction and conclusion, and not all the images in the poem are discussed. The intention is to demonstrate how interlinking imagery in a poem might be approached.)

One set of images traced throughout this poem are those of the world, the sun and the stars in space ('fragment of the sun'; 'world'; 'endless pulsations of space'; 'stars breaking the dark'; 'sun to sun'). These are significant because they suggest absolute freedom. The universe is infinitely huge, and there are no boundaries in space. Chief Luthuli was restricted throughout his life – first by the discriminatory laws of apartheid, and then later by his banning order, which placed him under house arrest and tried to end his political activism. The choice of images of freedom is thus particularly telling.

The first and last lines of the poem both use the sun as a metaphor, which links into this theme, but also operates on other levels. By describing Luthuli as a 'fragment of the sun' at the beginning of the poem, the speaker immediately conveys the sense that he is a source of warmth, light, and inspiration. At the end of the poem, however, the image has changed slightly; now it is suggested that Luthuli takes his place in the universe as a sun among suns ('Walk now father ... from sun to sun'). This could mean, first of all, that even after his death he remains a source of light and guidance; it also gives a sense of his stature and dignity. Finally, it could also mean his death has given him the freedom of the entire universe, in

implies gift or memorial

For Albert Luthuli (21.7.67) ← *date of death*

also means change →

You a ~~fragment of the sun~~ → *light, warmth*
←~~go turn~~ the ~~world~~ ← *world revolves around sun*
in the long strength
of your (fingers) *famous for 'knocking on a door'*

paradox

⎧Bounded
⎨you gave me
⎩knowledge of freedom

developed further

⎧Silenced
⎨you taught me
⎩how to speak

luthuli was killed in a train accident; also metaphor for a journey

Somewhere a (train)
has reached a destination
and tonight *contrast to sun*
the cold (fist) of winter *contrast to fingers (line 4): a fist is closed, potentially violent*

effect of luthuli's death {clenches around the world

freedom, no limits

But beyond it
the (endless) pulsations of (space)
grow louder
and stars breaking the dark *traditional image of hope*
grow large

significant, as luthuli was banned: death restores his freedom

Walk now father *close personal relationship, loving*
(unchecked)
from sun to sun → *takes his place in the universe*

sharp contrast to the restrictions he endured in life.

Another image that is developed involves hands. The speaker describes the 'long strength' of Luthuli's fingers; later we read that the 'cold <u>fist</u> of winter/ <u>clenches</u> around the world'. These images remind us of Luthuli's famous phrase 'knocking on a door'. We use our hands to knock, and so the power of Luthuli's words, which constantly 'knocked' at apartheid's door, are translated into an image of hands and strong fingers. The speaker considers the power of Luthuli's words/hands to be so great that they can 'turn' (or change) the world. This image of 'fingers' contrasts with the later image of a fist, which is used to describe the immediate impact of Luthuli's death. Unlike fingers, which can hold, point, guide or knock, a fist is closed, potentially violent and unable to give or receive. One interpretation of the 'cold fist of winter' is that it is a metaphor for apartheid and its violence; without the guiding light and warmth ('fragment of the sun') of Luthuli's leadership to combat it, apartheid 'clenches around the world' like a fist. This image also suggests the experience of being 'gripped' by grief and loss.

Writing poetry exams

A final word needs to be added about poetry exams. Many good students underperform simply because they reproduce prepared material in the exam, instead of answering the specific questions asked. Just as in the essay, it is vital that you read the question carefully, break it down into parts, and analyse it. For essay-type questions, it is essential that you spend the first five minutes of your allotted time for that question doing this. Next, work on a very short rough draft of your essay. Scribble down any thoughts you might have and see if you can organize them into a logical sequence. This is particularly important if you have been asked to present an argument, or to explain whether you agree or disagree with a criticism of a poem. Now is the time to draw a skeleton structure for your answer; this will help if your mind goes blank, or if you run out of ideas halfway through your essay. It is essential that you give yourself this time for planning in an exam. Do not be daunted by the sight of your fellow students around you scribbling as fast as they can; you will definitely benefit from taking a few extra minutes to plan your answer. Now work through the poem chronologically. If you are writing about the first stanza, and you suddenly get a fresh idea about an image in the fifth stanza, quickly jot this down on your rough structure, so that you will remember to include it once you are further along in your essay. The same rule applies to exam questions as to essays; try not to skip backwards and forwards in the poem. Leave plenty of space between paragraphs in case you think of something you want to add to an argument you have already made. Remember to add a conclusion, even if this is only one sentence summing up your point of view or your response to the poem. If you have time at the end of the exam, read through your answer to check for errors and to satisfy yourself that your meaning is clear.

Working through your exam question according to this system can help to control anxiety. More important, it increases your chances of doing justice to your careful preparation. Remember that when it comes to poetry, you are being asked to demonstrate a skill that you have mastered, rather than to repeat factual information contained in a syllabus.

Good luck!

Li Ho (791–817)

On the Frontier

A Tartar[1] horn tugs at the north wind,
Thistle Gate shines whiter than the stream.
The sky swallows the road to Kokonor.
On the Great Wall,[2] a thousand miles of moonlight.

5   The dew comes down, the banners drizzle,
Cold bronze rings the watches of the night.
The nomads' armour meshes serpents' scales.
Horses neigh, Evergreen Mound's[3] champed° white.   *chewed by horses*

In the still of autumn see the Pleiades.[4]
10 Far out on the sands, danger in the furze.°   *bushes*
North of their tents is surely the sky's end
Where the sound of the river streams beyond the border.

Li Ho was a great and original contributor to the 'golden age' of Chinese poetry (which reached its height during the eighth and ninth centuries). Although he died young, he was famous in his lifetime for his often unorthodox poems, which had a reputation for being moody and sensual.

Notes

1. War-like nomadic tribes that threatened the borders of the old Chinese empire.
2. Long, fortified wall built as a defence against the Tartars. It stretched for thousands of kilometres, and much of it still stands today.
3. Grave of a royal mistress and Tartar empress. According to legend, grass always grew on her grave.
4. Constellation of stars; their flickering was seen as an omen of Tartar attack.

Tu Mu (803–852)

The Gate Tower of Ch'i-an City[1]

The sound grates on the river tower, one blast of the horn.
Pale sunlight floods, sinking by the cold shore.
Pointless to lean on the balcony and look back miserably:
There are seventy-five post-stations from here to home.

To Judge Han Ch'o at Yang-chou

Over misted blue hills and distant water
In Chiang-nan at autumn's end the grass has not yet wilted.
By night on the Four-and-Twenty Bridges, under the full moon,
Where are you teaching a jade girl to blow tunes on your flute?

Talking points

You might like to compare Li Ho and Tu Mu's poems with Mao Tse-
Tung's 'Lou Mountain Pass' (p. 125) and Ezra Pound's 'A River
Merchant's Wife' (pp. 107–8), a very loose translation of a poem by
the great Chinese poet Li Po (*c.* 700–762). Do these poems have
features in common? Do you notice any points of style and imagery
that differ from 'Western' poems you have studied? You might also
enjoy Auden's 'Roman Wall Blues' (p.136), a very different treatment
of similar concerns.

Tu Mu spent time wandering between monasteries in the lovelier parts of
China, and his work closely observes and celebrates the natural beauty of the
Chinese landscape. He was particularly admired for his brief four-line poems
(called *chueh-chu*), of which two examples have been given here.

Tu Mu and Li Ho's poems were written at a time when China, ruled by the
Tang dynasty, was the largest empire in the world. Its flourishing and rich
civilization was constantly under threat of invasion by land-hungry and
nomadic tribes from Mongolia and inner Asia, who were feared for their
swiftness of attack and brilliance on horseback (which gave them a
significant military advantage). This is why the reference to horses in Li Ho's
'On the Frontier' (p. 1) conveys especial menace.

Some historians argue that it was pressure on the eastern borders of Europe
by these same tribes that led to the westward spread of the Germanic peoples.
Eventually, the force of the invaders (often referred to as Tartars or Mongols)
became too strong to resist, and China was conquered and itself colonized.

Notes

[1] Presumably an outpost on the Great Wall of China.

Anonymous (8th or 9th century)

The Viking[1] Terror

Fierce is the wind tonight,
It ploughs up the white hair of the sea
I have no fear that the Viking hosts°   *bands of fighting men*
Will come over the water to me.

Although composed two continents away, this short Irish poem (found
written on the margin of a religious manuscript) expresses the same anxiety
that we see in 'On the Frontier' (p. 1).

Notes

[1] Seafaring warriors from northern
Europe (Scandinavia); among the
Germanic tribes that repeatedly
raided (and eventually
conquered) the British Isles.

Geoffrey Chaucer (c. 1343–1400)

From The Canterbury Tales

The Pardoner's Prologue (*extracts*)

Lordinges° — quod° he — in chirches whan I preche,	*sirs / said*
I paine me° to han an hautein° speeche,	*I take pains / loud*
And ringe it out as round as gooth a belle,	
For I can° al by rote that I telle.	*know*
5 My theme is alway oon,° and evere° was:	*the same / always*
Radix malorum est cupiditas.[1]	
First I pronounce whennes° that I come,	*from where*
And thanne my bulles[2] shewe I alle and some:	
Oure lige lordes seel on my patente,[3]	
10 That shewe° I first, my body to warente,°	*show / protect*
That no man be so bold, ne° preest ne° clerk,	*neither / nor*
Me to destourbe of Cristes holy werk.[4]	
And after that thanne telle I forth my tales —	
Bulles° of popes and of cardinales,	*letters*
15 Of patriarkes° and bisshopes I shewe,	*church fathers*
And in Latin I speke a wordes fewe,	
To saffron with° my predicacioun,°	*spice up / preaching*
And for to stire hem° to devocioun.	*them*
Thanne shewe I forth my longe crystal stones,°	*glass jars*
20 Ycrammed ful of cloutes° and of bones —	*rags*
Relikes[5] been they, as weenen° they eechoon.°	*suppose / each one*
Thanne have I in laton° a shulder-boon°	*metal case / shoulder-bone*
Which that was of an holy Jewes sheep.	
'Goode men,' I saye, 'take of my wordes keep:° . . .	*notice*

Chaucer's fascination with the class structure of England, which he explores in his works, is hardly surprising considering his own upwardly mobile career. He himself was born into the new middle class that was changing the face of feudal medieval society (see Introductory notes, p. xv). He travelled to Europe as a soldier, established links with three successive royal courts, married into the aristocracy, and held a number of increasingly prestigious civil, diplomatic, and political posts. Nevertheless, he ran into difficulties of his own making; he was often in debt, and was once charged with rape.

In an uncertain and hectic age, Chaucer produced a significant amount of great writing. His works are extraordinary for their ability to capture the language and idiom of their time, while remaining open to contemporary interpretation and enjoyment.

Notes

[1] 'Avarice (or love of money) is the root of all evil' (1 Timothy: 6).

[2] Letters of authorization from a bishop.

[3] The papal seal on my license ('lige lorde' refers to the Pope).

[4] Try to stop me doing Christ's holy work.

[5] Relics supposed to have belonged to holy figures were very popular in medieval times; this led to widespread manufacture and sale of fake relics.

25	Goode men and wommen, oo° thing warne I you:	*one*
	If any wight° be in this chirche now	*person*
	That hath doon sinne horrible, that he	
	Dar nat for shame of it yshriven⁶ be,	
	Or any womman, be she yong or old,	
30	That hath ymaked hir housbonde cokewold,⁷	
	Swich° folk shal have no power ne no grace	*such*
	To offren° to my relikes in this place;	*make offerings*
	And whoso findeth him out of swich blame,	
	He wol come up and offre in Goddes name,	
35	And I assoile° him by the auctoritee°	*forgive / authority*
	Which that by bulle ygraunted was to me.'	
	By this gaude° have I wonne, yeer by yeer,	*trick*
	An hundred mark° sith° I was pardoner.	*pounds / since*
	I stonde lik a clerk in my pulpet,	
40	And whan the lewed° peple is down yset,°	*simple / sitting*
	I preche so as ye han herd bifore,	
	And telle an hundred false japes° more.	*jokes*
	Thanne paine I me to strecche forth the nekke,	
	And eest and west upon the peple I bekke⁸	
45	As dooth a douve,° sitting on a berne;°	*dove / barn*
	Mine handes and my tonge goon so yerne°	*quickly*
	That it is joye to see my bisinesse.	
	Of avarice and of swich cursednesse	
	Is al my preching, for to make hem free	
50	To yiven hir pens,° and namely unto me,	*pennies, money*
	For myn entente is nat° but for to winne,°	*nothing / gain*
	And no thing for correccion of sinne:	
	I rekke° nevere whan that they been beried°	*care / buried*
	Though that hir soules goon a-blakeberied.⁹	
55	For certes, many a predicacioun°	*good sermon*
	Comth ofte time of yvel entencioun:° . . .	*evil intention*

The 'Pardoner's Prologue' is an extract from the Prologue (or introduction) to a tale told by the Pardoner (a character in Chaucer's *The Canterbury Tales*) and shows Chaucer's concern with the abuses of the medieval church. Pardoners were minor members of the clergy who were licensed to travel from place to place, granting people absolution. In the Catholic faith (the only Christian religion in western Europe until the 1520s), this was the practice whereby people confessed their sins, and were given some kind of self-punishment called 'penance' to do to prove genuine contrition or regret. Unfortunately, money sometimes changed hands; the penitent might be urged to make a financial contribution to a holy cause, for example. This, combined with the sale of religious relics and the practice of paying for prayers to be said for the souls of the dead, led to widespread corruption and even extortion by some representatives of the church.

In the figure of the Pardoner, Chaucer launches a stinging attack on these

Notes

⁶ Confess and be forgiven.
⁷ Made her husband a cuckold (i.e., been unfaithful to him).
⁸ Nod my head.
⁹ Even if their souls go black-berrying (i.e., go to hell).

Thus spete° I out my venim under hewe°   *spit / disguise*
Of holinesse, to seeme holy and trewe.
But shortly myn entente° I wol devise:°   *intention / describe*
60 I preche of no thing but for coveitise;[10]
Therfore my theme is yit and evere was
Radix malorum est cupiditas.
     Thus can I preche again° that same vice   *against*
Which that I use, and that is avarice.
65 But though myself be gilty in that sinne,
Yit can I make other folk to twinne°   *turn*
From avarice, and sore to repente —
But that is nat my principal entente:°   *intention*
I preche no thing but for coveitise.
70 Of this matere it oughte ynough suffise.°   *to provide enough*
     Thanne telle I hem ensamples° many oon°   *moral stories / ones*
Of olde stories longe time agoon,
For lewed° peple loven tales olde —   *simple*
Swiche thinges can they wel reporte° and holde.°   *repeat / remember*
75 What, trowe ye° that whiles I may preche,   *do you think*
And winne gold and silver for° I teche,   *because*
That I wol live in poverte wilfully?
Nay, nay, I thoughte° it nevere, trewely,   *considered*
For I wol preche and begge in sondry° landes;   *many*
80 I wol nat do no labour with mine handes,
Ne make baskettes and live therby,[11]
By cause° I wol nat beggen idelly.°   *because / in vain*
I wol none of the Apostles countrefete.°   *imitate*
I wol have moneye, wolle,° cheese, and whete,   *wool*
85 Al were it yiven of the pooreste page,[12]
Or of the pooreste widwe° in a village —   *widow*
Al sholde hir children sterve for famine.[13]
Nay, I wol drinke licour of the vine
And have a joly wenche in every town.

---

practices. What is interesting is that he did so at a time when the church had enormous political, secular, and even legal power, and practised strict censorship. Its critics could even be executed for heresy (the religious equivalent of treason).

If the unfamiliar spelling makes this extract difficult to understand, read it aloud, pronouncing the words as they are spelled; Middle English spelling (in an age of many dialects and no dictionaries) is rather inconsistent, but much more phonetic than Modern English, i.e., words are spelled the way they sound. So 'preche' is 'preach', 'beried' is 'buried', 'trewe' is 'true', and so on. Also check whether any unfamiliar words resemble Afrikaans words you might know; because of the shared Germanic heritage, the meaning is often the same; 'sterve' for example, means to die in both Middle English and Afrikaans (and is obviously related to the English 'starve').

Notes

[10] I preach for no reason except greed.
[11] Nor make a living from weaving or handiwork (basket-making).
[12] Even if it was given by the poorest child.
[13] Even if her children died of hunger.

90	But herkneth,° lordinges, in conclusioun,	*hark*
	Youre liking° is that I shal telle a tale:	*wish*
	Now have I dronke a draughte of corny ale,°	*beer*
	By God, I hope I shal you telle a thing	
	That shal by reson been at youre liking;	
95	For though myself be a ful vicious man,	
	A moral tale yit I you telle can,	
	Which I am wont° to preche for to winne.	*likely*
	Now holde youre pees,° my tale I wol biginne.	*now keep quiet*

Talking points

1   Given the information provided here about the medieval church, what literary and narrative techniques does Chaucer use to 'get away with' his attack on the abuses within the church? In what ways does this extract differ from a pamphlet or letter he might have written making exactly the same criticisms?

2   If you have correctly identified irony* as one of the ways in which Chaucer gets his point across without explicitly attacking the institution, try working through the extract, identifying exactly where irony is located and how it operates. You might like to start by using the extract to draw up a list of all the ways in which a compassionate and sincere member of the clergy might be expected to act, especially towards the poor; next, list all the acts of the Pardoner that contradict these. The irony becomes even richer when we read the tale that follows the Prologue. You might like to consult a modern translation; Neville Coghill's version of *The Canterbury Tales* is a racy and easy read.

3   The Pardoner is an unforgettable study of an utterly corrupt and cynical human being. Some critics argue that he is a supreme hypocrite; others say that he at least recognizes his own depravity. What kind of emotional blackmail does he use? Are there modern equivalents of the Pardoner? During the late 1980s, 'televangelists' in the United States and elsewhere (now largely discredited) often hinted that prayers would be answered only if viewers gave them large donations. Corruption is of course not limited to religious figures; all professions that involve power (whether psychological, spiritual, political, or economic) over other people carry this risk. Growing awareness of the issues of sexual harassment and political corruption has alerted us to some of the dangers involved. How can people like the Pardoner be prevented from abusing their power?

4   You might also like to consider the effect of censorship on culture generally; were there similar levels of irony and satire* in resistance art during South Africa's period of state censorship? Can you think of any examples?

Anonymous (15th century)

Western Wind

Western wind, when will thou blow,
    The small rain down can rain?
Christ, if my love were in my arms
    And I in my bed again!

Talking points

We know nothing about the author, or the circumstances in which
this exquisite short poem was written. Perhaps the speaker is a
traveller or soldier far from home. In medieval Europe, soldiers who
were also poets were fairly common. Here is another particularly
lovely short poem, this time using an image of armour. It was written
in the twelfth century by a Spanish Moor (as the Arabs who
conquered Spain were known), Ab l-Qasim al-Man sh .

Rain Over The River

The wind does the delicate work
of a goldsmith
crimping water into mesh
for a coat of mail.

5   Then comes the rain
and rivets the pieces together
with little nails.

Short poems can be particularly effective and memorable. You might
want to turn to pp. 106–7 for further examples.

Anonymous (15th century)

I Sing of a Maiden

I sing of a maiden
   That is makéles;°   *matchless, mateless*
King of alle kingés
   To her son she ches.°   *chose*
5 He cam also stillé
   Ther His moder was,
As dew in Aprille
   That falleth on the gras.
He cam also stillé
10   To His moderes bowr,°   · *room or garden*
As dew in Aprille
   That falleth on the flowr.

'I Sing of a Maiden' is a lovely example of a lyric.* It uses simple, repetitive language and has a regular and musical rhythm. If you read it aloud, you will find it easy to imagine this poem being sung.

The poem takes the form of a prayer to Mary, the mother of Jesus (during the Middle Ages, the practice of honouring Mary was at its height, and was expressed in a variety of cultural forms – poetry, music, sculpture, tapestry, and even architecture). However, it also closely resembles much of the secular* love poetry typical of this time, which reflected the values of 'courtly love'. This began as an aristocratic game of manners in which women were set up as objects of adoration. The poet-lover (always male), following a strictly observed script, would praise his beloved extravagantly, claim to suffer greatly as a result of his love for her, and beg her to return his love, or at least show some sign of her favour. (Later on, as Renaissance values replaced medieval ones, many poets were to subvert or satirize* the tradition of courtly love; see Wyatt's 'My Lute, Awake!' [pp. 13–14] for a chilling example of how an apparently conventional courtly love poem is turned into a series of threats. Some of Shakespeare's sonnets [see pp. 23–25] also poke fun at the more formal and artificial features of courtly love poetry. See the OUP website for more examples of courtly love poems from medieval and Elizabethan times.)

Nevertheless, as an influence on art, culture, and social relations, the underlying attitudes of courtly love persist to this day. Concepts such as 'courtesy', 'chivalry', and 'gallantry' all stem from it, as do many traditional ideas about the roles and behaviour of women and men. The belief that men are active and direct in romantic affairs, while women are passive and perhaps manipulative, still persists. Many societies continue to accept the custom that men should court and women should be courted.

He cam also stillé
 Ther His moder lay,
15 As dew in Aprille.
 That falleth on the spray.
Moder and maiden
 Was never none but she;
Wel may swich° a lady   *such*
20 Godés moder be.

 You will notice that the simple but effective imagery of spring used in this poem refers, of course, to the northern hemisphere. The coming of spring in England must have seemed like a miracle after the darkness, hunger, and often life-threatening cold of winter, and it is not surprising that its symbolism was often used in religious poetry, usually to refer to the resurrection of Jesus from the dead, or the hope of life after death.

Anonymous (15th century)

The Unquiet Grave

'The wind doth blow today, my love,
    And a few small drops of rain;
I never had but one true-love,
    In cold grave she was lain.

5 'I'll do as much for my true-love
    As any young man may;
I'll sit and mourn all at her grave
    For a twelvemonth, and a day.'

The twelvemonth and a day being up,
10   The dead began to speak:
'Oh who sits weeping on my grave,
    And will not let me sleep?'

'T is I, my love, sits on your grave
    And will not let you sleep;
15 For I crave one kiss of your clay-cold lips,
    And that is all I seek.'

'You crave one kiss of my clay-cold lips,
    But my breath smells earthy strong;
If you have one kiss of my clay-cold lips,
20   Your time will not be long.

'T is down in yonder garden green,
    Love, where we used to walk,
The finest flower that e're° was seen   *ever*
    Is withered to a stalk.

25 'The stalk is withered dry, my love,
    So will our hearts decay;
So make yourself content, my love,
    Till God calls you away.'

'The Unquiet Grave' has many of the features of a ballad;* it tells a story, making use of dialogue, that resembles a folk-tale or fable, and involves a supernatural element. It also has a lilting rhythm and can be sung (the folk-singer Joan Baez has recorded a version); however, it does not have the 'chorus' or set of repeating lines that is typical of most ballads.

Talking points

Once you have read through this poem, turn to Christina Rossetti's 'Song' (p. 88). At first the poems may seem to have only superficial similarities; both deal with the separation (or potential separation) of lovers, one of whom is alive and mourning, the other dead and buried.

However, in 'The Unquiet Grave', it is clear that the conventions of elegy* are being gently mocked. The young lover is determined to behave in an appropriate (but not necessarily sincere) manner, and to do all the right and proper things: 'I'll do as much ... as any young man may'. His dead girlfriend is far more realistic and sensible, and points out that life must go on without her. 'Song', meanwhile, comes across at first as a sweet but rather sentimental and morbid love poem.

If you consider the following questions, you may find that your view of Rossetti's poem changes, and that you also see 'The Unquiet Grave' from a fresh perspective.

1   What do you think of the fact that both the speakers 'from the grave' are women? Is it usual to hear women's voices in love poems? What do you make of the fact that both women are dead or dying? Could the poets perhaps be using the grave as a platform from which women can have a voice or 'answer back'?

2   In real life, the dead cannot respond to the elegies that are said over their graves. Could these poets be making a point about sincerity? In Rossetti's poem, is there a harsher message? While the young woman in 'The Unquiet Grave' has plenty of sensible advice for her melodramatic lover, Rossetti's speaker seems to underline the sheer indifference of the dead to the living, and warns that once she is dead, the whole drama of mourning will be irrelevant to her. If you re-read this poem, do you pick up any darker overtones?

3   Why do you think Rossetti's poem has such a conventional form? You will notice imagery that is so traditional as to be almost clichéd. Could this be deliberate? Is it possible that poets sometimes use conservative and conventional techniques as a form of camouflage? Why would they do this? Under what circumstances are subversive messages likely to be disguised?

4   Look at 'The Unquiet Grave' again. Would you now agree that it makes the same basic point as 'Song'? However, its tone in expressing this message is quite different. Which is the more humorous poem? Which is more subtle?

5   Now compare these two poems with the elegiac poems from Tennyson's *In Memoriam* (see pp. 72–75). It should be clear that there is a significant difference between the two sets of poems. Tennyson's are true elegies; do you agree that the other two are poems that look like elegies, but are actually 'anti-elegy' in intention?

Sir Thomas Wyatt (1503–1542)

My Lute, Awake!

My lute, awake! Perform the last
Labour that thou and I shall waste,
And end that I have now begun;
For when this song is sung and past,
5 My lute, be still, for I have done.

As to be heard where ear is none,
As lead to grave° in marble stone,   *engrave*
My song may pierce her heart as soon.
Should we then sigh or sing or moan?
10 No, no, my lute, for I have done.

The rocks do not so cruelly
Repulse the waves continually
As she my suit° and affection.   *courtship*
So that I am past remedy,°   *curing, saving*
15 Whereby my lute and I have done.

Proud of the spoil° that thou hast got   *prizes, loot*
Of simple hearts, thorough° love's shot;   *through*
By whom, unkind, thou hast them won,
Think not he hath his bow¹ forgot,
20 Although my lute and I have done.

Vengeance shall fall on thy disdain
That makest but game on earnest pain.
Think not alone under the sun
Unquit° to cause thy lovers plain,   *unrequited*
25 Although my lute and I have done.

Thomas Wyatt was educated at Cambridge University and served as a
diplomat in various European countries, including Italy. Here he began
translating the sonnets of the Italian poet and philosopher Petrarch. His
career at the court of King Henry VIII was put at risk when his mistress, Anne
Boleyn, became Henry's queen. This, together with rumours of treason, led to
periods of imprisonment. His style (especially in his love poems) marks a
distinct shift away from the conventions of medieval verse to new,
innovative, and sometimes cynical kinds of poetry.

Notes

¹ Cupid, god of love, who shoots
his victims with a bow and
arrow.

Perchance thee lie withered and old
The winter nights that are so cold,
Plaining° in vain unto the moon.   *complaining*
Thy wishes then dare not be told.
30 Care then who list,° for I have done.   *likes*

And then may chance thee to repent
The time that thou hast lost and spent
To cause thy lovers sigh and swoon.
Then shalt thou know beauty but lent,
35 And wish and want as I have done.

Now cease, my lute. This is the last
Labour that thou and I shall waste,
And ended is that we begun.
Now is this song both sung and past;
40 My lute, be still, for I have done.

Talking points

1   Read the notes on courtly love poetry on p. 9. Do you agree that
    'My Lute, Awake!' looks like a courtly love poem? How does it
    outwardly resemble one?
2   In what ways is it an attack on the conventions of courtly love?
    How would the 'beloved' feel on hearing the speaker's words?
3   Identify the specific threats made in this poem. Does it still come
    across as a love poem? What emotions are being expressed by the
    speaker? Does this help you to track the tone of the poem?
4   Look closely at the structure of the poem. Note how the rhyme
    scheme operates; you will notice that the sound of the word 'done'
    echoes through the entire poem, and that most of the words at
    the end of the lines have one syllable only. How does this support
    the tone and meaning of the poem? You will also notice that the
    last line of each stanza acts as a kind of chorus. How do the small
    changes in each one shift and develop the meaning? Line 5 and
    the last line of the poem are identical; yet the meaning has been
    transformed. How has it changed by the time we read the last
    line?

Whoso List to Hunt

Whoso list° to hunt, I know where is an hind,°   *likes / female deer*
But as for me, helas,° I may no more.   *alas*
The vain travail° hath wearied me so sore,   *struggle*
I am of them that farthest cometh behind.
5   Yet may I by no means my wearied mind
Draw from the deer, but as she fleeth afore
Fainting I follow. I leave off therefore
Since in a net I seek to hold the wind.
Who list her hunt, I put him out of doubt,
10   As well as I may spend his time in vain.
And graven° with diamonds in letters plain   *engraved*
There is written her fair neck round about:
'*Noli me tangere*² for Caesar's° I am,   *the king's*
And wild for to hold though I seem tame.'

The new fascination with Italian literature that was a characteristic of the Renaissance led to a rebirth of the sonnet,* which was to flower in the hands of poets such as Sidney, Spenser, and Shakespeare. (See the OUP website for another example of a 'hunting' sonnet, this time by Spenser.) Wyatt was responsible for bringing the sonnets of the medieval Italian poet and philosopher Petrarch to England, and early attempts to master this new form were mostly adaptations or translations of his poems.

Notes

² 'Touch me not.' The last two lines probably refer to Wyatt's relationship with Anne Boleyn.

Sir Walter Raleigh (*c.* 1552–1618)

The Nymph's Reply to the Shepherd[1]

If all the world and love were young,
And truth in every shepherd's tongue,
These pretty pleasures might me move
To live with thee and be thy love.

5   Time drives the flocks from field to fold,
When rivers rage and rocks grow cold,
And Philomel[2] becometh dumb;
The rest complain of cares to come.

The flowers do fade, and wanton fields
10 To wayward winter reckoning yields;
A honey tongue, a heart of gall,°   *bitter liquid*
Is fancy's spring, but sorrow's fall.

Thy gowns, thy shoes, thy beds of roses,
Thy cap, thy kirtle,° and thy posies   *skirt*
15 Soon break, soon wither, soon forgotten,
In folly ripe, in reason rotten.

Thy belt of straw and ivy buds,
Thy coral clasps and amber studs,[3]
All these in me no means can move
20 To come to thee and be thy love.

The legend of how **Raleigh** laid his cloak in a puddle for Queen Elizabeth I to step on has given him a rather romantic image. In reality, like many Renaissance heroes, he combined sophisticated scholarship with exploits of war and colonization. He made a marriage considered unwise in an era when choice of spouse had significant political implications, and had to undertake daring missions to try to regain favour at court. He was thus one of the first Europeans to sail to both South and North America, carrying out a number of raids. Elizabeth's successor, King James I, nevertheless imprisoned Raleigh on false charges of treason. He was eventually freed to go back to South America in search of gold. The trip was a disaster, and he was executed on his return.

His writing (much of which was done in prison) included his scholarly *History of the World*. Unfortunately, only a few of his witty and intelligent poems survive.

Notes

[1] A response to Marlowe's 'The Passionate Shepherd to His Love' (see p. 19–20).
[2] Classical name given to the nightingale. In legend, Philomel was a princess who was raped. The gods turned her into a bird so that she could escape.
[3] Coral is a hard, reddish substance formed by sea-creatures; amber is gold-coloured fossilized sap. Both are used in making jewellery.

But could youth last and love still breed,
Had joys no date nor age no need,
Then these delights my mind might move
To live with thee and be thy love.

Sir Philip Sidney (1554–1586)

Sonnet: Who Will in Fairest Book of Nature Know

Who will in fairest book of Nature know
How virtue may best lodged in beauty be,
Let him but learn of love to read in thee,
Stella, those fair lines which true goodness show.
5 There shall he find all vices' overthrow,
Not by rude force, but sweetest sovereignty
Of reason, from whose light those night birds[1] fly,
That inward sun in thine eyes shineth so.
And, not content to be perfection's heir
10 Thyself, dost strive all minds that way to move,
Who mark° in thee what is in thee most fair.   *notice*
So while thy beauty draws the heart to love,
    As fast thy virtue bends that love to good.
    'But ah,' Desire still cries, 'give me some food.'

Sidney belonged to a generation of Renaissance scholar-soldiers who prided themselves on being equally skilled with both the pen and sword. Born into a noble and literary family, he was a successful diplomat who travelled and studied in Europe. His writings included the critical work *Defence of Poesy*, as well as poetry that, while experimenting with classical forms, established a unique English identity that was to influence both Shakespeare and Spenser. He died young after being wounded in battle, and is supposed to have gallantly handed his water bottle to a dying man as he was carried off the field. His sister Mary, Countess of Pembroke, herself a gifted writer, translator, and patron of the arts, completed and published his unfinished works, including his famous *Arcadia*.

'Who Will in Fairest Book of Nature Know' is taken from the sonnet sequence *Astrophel and Stella* ('star-lover' and 'star'), supposedly inspired by Sidney's love for a woman who married someone else. It deals with an age-old problem for lovers: the tension between chaste love and lust. This theme was inventively explored by many later poets, especially the generation that followed on immediately after the sixteenth century. You might like to read Andrew Marvell's 'To His Coy Mistress' (see pp. 40–41), which takes the complaint in Sidney's sonnet and gives it a marvellous twist. How many other poems can you find in this anthology that deal with this topic?

Notes

[1] Symbols of wickedness.

Christopher Marlowe (1564–1593)

The Passionate Shepherd to His Love[1]

Come live with me and be my love,
And we will all the pleasures prove
That valleys, groves, hills and fields,
Woods, or steepy mountain yields.

5   And we will sit upon the rocks,
Seeing the shepherds feed their flocks
By shallow rivers, to whose falls
Melodious birds sing madrigals.°   *songs*

And I will make thee beds of roses
10 And a thousand fragrant posies;
A cap of flowers, and a kirtle°   *skirt*
Embroidered all with leaves of myrtle;°   *evergreen shrub*

A gown made of the finest wool
Which from our pretty lambs we pull;
15 Fair linèd slippers for the cold,
With buckles of the purest gold;

Marlowe was educated at Cambridge University and was widely admired for his powerful dramatic tragedies*, which strongly influenced Shakespeare's plays. His life was surrounded by intrigue of the shadier kind; it is likely that he was involved in spying and fraud. He was also mixed up in a street fight in which a man died. He himself was killed (at the age of twenty-nine) in suspicious circumstances, shortly before he was due to be tried on mysterious charges.

'The Passionate Shepherd to His Love' is an excellent example of the classical pastoral* tradition revived by Sidney and other Renaissance poets. Pastoral poetry was based on an extremely artificial and idealistic view of rural life, in which shepherds, shepherdesses, and their unrealistically co-operative flocks played together against a backdrop of eternal spring (as Raleigh [pp. 16–17] suggests, the nitty-gritty of winter mud or sheep-shearing are never shown). The poet was concerned with the creation of beauty rather than with realism.

Notes

[1] This poem inspired a response by Sir Walter Raleigh (see pp. 16–17). Other poets who wrote humorous replies were John Donne and, more recently, Cecil Day-Lewis (father of the actor Daniel Day-Lewis).

A belt of straw and ivy buds,
With coral clasps and amber studs:[2]
And if these pleasures may thee move,
20   Come live with me and be my love.

The shepherds' swains° shall dance and sing   *lovers*
For thy delight each May morning:
If these delights thy mind may move,
Then live with me and be my love.

Talking points

Although this poem can stand alone (and lends itself very well to
close analysis), it is probably more enjoyable when compared with
Raleigh's 'The Nymph's Reply to the Shepherd' (see pp. 16–17).
Perhaps your class or study group could split into two groups, with
each discussing and analysing one poem. After twenty minutes or so,
each group could then report back to the other to 'combine' the
debate, and to see how the conclusions reached about one poem
enrich the understanding of the other. You might also like to try to
find the other 'replies' to this poem (by John Donne and Cecil
Day-Lewis) in a library or on the Internet.

Notes

[2] See footnote 3, p. 16.

Chidiock Tichborne (*c.* 1568–1586)

Tichborne's Elegy

Elegy Written with His Own Hand in the Tower before His Execution

My prime of youth is but a frost of cares,
　My feast of joy is but a dish of pain,
My crop of corn is but a field of tares,°　　　　　　　　　　　　　　*weeds*
　And all my good is but vain hope of gain;
5　The day is past, and yet I saw no sun,
And now I live, and now my life is done.

My tale was heard, and yet it was not told,
　My fruit is fall'n, and yet my leaves are green,
My youth is spent, and yet I am not old,
10　I saw the world, and yet I was not seen;
My thread is cut, and yet it is not spun,
And now I live, and now my life is done.

I sought my death, and found it in my womb,
　I looked for life, and saw it was a shade,
15　I trod the earth, and knew it was my tomb,
　And now I die, and now I was but made;
My glass° is full, and now my glass is run,　　　　　　　　　　　　*hourglass*
And now I live, and now my life is done.

We know almost nothing about **Tichborne** other than the fact that he was Catholic, and became involved in a plot to assassinate the Protestant queen Elizabeth I. He was arrested and sentenced to a gruesome death along with the other conspirators.

The only poem that Tichborne is known for is this elegy* he wrote for himself, the night before his execution. Although poetry is not necessarily autobiographical, the force of this poem comes from the honesty with which the poet writes about his own desperate situation. It has an impact that is quite different from any of the other elegies in this anthology (see Jonson's two poems [p. 31]; Tennyson's *In Memoriam* poems [pp. 72–75]; Jack Cope and Sally Bryer's poems in memory of Ingrid Jonker [pp. 140 and 212]; and Jennifer Davids' 'For Albert Luthuli (21.7.67)' [discussed on p. xxxvii]). This is no doubt because this elegy was written by the doomed man himself. He was only eighteen at the time; one critic has noted that there is a line of poetry for each year of his life.

　In terms of South Africa's recent history, Tichborne would have been a 'political prisoner' facing the death penalty for taking part in an 'armed struggle' or 'revolutionary violence'. Can you find any poems, speeches, letters, or stories by South Africans in similar situations?

William Shakespeare (1564–1616)

Song: Full Fathom Five Thy Father Lies

Full fathom[1] five thy father lies;
   Of his bones are coral[2] made;
Those are pearls that were his eyes:
   Nothing of him that doth fade,
5   But doth suffer a sea-change
Into something rich and strange.
Sea-nymphs hourly ring his knell:
       Ding-dong.
Hark! now I hear them — Ding-dong, bell.

Little is known about **Shakespeare's** life. He did not receive much formal education, married and had three children, and joined a theatrical company in London in the 1590s. He wrote, directed, and acted in his own plays (over thirty-five in all), which included histories, comedies*, tragedies,* and romances.* Because they were produced directly for the stage, his plays were often not published until long after they had been performed; the sometimes uncertain status of their scripts remains a subject of lively debate.

Shakespeare was recognized while he lived as the best dramatist of his age. His memorable characters, unrivalled skill with language, and ability to entertain all levels of society mark him as the most famous playwright in the English language. His output of poetry was also considerable, and his sonnets are ranked among the finest examples of their kind. Ben Jonson described him (prophetically) as 'not of our age, but of all time'.

In the play *The Tempest*, the spirit Ariel sings the song '**Full Fathom Five Thy Father Lies**' to a prince who believes that his father has been drowned at sea. Unknown to the prince, his father has survived. Critics argue about whether the words are cruel or strangely comforting, given the beauty of the images used.

The Tempest is itself a particularly interesting play, because its story (of exiled nobles who land on an island and take it over, enslaving the original inhabitants) lends itself to lively post-colonial* analysis. The poem 'Miranda' on p. 184, also inspired by the play, is a good example of this kind of commentary.

Notes

[1] Measurement used to judge depth of water.
[2] See footnote 3, p. 16.

Sonnet: Let Me Not to the Marriage of True Minds

Let me not to the marriage of true minds
Admit impediments. Love is not love
Which alters when it alteration finds,
Or bends with the remover to remove.
5 O, no! it is an ever-fixèd mark
That looks on tempests and is never shaken;
It is the star to every wand'ring bark,°   *ship*
Whose worth's unknown, although his height be taken.[3]
Love's not Time's fool, though rosy lips and cheeks
10 Within his bending sickle's[4] compass come;
Love alters not with his brief hours and weeks,
But bears it out even to the edge of doom.
    If this be error and upon me proved,
    I never writ, nor no man ever loved.

'Let Me Not to the Marriage of True Minds' was written at a time of renewed exploration by sea and increasingly sophisticated navigation. The image of the ship and star in lines 7 and 8 is therefore significant. Without modern radar, sixteenth-century sailors relied heavily on the position of stars and constellations to guide them. (Find out if any of your friends know how to work out the position of the South Pole by looking at the stars, or check in an encyclopaedia or on the Internet. If you can imagine being on a boat in the middle of the ocean without any landmarks to indicate where you are, or what direction you are going, you can appreciate the security that stars offer sailors!)

The reference to Time in lines 9 and 10 draws on the common medieval and Renaissance personification of both death and time as a reaper who uses his sickle to harvest souls (or, in the case of time, youth) rather than crops. This image of the 'grim reaper' has become popular in recent fantasy writing, including the humorous books by Terry Pratchett.

Notes

[3] Reference to the measurements of a ship, in particular the height of the mast.

[4] Curved knife used for harvesting or cutting crops.

Sonnet: Shall I Compare Thee to a Summer's Day?

Shall I compare thee to a summer's day?
Thou art more lovely and more temperate:°   *moderate*
Rough winds do shake the darling buds of May,
And summer's lease hath all too short a date;
5   Sometime too hot the eye of heaven shines,
And often is his gold complexion dimmed;
And every fair from fair sometime declines,
By chance or nature's changing course untrimmed:
But thy eternal summer shall not fade
10   Nor lose possession of that fair thou ow'st;°   *own*
Nor shall Death brag thou wand'rest in his shade,
When in eternal lines to time thou grow'st;
     So long as men can breathe or eyes can see,
     So long lives this, and this gives life to thee.

Both 'Shall I Compare Thee to a Summer's Day' and 'My Mistress' Eyes
Are Nothing Like the Sun' undermine the Petrarchan tradition in which
extravagant and unrealistic comparisons were made between a woman's
appearance and a list of beautiful objects; for example, eyes were like
'sapphires', teeth were like 'pearls', hair was 'spun gold'; necks were 'ivory

Sonnet: My Mistress' Eyes Are Nothing Like the Sun

My mistress' eyes are nothing like the sun;
Coral[5] is far more red than her lips' red;
If snow be white, why then her breasts are dun;°   *yellowish-brown*
If hairs be wires, black wires grow on her head.
5   I have seen roses damasked,° red and white,   *mixed, patterned*
But no such roses see I in her cheeks;
And in some perfumes is there more delight
Than in the breath that from my mistress reeks.
I love to hear her speak, yet well I know
10 That music hath a far more pleasing sound;
I grant I never saw a goddess go;
My mistress, when she walks, treads on the ground.
    And yet, by heaven, I think my love as rare
    As any she belied° with false compare.°   *lied about / comparisons*

Talking points

1 In 'My Mistress' Eyes', what word in the first line alerts us to the fact that this poem is not going to follow the conventional formula?

2 A careful reading of this sonnet gives two very different pictures: one of the ideal Petrarchan woman, and one of Shakespeare's lover. Work through the poem, sorting out their different sets of characteristics. How does the poet feel about the Petrarchan criteria for beauty in women? Do these criteria still exist? Where do we find them being promoted? How do you feel about them? Is there still a difference in value between the descriptions 'blonde' and 'brunette'? What about 'fat' and 'thin'? Why do you think this is so? Do similar criteria exist for men? Are there racial implications as well?

3 At times, the poet's picture of his girlfriend seems quite cruel, even if funny. How do we know that this is a love poem? In sonnets, the last two lines usually sum up the message underlying the whole poem. What happens to this poem if we leave the last couplet out?

towers', and so on. The first sonnet simply takes one comparison and turns its failure to adequately describe the beloved into a serious and serene love poem. The second is far more realistic, irreverent, and humorous. However, they both use the same logical reasoning.

Notes

[5] See footnote 3, p. 16.

John Donne (1572–1631)

The Sun Rising

Busy old fool, unruly sun,
Why dost thou thus,
Through windows and through curtains, call on us?
Must to thy motions lovers' seasons run?
5   Saucy pedantic wretch, go chide
Late schoolboys, and sour prentices,°   *apprentices*
Go tell court-huntsmen that the King will ride,
Call country ants to harvest offices;
Love, all alike, no season knows, nor clime,°   *climate*
10 Nor hours, days, months, which are the rags of time.

Thy beams, so reverend and strong
Why shouldst thou think?
I could eclipse and cloud them with a wink,
But that I would not lose her sight so long:
15   If her eyes have not blinded thine,
Look, and tomorrow late, tell me,
Whether both th' Indias of spice and mine[1]
Be where thou left'st them, or lie here with me.
Ask for those kings whom thou saw'st yesterday,
20 And thou shalt hear, All here in one bed lay.

She's all states, and all princes, I,
Nothing else is.
Princes do but play us; compared to this,
All honour's mimic, all wealth alchemy.[2]

John Donne (pronounced Dun) studied at Oxford University but was not allowed to graduate because he came from a Catholic family. Ambitious and brilliant, he trained as a lawyer and established contacts in powerful circles. He was much in demand socially, and had many affairs. On the brink of a prestigious career as a Member of Parliament, he fell deeply in love, and married secretly, a politically unpopular step that forced him to retire from public life. Later, he made a sincere conversion to the Anglican faith, and became a celebrated preacher. He was eventually made Dean of St Paul's, the biggest church in London.

He was one of the first great metaphysical* poets, and his poems are typically witty and rich in their inventive use of comparisons. He is especially known for his passionate expression of both secular and sacred love.

Notes

[1] Reference not just to India, but also South-east Asia, which was seen as a mysterious and exotic source of spices, jewels, and precious metals.
[2] The medieval art, part chemistry, part magic, of trying to create gold; widely discredited by Donne's time.

25　　Thou, sun, art half as happy as we,
　　　　In that the world's contracted thus;
　　Thine age asks ease, and since thy duties be
　　To warm the world, that's done in warming us.
　　Shine here to us, and thou art everywhere;
30　This bed thy centre is, these walls, thy sphere.

Talking points

1　In 'The Sun Rising', the title and the first line are fairly unusual,
　　given that this is a love poem. What tone is established in the
　　first line? Why is it so surprising? Does it make more sense once
　　you have read through the entire poem?
2　Throughout the poem, the speaker sets himself and his lover
　　apart from other inhabitants of the world. What tone is used to
　　refer to others 'out there', and who exactly are these people?
　　Could this be related to Donne's own experience of social and
　　political downfall after he fell in love and married? Even if the
　　answer can only be speculative, do you agree that the poem's
　　personal tone makes it especially moving?
3　As is typical of metaphysical poetry, the poet establishes an
　　image, and then transforms it, or 'stretches' it to even more
　　inventive limits. In this poem, the two lovers are first set apart
　　from the world; they then become the world itself, effectively
　　replacing the globe. Trace the exact development of these images
　　throughout the poem; where does the change take place?
4　Look closely at how the poet structures his lines and syntax. For
　　example, read the first two lines of the third stanza, and check
　　the positioning of the pronouns as well as the nouns to which
　　they are linked. How does this emphasize the message that the
　　first-person speaker and his lover mean the world to each other?

Donne's poems are full of references to the new inventions and sciences of his age, including an awareness of the newly explored globe. In 'The Sun Rising', he makes use of the belief that the sun revolved around the earth (although astronomers were discovering for the first time that it happened the other way round) as the central metaphor or 'conceit' of this poem. A 'conceit' is a particular kind of image used by the metaphysical poets, and refers to a comparison that is striking because it is original or unusual, rather than apt or accurate.

Holy Sonnet: Batter My Heart, Three-Personed God[3]

Batter my heart, three-personed God; for You
As yet but knock, breathe, shine, and seek to mend;
That I may rise, and stand, o'erthrow me, and bend
Your force, to break, blow, burn, and make me new.
5   I, like an usurped° town, to another due,   *taken over*
Labour to admit You, but O, to no end;
Reason, your viceroy° in me, me should defend,   *surrogate ruler*
But is captivated, and proves weak or untrue.
Yet dearly I love You, and would be loved fain,°   *gladly*
10 But am betrothed° unto Your enemy.[4]   *married*
Divorce me, untie, or break that knot again,
Take me to You, imprison me, for I,
Except You enthrall° me, never shall be free,   *captivate*
Nor ever chaste, except You ravish me.

To His Mistress Going to Bed

Come, madam, come, all rest my powers defy,
Until I labour, I in labour lie.
The foe oft-times, having the foe in sight,
Is tired with standing though they never fight.
5   Off with that girdle, like heaven's zone[5] glistering,
But a far fairer world encompassing.
Unpin that spangled breastplate which you wear,
That the eyes of busy fools may be stopped there.
Unlace yourself, for that harmonious chime
10 Tells me from you that now 'tis your bed time.
Off with that happy busk,° which I envy,   *corset, undergarment*
That still can be, and still can stand so nigh.
Your gown's going off such beauteous state reveals,
As when from flowry meads° the hill's shadow steals.   *meadows*

Notes

[3] Reference to the Christian belief in the Trinity.
[4] Sin or Satan.
[5] Probably the Milky Way (a broad, dense band of stars).

15 Off with that wiry coronet° and show   *headdress*
The hairy diadem° which on you doth grow: *crown (of hair)*
Off with those shoes, and then safely tread
In this love's hallowed temple, this soft bed.
In such white robes heaven's angels used to be
20 Received by men; thou, Angel, bring'st with thee
A heaven like Mahomet's° Paradise; and though   *Mohammed's*
Ill spirits walk in white, we easily know
By this these angels from an evil sprite:°   *spirit*
Those set our hairs, but these our flesh upright.
25   License my roving hands, and let them go
Behind, before, between, above, below.
O my America! my new found land,
My kingdom, safeliest when with one man manned,
My mine of precious stones, my empery°,   *empire*
30 How blest am I in this discovering thee!
To enter in these bonds is to be free;
Then where my hand is set, my seal shall be.
    Full nakedness, all joys are due to thee.
As souls unbodied, bodies unclothed must be
35 To taste whole joys.⁶ Gems which you women use
Are like Atalanta's balls,⁷ cast in men's views,
That when a fool's eye lighteth on a gem,
His earthly soul may covet theirs, not them.
Like pictures, or like books' gay coverings made
40 For laymen, are all women thus arrayed;
Themselves are mystic books, which only we
(Whom their imputed grace will dignify)
Must see revealed. Then, since I may know,
As liberally as to a midwife, show
45 Thyself: cast all, yea, this white linen hence,
Here is no penance, much less innocence.⁸
    To teach thee, I am naked first; why than,°   *then*
What needst thou have more covering than a man?

Notes

6   Donne suggests that nudity is, literally, heavenly.
7   Goddess, who in classical legend was distracted in an important race by golden apples dropped in her path.
8   Wearing white usually signified innocence or repentance.

Talking points

All three poems given here demonstrate Donne's ability to write love poems that differ dramatically in style, tone, and content. 'Batter My Heart, Three-Personed God' uses sexual imagery to convey religious fervour or passion, while 'To His Mistress Going to Bed' is a frankly erotic and funny seduction poem, completely different once again from 'The Sun Rising'. Yet Donne uses a similar set of images in both 'Batter My Heart' and 'To His Mistress'; can you identify these?

If you have difficulty in pinning down exactly what is meant by tone, a comparison of all three poems might be a useful way of seeing how tone can differ dramatically in works that might seem to deal with similar topics, and even use the same images.

Ben Jonson (1572–1637)

On My First Daughter

Here lies, to each her parents' ruth,°   *sorrow, pity*
Mary, the daughter of their youth;
Yet, all heaven's gifts being heaven's due,
It makes the father less to rue.
5   At six months' end she parted hence
With safety of her innocence;
Whose soul heaven's Queen (whose name she bears),
In comfort of her mother's tears,
Hath placed amongst her virgin train;°   *company*
10 Where, while that severed doth remain,
This grave partakes the fleshly birth;[1]
Which cover lightly, gentle earth.

On My First Son

Farewell, thou child of my right hand,[2] and joy;
    My sin was too much hope of thee, loved boy.
Seven years thou wert lent to me, and I thee pay,
    Exacted by thy fate, on the just day.
5   Oh, could I lose all father now! For why
    Will man lament the state he should envy?
To have so soon 'scaped world's and flesh's rage,
    And, if no other misery, yet age?
Rest in soft peace, and, asked, say here doth lie
10   Ben Jonson his best piece of poetry;
For whose sake, henceforth, all his vows be such,
    As what he loves may never like too much.[3]

Jonson's life was a colourful one. He was well educated, distinguished himself as a soldier, and then joined a company of travelling entertainers both as an actor and a writer. His part in a slanderous play landed him in jail, and he narrowly avoided execution after killing a fellow actor in a duel. Shakespeare acted in his first play, and his career blossomed until another defamatory play got him into trouble with King James I. However, the king eventually granted him a pension, which made him the first Poet Laureate (someone officially employed by the court or state to write poetry). His friends included Donne and Shakespeare, as well as several younger poets who called themselves the 'sons' or 'tribe of Ben'. His vigorous poetry and plays, together with his forceful personality, made him one of the most important literary figures of his time.

Notes

1   Reference to the belief that the body would eventually be physically resurrected ('fleshly birth') from the grave and reunited with the soul.
2   This is the literal meaning of the name 'Benjamin', shared by father and son.
3   The poet seems to be hoping that he will never love selfishly.

Talking points

In an age of high infant mortality, it was certainly not unusual to lose more than one child. Centuries later, this is unfortunately still something thousands of southern African families suffer, and with the arrival of the HIV/Aids pandemic, the situation is likely to grow even more serious.

You might like to compare, first of all, the poems that Jonson wrote on the deaths of his daughter and son. Try to establish what similarities there are, as well as what differences. What lies behind these differences?

Now turn to de Kok's 'Small Passing' (pp. 221–3) and read it closely. At first it may seem very different to Jonson's poems; how do you think the gender of the poets shapes these differences? Can you find any similarities? Are there aspects of the tragedy of losing a child that transcend gender and historical period, and can you identify these in the poems? Interestingly enough, all three poems deal with the moral implications of mourning, and whether this is selfish or not. What different conclusions do Jonson and de Kok reach? Can you identify with both positions?

You might also want to look at the other elegies in this book (listed on p. 21) and look at how these (which mourn the loss of adults) compare with the ones discussed here, which describe the loss of babies or small children.

Robert Herrick (1591–1674)

To the Virgins, to Make Much of Time

Gather ye rosebuds while ye may,
    Old time is still a-flying;
And this same flower that smiles today
    Tomorrow will be dying.

5   The glorious lamp of heaven, the sun,
    The higher he's a-getting,
The sooner will his race be run,
    And nearer he's to setting.

That age is best which is the first,
10   When youth and blood are warmer;
But being spent, the worse, and worst
    Times still succeed the former.

Then be not coy, but use your time,
    And while ye may, go marry:
15   For having lost but once your prime,
    You may for ever tarry.°   *wait*

Initially an apprentice goldsmith, **Herrick** studied at Cambridge University and moved in literary circles in London, where he came under the influence of Ben Jonson. He was eventually ordained as a country priest, but remained unconventional – he kept a pet pig and regularly escaped to London, where he had a mistress twenty-seven years his junior. He is counted as one of the 'Cavalier' poets – a group of poets loyal to the monarchy during and after the Civil War (see the entries under Milton and Marvell, pp. 37 and 40, for more details). They specialized in elegant lyrics* and gallant love poems. Herrick in particular was known for secular* love lyrics that emphasized the sweetness and shortness of life.

'To the Virgins to Make Much of Time' is a famous example of a *carpe diem* poem. This Latin phrase, first used by the Roman poet Horace, literally means 'seize the day', and urges that pleasure should never be postponed, given the shortness of life. This theme was skilfully developed by several seventeenth-century poets; see, for example, Marvell's 'To His Coy Mistress' (pp. 40–1). The *carpe diem* philosophy was popularized in the Hollywood film *Dead Poets' Society*.

George Herbert (1593–1633)

Virtue

Sweet day, so cool, so calm, so bright,
The bridal° of the earth and sky: *marriage, union*
The dew shall weep thy fall tonight,
          For thou must die.

5   Sweet rose, whose hue, angry° and brave,°   *red / bright*
Bids the rash gazer wipe his eye:
Thy root is ever in its grave,
          And thou must die.

Sweet spring, full of sweet days and roses,
10 A box where sweets° compacted lie: *perfumes*
My music shows ye have your closes,[1]
          And all must die.

Only a sweet and virtuous soul,
Like seasoned timber, never gives;
15 But though the whole world turn to coal,[2]
          Then chiefly lives.

George Herbert was born into a prominent family and performed brilliantly at Cambridge, becoming public orator of the university. At first he had political ambitions, and with his connections, a career at court seemed certain. However, he experienced a deep religious calling, and was ordained as a priest in the Anglican church. He performed his spiritual duties with great humility and sincerity, and wrote what is widely recognized as some of the finest devotional* poetry in the English language.

Notes
[1] Musical term for conclusions.
[2] Reference to the end of the world in flames, as prophesied in the Bible.

The Flower

How fresh, oh Lord, how sweet and clean
Are thy returns! even as the flowers in spring;
   To which, besides their own demean,°   *demeanour*
The late-past frosts tributes of pleasure bring.
        Grief melts away
        Like snow in May,
   As if there were no such cold thing.

Who would have thought my shrivelled heart
Could have recovered greenness? It was gone
   Quite underground; as flowers depart
To see their mother-root, when they have blown°   *bloomed*
        Where they together
        All the hard weather,
   Dead to the world, keep house unknown.

These are thy wonders, Lord of power,
Killing and quickening,° bringing down to hell·   *bringing to life*
   And up to heaven in an hour;
Making a chiming of a passing-bell°   *bell announcing death*
        We say amiss
        This or that is:
   Thy word is all, if we could spell.

Oh that I once past changing were,
Fast in thy Paradise, where no flower can wither!
   Many a spring I shoot up fair,
Offering° at heaven, growing and groaning thither;   *aiming*
        Nor doth my flower
        Want a spring shower,
   My sins and I joining together.

But while I grow in a straight line,
Still upwards bent, as if heaven were mine own,
   Thy anger comes, and I decline:
What frost to that? what pole is not the zone
        Where all things burn,
        When thou dost turn,
   And the least frown of thine is shown?

And now in age I bud again,
After so many deaths I live and write;
   I once more smell the dew and rain,
And relish versing. Oh, my only light,
40   It cannot be
        That I am he
On whom thy tempests fell all night.

These are thy wonders, Lord of love,
To make us see we are but flowers that glide;
45   Which when we once can find and prove,
Thou hast a garden for us where to bide;
        Who would be more,
        Swelling through store,°   *wealth*
Forfeit their Paradise by their pride.

Talking points

You might find it interesting to compare 'The Flower' with Hopkins'
'No Worst, There Is None' (p. 93). Both deal with depression and
spiritual alienation, but while Hopkins' poem seems to spring from
the depths of misery (psychiatrists agree it is a textbook account of
the symptoms of clinical depression), Herbert's speaks of surviving
the ordeal and experiencing a sense of rebirth. Herbert's skill lies in
his ability to use ordinary and natural imagery to describe a common
human experience in fresh and accessible terms, in sharp contrast to
the vivid, nightmarish images Hopkins packs into his tortured poem.
Yet both describe similar emotional conditions.

   Both poems lend themselves very well to close critical analysis; here
again, you might like to split into two groups, each discussing and
analysing one poem, then getting together to report back. You will
discover that both poems are extremely rich in possible meanings (the
apparent simplicity of the Herbert poem is deceptive), and should
provoke some interesting debates. Although both speakers explore
their relationships with God in explicitly Christian terms, the power
of both poems is that the emotional territory they chart is familiar to
members of all faith traditions, as well as agnostics.

John Milton (1608–1674)

On His Blindness

When I consider how my light is spent,°   *wasted*
    Ere half my days, in this dark world and wide,
    And that one talent which is death to hide[1]
    Lodged with me useless, though my soul more bent
5 To serve therewith my Maker, and present
    My true account, lest He returning chide;
    'Doth God exact day-labour, light denied?'
    I fondly° ask. But Patience, to prevent   *foolishly*
That murmur, soon replies, 'God doth not need
10   Either man's work or his own gifts. Who best
    Bear his mild yoke, they serve him best. His state
Is kingly: thousands at his bidding speed
    And post° o'er land and ocean without rest;   *travel*
    They also serve who only stand and wait.'

Milton was educated at Cambridge University, and studied further to prepare himself for a career either as a poet or a priest. He soon gained a reputation as a writer of vivid imagination and skill. He travelled in Europe, meeting intellectuals and scientists such as Galileo, before returning to find England in a state of civil war between supporters of the monarchy and Cromwell's parliamentarians (see Introductory notes, p. xviii). Milton was an ardent supporter of the new Puritan regime under Cromwell, and worked hard publishing pamphlets and tracts in favour of the new government, even though this contributed to his going blind. After the restoration of the monarchy, he returned to writing poetry and produced his most famous work, the monumental *Paradise Lost*, in which he set out to 'justify the ways of God to man'. His use of blank verse (poetry with no end-rhymes, previously found only in drama) was to influence the course of English poetry; he is also recognized for his contribution to the art of sonnet-writing.

Notes

[1] Reference to the parable of the talents told by Jesus (Matthew 25:14–30). This warns that it is spiritually essential to make use of the gifts granted to one.

Anne Bradstreet (*c.* 1612–1672)

The Author to Her Book

Thou ill-formed offspring of my feeble brain,
Who after birth didst by my side remain,
Till snatched from thence by friends, less wise than true,
Who thee abroad exposed to public view,
5   Made thee in rags,[1] halting° to th' press to trudge,   *limping, faltering*
Where errors were not lessened (all may judge).
At thy return my blushing was not small,
My rambling brat (in print) should mother call;
I cast thee by as one unfit for light,
10   Thy visage was so irksome in my sight;
Yet being mine own, at length affection would
Thy blemishes amend, if so I could:
I washed thy face, but more defects I saw,
And rubbing off a spot still made a flaw.
15   I stretched thy joints to make thee even feet,[2]
Yet still thou run'st more hobbling than is meet;
In better dress to trim thee was my mind,
But nought save homespun cloth i' th' house I find.
In this array 'mongst vulgars may'st thou roam;
20   In critic's hands beware thou dost not come,
And take thy way where yet thou are not known;
If for thy father asked, say thou hadst none;
And for thy mother, she alas is poor,
Which caused her thus to send thee out of door.

Bradstreet was born in England, but emigrated to the new colony of
Massachusetts in North America at the age of eighteen, together with her
father (who became governor of the colony) and her husband. Her family
were among the first Puritan settlers who left for the New World to escape
religious repression at home. She had eight children, and suffered from ill
health throughout her life. A relative took her poetry to London to be
published; as a result, she was recognized as the first poet of the North
American colonies.

Notes

1 Paper used to be made out of cloth and rags.
2 This pun refers to the metre of poetry; feet are units made up of one stressed (or 'strong') syllable together with one or more unstressed syllables.

Talking points

1   Although today it is not so unusual for a writer to compare a book with a baby, this poem is probably one of the first to have done so. The author develops and elaborates on this central comparison in a way that is characteristic of the metaphysical* poets; can you trace this development? (You might like to read the notes and Talking points for Donne's 'The Sun Rising' [pp. 26–27] first.)

2   As you will have noticed, the poet draws on her practical experience as a parent to create effective imagery. What images are specifically maternal? The speaker explicitly identifies herself as a woman; why is she so 'upfront' about her gender?

3   The speaker struggles with two conflicting emotions throughout the poem; what are they? At times, one dominates, then the other overcomes it; can you trace these swings in her feelings? How do they contribute to the tone of the poem?

4   The poet makes clever use of words that have a double meaning, especially when applied separately to a book and a child; can you identify some of these words?

5   What final motive does the speaker give for publication? How does this change the conventional picture of the poet who writes only 'when inspiration strikes'? Can writing be 'hard labour'?

Andrew Marvell (1621–1678)

To His Coy Mistress

Had we but world enough, and time,
This coyness, Lady, were no crime.
We would sit down, and think which way
To walk, and pass our long love's day.
5   Thou by the Indian Ganges'¹ side
Shouldst rubies find: I by the tide
Of Humber² would complain. I would
Love you ten years before the Flood;³
And you should, if you please, refuse
10   Till the conversion of the Jews.⁴
My vegetable° love should grow   *plant-like*
Vaster than empires, and more slow;
An hundred years should go to praise
Thine eyes, and on thy forehead gaze;
15   Two hundred to adore each breast,
But thirty thousand to the rest.
An age at least to every part,
And the last age should show your heart.
For, Lady, you deserve this state,°   *dignity*
20   Nor would I love at lower rate.
        But at my back I always hear
Time's wingéd chariot hurrying near;
And yonder all before us lie
Deserts of vast eternity.
25   Thy beauty shall no more be found;
Nor, in thy marble vault, shall sound
My echoing song: then worms shall try
That long-preserved virginity:
And your quaint⁵ honour turn to dust,
30   And into ashes all my lust:
The grave's a fine and private place,
But none, I think, do there embrace.

One of the last great metaphysical* poets, **Marvell** graduated from
Cambridge University and travelled in Europe during the English Civil War. On
returning, he moved in literary circles among both parliamentarians and those
loyal to the monarchy. He was friends with Milton, and the two supported
each other through unsettling political changes. Marvell became the
unofficial laureate to the Puritan leader Cromwell, who ruled England
temporarily after the war. During his lifetime, he had a reputation as a sharp
satirist; today, he is best remembered for his lyrical poems.

Notes

¹ Holy river in the north of India.
² River beside Hull, Marvell's home
  town in the north of England.
³ The great flood described in the
  Old Testament.
⁴ This conversion (to Christianity)
  would supposedly be a sign that
  the world was ending.

Now therefore, while the youthful hue
Sits on thy skin like morning glew,°   *glow, warmth*
35 And while thy willing soul transpires°   *breathes*
At every pore with instant fires,
Now let us sport us while we may;
And now, like amorous birds of prey,
Rather at once our time devour,
40 Than languish in his slow-chapped[6] power.
Let us roll all our strength, and all
Our sweetness, up into one ball:
And tear our pleasures with rough strife
Thorough° the iron gates of life: *through*
45 Thus, though we cannot make our sun
Stand still, yet we will make him run.

Talking points

1 How exactly does the poet use (or misuse) logic in this poem? Try to paraphrase Marvell's line of argument into a short paragraph.
2 You will notice that the poem is divided into three parts. Find where these breaks occur, and note at what stage of the argument they take place. How does the rhythm and pace of the poem change from section to section? (You will need to read the poem aloud at this point.) How do these changes reinforce the speaker's reasoning?
3 Now examine the images used in each section. What atmosphere and tone do they create, and how does this alter from section to section? What effect does the pace and tone of the last section have, coming after the first two?

'To His Coy Mistess' is one of the best-known *carpe diem* poems in the English language (you might like to compare it with Herrick's 'To the Virgins, to Make Much of Time', p. 33). It is also an excellent example of the metaphysical delight in manipulating logic. For another example of a seduction poem that shamelessly twists logical argument, you might like to try to find Donne's 'The Flea' in a library or on the Internet.

Notes

5 A bawdy pun; since Chaucer's time, 'quaint' had been affectionate slang for female genitals (today degraded to the deeply offensive 'cunt').
6 Chaps are jaws; time is presented as slowly consuming human beings.

Lady Mary Chudleigh (1656–1710)

To the Ladies

Wife and servant are the same,
But only differ in the name:
For when that fatal knot is tied,
Which nothing, nothing can divide,
5   When she the word *Obey* has said,
And man by law supreme has made,
Then all that's kind is laid aside,
And nothing left but state° and pride.   *formality, display*
Fierce as an eastern prince he grows,
10 And all his innate rigour shows:
Then but to look, to laugh, or speak,
Will the nuptial° contract break.   *marital*
Like mutes,[1] she signs alone must make,
And never any freedom take,
15 But still be governed by a nod,
And fear her husband as her god:
Him still must serve, him still obey,
And nothing act, and nothing say,
But what her haughty lord thinks fit,
20 Who, with the power, has all the wit.
Then shun,° oh! shun that wretched state,   *avoid*
And all the fawning flatterers hate.
Value yourselves, and men despise:
You must be proud, if you'll be wise.

Chudleigh married young. Most of her life was spent in solitude on her husband's country estate, but she read widely and corresponded with other writers, including early feminists, and formulated progressive views of her own. Several editions of her poems were published in her lifetime; her work also includes plays and translations.

'To the Ladies' is an unusually polemic* poem that was written at a time when the status of women under British law meant that they were considered the property first of their fathers, then of their husbands. On marrying, they became legal minors, and had no rights to land, wealth, income, or even their own children (their husbands assumed full control over all these). This situation lasted from the first codifying of laws in Britain (in 1215) until the late nineteenth century. Today there are still many countries in which women are, if not legally, then socially and economically second-class citizens. In recent years, there has been an alarming trend in certain societies or countries (Afghanistan, for example) towards stripping women of the few political and even human rights that they have. For many, the concerns raised in Chudleigh's poem are as pressing as ever.

Notes

1 Those physically unable to speak.

Alexander Pope (1688–1744)

A Little Learning

A little learning is a dangerous thing;
Drink deep, or taste not the Pierian spring:[1]
There shallow draughts intoxicate the brain,
And drinking largely sobers us again.
5 Fired at first sight with what the Muse[2] imparts,
In fearless youth we tempt the heights of Arts;
While from the bounded° level of our mind   *restricted*
Short views we take, nor see the lengths behind,
But, more advanced, behold with strange surprise
10 New distant scenes of endless science rise!
So pleased at first the towering Alps[3] we try,
Mount o'er the vales, and seem to tread the sky;
The eternal snows appear already past,
And the first clouds and mountains seem the last:
15 But those attained, we tremble to survey
The growing labours of the lengthened way;
The increasing prospect tires our wandering eyes,
Hill peep o'er hills, and Alps on Alps arise!

A childhood illness left **Pope** handicapped and in constant poor health, but he compensated for physical weakness with mental brilliance. His translation of Homer's **Iliad** and **Odyssey** (classical Greek epic poems – see notes on p. 71) brought him recognition and financial independence. Meanwhile, he earned a reputation as one of the best writers of satire* of his time, even though the accuracy of his barbs often made him most unpopular. Most of his poetry is written in rhyming couplets, an astonishing testimony to his technical skill. Today he is best remembered as the author of the mock-heroic* poem 'The Rape of the Lock'.

Notes

[1] Fountain reputed to be the source of wisdom and inspiration.
[2] Classical goddess supposed to prompt inspiration.
[3] Highest mountain range in western Europe.

Lady Mary Wortley Montagu (1689–1762)

An Answer to a Love-Letter in Verse

Is it to me, this sad lamenting strain?
Are Heaven's choicest gifts bestowed in vain?
A plenteous fortune, and a beauteous bride,
Your love rewarded, and content your pride:
5 Yet leaving her – 'tis me that you pursue,
Without one single charm but being new.
     How vile is man! how I detest the ways
Of artful falsehood, and designing praise!
Tasteless, an easy happiness you slight,
10 Ruin your joy, and mischief your delight.
Why should poor pug[1] (the mimic of your kind)
Wear a rough chain, and be to box confined?
Some cup, perhaps, he breaks, or tears a fan,
While moves unpunished the destroyer, man.
15 Not bound by vows, and unrestrained by shame,
In sport you break the heart, and rend the fame.
Not that your art can be successful here,
Th' already plundered need no robber fear:
Nor sighs, nor charms, nor flattery can move,
20 Too well secured against a second love.
Once, and but once, that devil charmed my mind;
To reason deaf, to observation blind,
I idly hoped (what cannot love persuade?)
My fondness equalled, and my truth repaid:
25 Slow to distrust, and willing to believe,
Long hushed my doubts, and would myself deceive;
But oh! too soon – this tale would ever last;
Sleep, sleep my wrongs, and let me think 'em past.
     For you, who mourn with counterfeited grief,
30 And ask so boldly like a begging thief,
May soon some other nymph° inflict the pain   *beautiful girl*
You know so well with cruel art to feign.
Though long you've sported with Dan Cupid's dart,[2]
You may see eyes, and you may feel a heart.

Montagu was the daughter of a duke, and moved in sophisticated social and literary circles throughout her life. She married Edward Wortley Montagu secretly and went with him to Turkey. On her return, she introduced the practice of inoculating against the deadly disease of smallpox into England. She was a close associate of Pope's until a public quarrel ended the friendship. She spent much of her later life in continental Europe. She is best remembered for her witty letters, although her poems are also interesting.

Notes

[1] Pet monkey.
[2] The arrow with which Cupid (the god of love) was supposed to strike.

35   So the brisk wits, who stop the evening coach,[3]
        Laugh at the fear that follows their approach;
        With idle mirth, and haughty scorn, despise
        The passenger's pale cheek and staring eyes:
        But seized by Justice, find a fright no jest,
40   And all the terror doubled in their breast.

English poetry since the Middle Ages has included hundreds of love poems written by men urging the woman of their dreams to return their love and begin an affair with them. 'An Answer to a Love-Letter in Verse' gives us a rare glimpse of what it meant to be on the receiving end of one of these pleas. The speaker in Montagu's poem assumes that her would-be lover is completely insincere; how many love poems or seduction poems can you find in this anthology that you suspect of falling into this category?

Notes

3 Reference to highwaymen, who held up and robbed travelling coaches.

Samuel Johnson (1709–1784)

A Short Song of Congratulation

Long-expected one and twenty,
Lingering year at last is flown:
Pomp and pleasure, pride and plenty,
Great Sir John, are all your own.

5   Loosened from the minor's tether,
Free to mortgage[1] or to sell,
Wild as wind, and light as feather,
Bid the slaves of thrift farewell.

Call the Betties, Kates, and Jennies,
10   Every name that laughs at care,
Lavish of your grandsire's guineas,
Show the spirit of an heir.

All that prey on vice and folly
Joy to see their quarry fly,
15   Here the gamester° light and jolly,   *gambler*
There the lender grave and sly.

Wealth, Sir John, was made to wander,
Let it wander as it will;
See the jockey, see the pander,°   *pimp*
20   Bid them come and take their fill.

Johnson's early years were marked by poverty and illness. Although he was a good scholar, lack of money forced him to leave Oxford University. He spent nine years writing the first dictionary in the English language, and its publication confirmed his growing status in literary circles. His writing included essays, reviews, political articles, biographies, and a novel, as well as poetry. His close friend Boswell wrote an extremely popular biography celebrating Johnson's achievements, and this ensured the fame of both men.

'A Short Song of Congratulation' refers to Sir John Lade, the nephew of one of Johnson's friends, who wasted the fortune he inherited. Underlying its witty sarcasm is a very real concern for the laws of inheritance that allowed such irresponsibility. During the eighteenth century, the role of the 'landed gentry' (minor aristocrats who inherited estates and lived off the income generated by farming or renting their land) became the subject of much debate and criticism, and responsible management was strongly urged.

Notes

[1] Borrow money against land or property.

When the bonny blade° carouses,   *young man*
Pockets full, and spirits high,
What are acres? What are houses?
Only dirt, or wet or dry.

25   If the guardian or the mother
Tell the woes of wilful waste,
Scorn their counsel, scorn their pother:°   *bother, anxiety*
You can hang or drown at last!

Talking points

You might like to compare Johnson's poem with one on a similar
topic (but which presents a very different perspective) by Eva Gore-
Booth: 'The Land to the Landlord' (pp. 101–2). Part of the interest
comes from the fact that the two poets are polar opposites, which
gives us an opportunity to look at how gender and political
orientation influence poetical argument. (The word 'carouses' – line
21 – means to enjoy a noisy drinking party.)

William Cowper (1731–1800)

The Negro's Complaint

Forc'd from home, and all its pleasures,
Afric's coast I left forlorn;
To increase a stranger's treasures,
O'er the raging billows° borne.   *waves*
5   Men from England bought and sold me,
Paid my price in paltry gold:
But, though theirs they have enroll'd me,
Minds are never to be sold.

Still in thought as free as ever,
10   What are England's rights, I ask,
Me from my delights to sever,
Me to torture, me to task?
Fleecy locks, and black complexion
Cannot forfeit nature's claim;
15   Skins may differ, but affection
Dwells in white and black the same.

Why did all-creating Nature
Make the plant for which we toil?
Sighs must fan it, tears must water,
20   Sweat of ours must dress the soil.
Think, ye masters, iron-hearted,
Lolling at your jovial boards;°   *tables*
Think how many backs have smarted°   *to throb or sting with pain*
For the sweets your cane affords.

25   Is there, as ye sometimes tell us,
Is there one who reigns on high?
Has he bid you buy and sell us,
Speaking from his throne the sky?

Cowper (pronounced Cooper) was a retiring and delicate soul. After an
unhappy school career, he trained as a lawyer, but was too mentally fragile to
practice. He led a quiet life, troubled by bouts of depression during which he
wrote often morbid or manic poetry. Fortunately, his friends and fiancée (to
whom he was engaged for nearly thirty years!) supported him, and when in
good health, he produced fine hymns, poems, and comic writing, as well as
delightful letters and competent translations. He was greatly influenced by
clergy of the Evangelical church, who enlisted him in the anti-slavery cause.

In 'The Negro's Complaint', Cowper attacks the slave trade, an issue that
was beginning to trouble the consciences of many. Britain held vast and

Ask him, if your knotted scourges,
30 Matches, blood-extorting screws,
Are the means which duty urges
Agents of his will to use? . . .

By our blood in Afric wasted,
Ere our necks receiv'd the chain;
35 By the mis'ries we have tasted,
Crossing in your barks° the main;   *ships*
By our suff'rings since ye brought us
To the man-degrading mart;
All sustain'd by patience, taught us
40 Only by a broken heart:

Deem our nation brutes no longer
Till some reason ye shall find
Worthier of regard and stronger
Than the colour of our kind.
45 Slaves of gold, whose sordid dealings
Tarnish all your boasted pow'rs,
Prove that you have human feelings,
Ere you proudly question ours!

Talking points

Compare this poem with Grace Nichol's 'Taint' (p. 220); together
they paint a devastating picture of the horrors of slavery. It is
interesting to compare this urgent eighteenth-century plea to end
slavery with a modern poem reflecting back on the long-term damage
that has been its legacy. Although slavery has been officially abolished
for nearly two centuries, it is on the rise throughout the globe in
various illicit forms. You and your classmates might like to investigate
this topic, or make it the focus of a writing project. What kinds of
slavery exist today? Can you think of any examples of labour practices
that are close to slavery?

hugely profitable sugar plantations in the West Indies, but these depended on
slave labour. Slaves had no rights whatsoever, and it was completely legal to
use torture to punish them or force them to work harder, as we see in the
fourth stanza (scourges were whips or lashes with knots tied in them, and
screws were clamps applied to the fingers or genitals and tightened). A
vigorous movement denouncing the cruelty of slavery and calling for its
abolition gained momentum towards the end of the eighteenth century, and
this poem (which was sung to a well-known tune) was one of several protests
circulated as pamphlets and in the press. Although some of the phrases
reflect a rather sentimental (and sometimes patronizing) view of the African
slave, the plea for racial understanding and equity is surprisingly modern.

William Blake (1757–1827)

London

I wander thro' each charter'd[1] street,
Near where the charter'd Thames[2] does flow.
And mark in every face I meet
Marks of weakness, marks of woe.

5   In every cry of every Man,
In every Infant's cry of fear,
In every voice: in every ban,[3]
The mind-forg'd manacles° I hear   *chains*

How the Chimney-sweeper's cry
10   Every blackning Church appalls,
And the hapless Soldier's sigh
Runs in blood down Palace walls

But most thro' midnight streets I hear
How the youthful Harlot's curse[4]
15   Blasts the new-born Infant's tear
And blights with plagues the Marriage hearse.

Blake is a classic example of a genius born before his time. He had no formal education, but was trained as an engraver (book illustrator). He developed a unique artistic style, opened a print shop in London, and produced books written and illustrated by himself. These introduced his energetic and often socially critical poetry and his visionary art to the public. However, his mystic philosophies, condemnation of conventional religion, and passion for justice meant that most of his contemporaries considered him insane. After his death, he was to have a growing influence on poets and artists who were inspired by his revolutionary ideas.

Blake was one of the first writers to voice his horror and concern at the effect the Industrial Revolution was having on the social fabric of England. In 'London' he addresses the problems of rapid urbanization. The new drive for industrialization, and the migration of poor people from the countryside to the cities in search of jobs, led to appalling living conditions and gross exploitation. There were no laws, for example, governing labour conditions. The 'Chimney-sweepers' in line 9, for example, were small boys (the younger

Notes

[1] Mapped out; also legally defined or restricted.
[2] River running through central London.
[3] Legal prohibition or punishment; possibly also a pun on 'bann' (marriage announcement).
[4] Swearing; also a reference to the sexually transmitted disease syphilis; babies born to infected women were often blind or deformed (see line 15).

The Sick Rose

O Rose, thou art sick.
The invisible worm,
That flies in the night
In the howling storm:

5   Has found out thy bed
Of crimson joy:
And his dark secret love
Does thy life destroy.

---

the better) who were made to climb up inside chimneys to clean them; many suffocated. Forced child labour was perfectly legal. The reference to the 'hapless Soldiers' (line 11), meanwhile, possibly refers to conscription. And the description of the 'Harlot' (prostitute) as 'youthful' (line 14) may be a reference to the fact that desperately poor families sometimes sold their daughters (many of them scarcely teenagers) into prostitution. (Then, as now, virgins were much in demand in the sex trade, as they were believed to be 'cleaner'.)

Perhaps Blake is most radical in his frank references in both these poems to the sexually transmitted diseases that were spreading as a result of urban prostitution. Until the discovery of antibiotics in the mid-twentieth century, syphilis was incurable and almost as deadly as HIV/Aids is today. Very often, the middle-class men who visited prostitutes would take the disease home to their wives, leading to suffering, sterility, and sometimes death – a tragic pattern referred to in the last line of 'London'.

Talking points

After a careful reading of 'London', turn to Serote's 'Alexandra' and 'City Johannesburg' (pp. 207–9). You will find that both poets, although writing from different centuries and continents, share a passionate concern for those social injustices that are heightened and worsened by urbanization.

The following questions will enable you to explore this connection further.

1   Both poets write in judgement of particular cities. However, in 'Alexandra', Serote's indictment of his home township is mixed with other emotions. Can you identify some of these?

2   If you work through both 'London' and 'City Johannesburg', what specific social and political evils do you find listed by each poet?

3   Now that you have established exactly what Blake criticizes in urban society, note how economically he uses serious puns and words with double meanings to get his message across. The footnotes already identify two 'double' words; can you find any others? (Look closely at line 10.) Serote, however, makes use of colourful images rather than loaded words in his poems, although there is one very clever pun in 'City Johannesburg'. (Check line 27.) What central metaphor* does he develop throughout 'Alexandra'? In what way is it unusual? In 'City Johannesburg', try to locate each metaphor and simile.* How does each one work, and which do you find the most effective? Debate these with your classmates. (Remember that there are no 'correct' answers.)

4   Bearing in mind your answers to question 2, can you identify any specific social and political problems or structures that were the same or similar in London in the 1790s and South African cities under apartheid?

5   Blake is particularly concerned with the problem of prostitution. Do you feel he is giving a lecture on morality? Or is his treatment of the issue more complex? How does he present it as a social, rather than a moral problem? Can you think of present-day parallels? (Look at the work done in South African cities by SWEAT – the organization that works with and represents sex workers, as many prostitutes prefer to be known.)

6   Do you feel that the criticisms both poets make are effective? Why? How does their treatment of these issues differ from the way they might be handled by a politician or an activist? Does this suggest any further insights on the role of poetry?

7   'The Sick Rose' touches on similar issues to those raised in question 5. This poem acts as a mini-allegory* on many subjects: but the phallic (penis-like) image of the worm means that it is most often interpreted as a comment on sexual betrayal. In 'London', we have already seen Blake's concern for the social and gender injustices underlying the problem of sexually transmitted disease. The most astonishing thing about 'The Sick Rose', however, is the way it seems to anticipate HIV/Aids. This is a poem that, tragically, fits our own times only too well.

Robert Burns (1759–1796)

John Anderson, My Jo

John Anderson my jo,° John,	*dear*
When we were first acquent;°	*acquainted*
Your locks were like the raven,	
Your bonie° brow was brent;°	*bonny / smooth*
5 But now your brow is beld,° John,	*bald*
Your locks are like the snaw;°	*snow*
But blessings on your frosty pow,°	*head*
John Anderson, my Jo.	
John Anderson my jo, John,	
10 We clamb° the hill the gither;°	*climb / together*
And mony° a canty° day, John,	*many / merry*
We've had wi' ane° anither:	*one*
Now we maun° totter down, John,	*must*
And hand in hand we'll go;	
15 And sleep the gither at the foot,	
John Anderson, my jo.	

Burns was a patriotic Scottish poet, and his birthday is still celebrated by the Scots. Raised to be a farmer, he struggled financially and was about to emigrate to Jamaica when his first book of poems, many in the Scottish dialect, was published. It was an immediate success, and guaranteed his popularity in society, and this in turn led to a string of romantic affairs. He also embarked on the task of collecting and thus preserving local Scottish songs. He died at the relatively young age of thirty-seven; his lively poems are still popular today.

William Wordsworth (1770–1850)

Three Years She Grew

Three years she grew in sun and shower,
Then Nature said, 'A lovelier flower
On earth was never sown;
This Child I to myself will take;
5   She shall be mine, and I will make
A Lady of my own.

'Myself will to my darling be
Both law and impulse: and with me
The Girl, in rock and plain,
10   In earth and heaven, in glade and bower°,   *enclosed garden*
Shall feel an overseeing power
To kindle or restrain.

'She shall be sportive° as the fawn   *playful*
That wild with glee across the lawn
15   Or up the mountain springs;
And hers shall be the breathing balm,
And hers the silence and the calm
Of mute insensate° things.   *without feeling*

Wordsworth was born in the Lake District, a beautiful part of England later celebrated in his poetry. After graduating from Cambridge University he spent a year in France, where he passionately supported the French Revolution, then at its height. He also fell in love with a French woman with whom he had a daughter. Back home, he was horrified when England declared war on France; he also found his radical principles challenged by the violent excesses of the Revolution, and became deeply depressed. A retreat to the countryside to live with his adoring sister Dorothy, together with an inspiring friendship with the poet Coleridge, helped him to recover. Together with Coleridge, he produced work that was to establish the foundations of a new era in English poetry, that of Romanticism. Their concept of Nature and its beauties as a source of comfort and moral guidance was perhaps inevitable in a rapidly industrializing country; it shapes our aesthetic* perceptions to this day. Later in life, Wordsworth was appointed Poet Laureate.

'Three Years She Grew' is interesting for its presentation both of Nature and the 'feminine'. One of the basic principles of Romantic poetry was to place the poet as a first-person speaker ('I') reflecting on the comfort and inspiration of Nature – which was usually given female characteristics. The poem would often go on to establish a relationship between the male poet

'The floating clouds their state shall lend
20   To her; for her the willow bend;
Nor shall she fail to see
Even in the motions of the Storm
Grace that shall mould the Maiden's form
By silent sympathy.

25   'The stars of midnight shall be dear
To her; and she shall lean her ear
In many a secret place
Where rivulets° dance their wayward round,   *small streams*
And beauty born of murmuring sound
30   Shall pass into her face.

'And vital feelings of delight
Shall rear her form to stately° height   *dignified*
Her virgin bosom swell;
Such thoughts to Lucy I will give
35   While she and I together live
Here in this happy dell.'°   *forest clearing*

Thus Nature spake – The work was done –
How soon my Lucy's race was run!
She died, and left to me
40   This heath,° this calm, and quiet scene;   *moor*
This memory of what has been,
And never more will be.

---

and female Nature. (This meant that it was difficult at first for women to write Romantic poetry, as they found themselves in the awkward position of being both speaker [subject] and spoken about [object]. Later, however, many Victorian women poets were to adapt the Romantic formula for writing nature poetry in creative ways. You might want to look at Dickinson's 'I Taste a Liquor Never Brewed' [p. 86] for an example of a startlingly unusual 'Nature poem'.)

In this poem, Wordsworth takes both a female figure and Nature and describes how one is absorbed into the other; at the end of the poem, we realize that it is also an elegy.* It is this use of natural imagery as a convention of mourning that Rossetti's speaker rejects in 'Song' (p. 88). A number of poems in this anthology make powerful or innovative use of this tradition, nevertheless; see Tennyson's 'It is the day when he was born' (CVII, pp. 74–5) and 'Thy voice is on the rolling air' (CXXX, p. 75), and Cope's 'The Flying Fish' (p. 140). Can you find any others?

I Wandered Lonely As a Cloud

I wandered lonely as a cloud
That floats on high o'er vales and hills,
When all at once I saw a crowd,
A host, of golden daffodils;
5 Beside the lake, beneath the trees,
Fluttering and dancing in the breeze.

Continuous as the stars that shine
And twinkle on the milky way,[1]
They stretched in never-ending line
10 Along the margin of a bay:
Ten thousand saw I at a glance,
Tossing their heads in sprightly° dance.   *lively*

The waves beside them danced; but they
Out-did the sparkling waves in glee:
15 A poet could not but be gay,
In such a jocund° company: *jolly*
I gazed – and gazed – but little thought
What wealth the show to me had brought:

For oft,° when on my couch I lie   *often*
20 In vacant or in pensive mood,
They flash upon that inward eye
Which is the bliss of solitude;
And then my heart with pleasure fills,
And dances with the daffodils.

Although in recent times the intense romanticism of 'I Wandered Lonely As a Cloud' has sometimes been mocked, it is a classic example of how the Romantic philosophy of beauty in Nature operates. The poet sees a vision of natural beauty, which he mentally photographs and describes in a poem. This image of beauty is then recalled at later moments to induce happiness. (In order to fully appreciate this poem, it is necessary to know that the part of the stem to which the daffodil flower is attached is very flexible; the flower thus bobs and 'dances' up and down in the slightest breeze.)

Another interesting fact about this poem is that it is one that Wordsworth 'plagiarized' from his sister Dorothy's diary. She would often write vivid prose descriptions of beautiful sights she had seen, and then show these to her brother; he would then sometimes rewrite her piece in the form of a poem. Scholars have recently begun to investigate the extent to which she was a 'co-author' of some of Wordsworth's more famous poems.

Notes

1 Broad, dense band of stars.

Composed upon Westminster Bridge, September 3, 1802

Earth has not anything to show more fair:
Dull would he be of soul who could pass by
A sight so touching in its majesty:
This City now doth, like a garment, wear
5   The beauty of the morning; silent, bare,
Ships, towers, domes, theatres, and temples lie
Open unto the fields, and to the sky;
All bright and glittering in the smokeless air.
Never did sun more beautifully steep
10 In his first splendour, valley, rock, or hill;
Ne'er saw I, never felt, a calm so deep!
The river glideth at his own sweet will:
Dear God! the very houses seem asleep;
And all that mighty heart is lying still!

Talking points

'Composed upon Westminster Bridge' describes the view from a
central bridge over the Thames River in London. This poem is in
sharp contrast to Blake's 'London' (p. 50). Nevertheless, together the
two poems encompass the main characteristics of Romantic poetry: a
passionate concern about injustice, and a deep emotional and even
spiritual response to scenes of beauty.

Samuel Taylor Coleridge (1772–1834)

Kubla Khan
OR, A VISION IN A DREAM, A FRAGMENT

In Xanadu did Kubla Khan[1]
A stately pleasure-dome decree:
Where Alph, the sacred river, ran
Through caverns measureless to man
5   Down to a sunless sea.
So twice five miles of fertile ground
With walls and towers were girdled° round: *encircled*
And there were gardens bright with sinuous rills,°   *streams*
Where blossomed many an incense-bearing tree;
10 And here were forests ancient as the hills,
Enfolding sunny spots of greenery.

But oh! that deep romantic chasm which slanted
Down the green hill athwart° a cedarn° cover!   *across / cedar*
A savage place! as holy and enchanted
15 As e'er beneath a waning moon was haunted
By woman wailing for her demon-lover!
And from this chasm, with ceaseless turmoil seething,
As if this earth in fast thick pants were breathing,
A mighty fountain momently° was forced: *at intervals*
20 Amid whose swift half-intermitted burst
Huge fragments vaulted like rebounding hail,
Or chaffy grain beneath the thresher's flail:
And 'mid these dancing rocks at once and ever
It flung up momently the sacred river.
25 Five miles meandering with a mazy motion
Through wood and dale° the sacred river ran,   *valley*
Then reached the caverns measureless to man,

Coleridge was a gifted but tormented person. Although he was a brilliant student at Cambridge University, his academic career was wrecked by drink, involvement in revolutionary politics, and turbulent affairs. Later he became addicted to opium, quarrelled with his close friends, struggled with depression, and made his marriage unhappy by falling hopelessly in love with another woman. He was nevertheless both politically active and a prolific writer, one of the greatest literary critics and poets of his age. He enjoyed creative friendships with a number of other writers, including Wordsworth, under whose influence he wrote his best poetry. No matter how chaotic Coleridge's personal affairs became, he remained energetic throughout his life, and was to significantly influence a band of younger writers (including Byron).

Notes

[1] Kubla was the first Mongol ruler, or 'Khan' of China. Coleridge invents the name of the capital city, calling it 'Xanadu'.

And sank in tumult to a lifeless ocean:
And 'mid this tumult Kubla heard from far
30   Ancestral voices prophesying war!

The shadow of the dome of pleasure
Floated midway on the waves;
Where was heard the mingled measure
From the fountain and the caves.
35   It was a miracle of rare device,
A sunny pleasure-dome with caves of ice!

A damsel with a dulcimer°   *harp*
In a vision once I saw:
It was an Abyssinian maid,
40   And on her dulcimer she played,
Singing of Mount Abora.²
Could I revive within me
Her symphony and song,
To such a deep delight 'twould win me,
45   That with music loud and long,
I would build that dome in air,
That sunny dome! those caves of ice!
And all who heard should see them there,
And all should cry, Beware! Beware!
50   His flashing eyes, his floating hair!

Weave a circle round him thrice,
And close your eyes with holy dread,
For he on honey-dew hath fed,
And drunk the milk of Paradise.

'Kubla Khan' is an extraordinary fantasy that was 'revealed' to the poet during a hallucination or dream induced by opium. It is apparently only part of what was meant to be a much longer work; Coleridge himself describes how, while writing down his vision, he was interrupted by a visitor; after their business was completed, the poet tried to continue with the poem, only to discover that he could no longer recall his dream.

Notes

²   Possible reference to Amara, supposed to be the location of paradise.

George Gordon, Lord Byron (1788–1824)

When We Two Parted

When we two parted
    In silence and tears,
Half broken-hearted
    To sever° for years,   *cut, separate*
5 Pale grew thy cheek and cold,
    Colder thy kiss;
Truly that hour foretold
    Sorrow to this.

The dew of the morning
10   Sunk chill on my brow –
It felt like the warning
    Of what I feel now.
Thy vows are all broken,
    And light° is thy fame;   *cheap*
15 I hear thy name spoken,
    And share in its shame.

They name thee before me,
    A knell to mine ear;
A shudder comes o'er me –
20   Why wert thou so dear?
They know not I knew thee,
    Who knew thee too well –
Long, long shall I rue° thee,   *regret*
    Too deeply to tell.

Byron was one of the rare poets who achieved fame (or perhaps notoriety) in his own lifetime. While young, he established himself both as a promising politician and as the leader of the younger generation of Romantic poets, who wrote passionate poetry and cultivated defiant and glamorous images, rather like rock stars towards the end of the twentieth century. He had several theatrical affairs, but went too far when he fell in love with his half-sister. After she gave birth to a child, public outrage, together with his own disillusion, compelled him to leave England. He stayed with the Shelleys (see p. 62) in Switzerland and travelled in Italy, continuing to write innovative and daring poetry while living as riotously as ever. He died (in appropriately dramatic circumstances) while fighting alongside Greek nationalists in their struggle for independence from the Turkish Empire.

25   In secret we met –
            In silence I grieve,
      That thy heart could forget,
            Thy spirit deceive.
      If I should meet thee
30   After long years,
      How should I greet thee?
            With silence and tears.

Percy Bysshe Shelley (1792–1822)

Ozymandias[1]

I met a traveller from an antique land,
Who said: Two vast and trunkless legs of stone
Stand in the desert . . . Near them, on the sand,
Half sunk, a shattered visage° lies, whose frown,   *face*
5   And wrinkled lip, and sneer of cold command,
Tell that its sculptor well those passions read°   *understood*
Which yet survive, stamped on these lifeless things,
The hand that mocked them, and the heart that fed:
And on the pedestal these words appear:
10   'My name is Ozymandias, king of kings:
Look on my Works, ye Mighty, and despair!'
Nothing beside remains. Round the decay
Of that colossal wreck, boundless and bare
The lone and level sands stretch far away.

Shelley, whose poetry combines lyrical beauty with passion, was a born rebel. He was expelled from Oxford for writing a pamphlet on the need for atheism; next he eloped with a girl of sixteen. A vegetarian and political radical, he led a nomadic life as a writer before abandoning his family to run away to Europe with seventeen-year-old Mary Godwin (daughter of the feminist writer Mary Wollstonecraft). He later married her, after his first wife committed suicide. Together with Byron, they were part of a circle of eccentric but creative artists. (Mary Shelley was the author of the famous horror novel *Frankenstein*.) Because of Shelley's affairs, his marriage became increasingly unhappy. He drowned at the age of twenty-nine, after deliberately setting sail in an unsafe boat during a storm.

Notes

[1] Greek name for the Egyptian king Ramses II, who had a huge statue of himself built as a monument to his power.

England in 1819

An old, mad, blind, despised, and dying king, —
Princes, the dregs of their dull race, who flow
Through public scorn, — mud from a muddy spring;
Rulers who neither see, nor feel, nor know,
5   But leech-like to their fainting country cling,
Till they drop, blind in blood, without a blow;
A people starved and stabbed in the untilled° field —   *unploughed*
An army, which liberticide[2] and prey
Makes as a two-edged sword to all who wield;
10 Golden and sanguine° laws which tempt and slay;   *bloody*
Religion Christless, Godless — a book sealed; .
A Senate, — Time's worst statute° unrepealed[3] —   *law*
Are graves, from which a glorious Phantom° may   *spirit, ghost*
Burst, to illumine our tempestuous day.

In 'England in 1819' Shelley expresses his scorn at the political state of
England, seventeen years after Wordsworth wrote a similar sonnet* (see the
OUP website). The 'dying king' is George III, one of the Hanoverian (German)
line of kings that had been installed on the English throne in the eighteenth
century. His illness made him insane, and in the final years of his life his
sons, the 'princes' (who were neither popular nor respected), had to manage
affairs of state.

Notes

2   Destruction of liberty.
3   Probably the Act of Union, which
    legally bound Ireland under
    English rule.

John Keats (1795–1821)

When I Have Fears That I May Cease To Be

When I have fears that I may cease to be
    Before my pen has glean'd° my teeming brain,   *harvested*
Before high piled books, in charactry,°   *letters of the alphabet*
    Hold like rich garners° the full ripen'd grain;   *storehouses*
5 When I behold, upon the night's starr'd face,
    Huge cloudy symbols of a high romance,
And think that I may never live to trace
    Their shadows, with the magic hand of chance;
And when I feel, fair creature of an hour,
10   That I shall never look upon thee more,
Never have relish in the faery° power   *magic*
    Of unreflecting love; – then on the shore
Of the wide world I stand alone, and think
Till love and fame to nothingness do sink.

As a young man **Keats** studied medicine and became a licensed chemist, a career he gave up to concentrate on poetry. Although he moved in circles that included Shelley and Wordsworth, his writing was at first denounced by critics. In spite of financial difficulties, he continued writing significant amounts of poetry, which was to earn him a reputation as one of the greatest younger Romantic poets. After nursing his brother, who was dying of tuberculosis, Keats also contracted the disease. His deteriorating health eventually drove him to the warmer climate of Italy, where he died at the age of only twenty-six.

Keats wrote 'When I Have Fears That I May Cease To Be' in 1818, the same year that he was diagnosed as having tuberculosis. His response was to plunge into intense creative and romantic activity. During this year, he wrote some of his best poetry and also became engaged.

La Belle Dame sans Merci

O, what can ail thee, knight-at-arms,
    Alone and palely loitering?
The sedge° has withered from the lake   *grass-like water plant*
    And no birds sing!

5   O, what can ail thee, knight-at-arms,
    So haggard and so woe-begone?
The squirrel's granary is full,
    And the harvest's done.

I see a lily on thy brow,
10   With anguish moist and fever dew
And on thy cheek a fading rose
    Fast withereth too.

I met a lady in the meads,°   *meadows*
    Full beautiful, a fairy's child,
15   Her hair was long, her foot was light,
    And her eyes were wild.

I made a garland for her head,
    And bracelets too, and fragrant zone;°   *belt of flowers*
She looked at me as she did love,
20   And made sweet moan.

I set her on my pacing steed,
    And nothing else saw all day long;
For sidelong would she bend, and sing
    A fairy's song.

25   She found me roots of relish sweet,
    And honey wild, and manna° dew;   *bread-like*
And sure in language strange she said,
    'I love thee true'.

She took me to her elfin grot,°   *cave*
30   And there she wept, and sighed full sore,
And there I shut her wild wild eyes
    With kisses four.

And there she lulléd me asleep,
    And there I dreamed, Ah Woe betide!
35 The latest° dream I ever dreamt   *last*
    On the cold hill side.

I saw pale kings, and princes too,
    Pale warriors, death-pale were they all;
They cried – 'La belle dame sans merci
40   Hath thee in thrall!'°   *hypnotized, enslaved*

I saw their starved lips in the gloam°   *dusk*
    With horrid warning gapéd wide,
And I awoke, and found me here
    On the cold hill's side.

45 And this is why I sojourn° here,   *stay*
    Alone and palely loitering,
Though the sedge is withered from the lake,
    And no birds sing.

Talking points

1 In 'La Belle Dame sans Merci' – which translates as 'the beautiful woman without pity' – the poet sets out to create a 'medieval' atmosphere. Many Romantic (and later, Victorian) artists attempted a nostalgic recreation of medieval culture in their works. To begin with, the poem takes the form of a ballad.* How do we know this? What other 'medieval' features are used?

2 How does the question and answer format function in the poem? (Note how the very first question in the opening two lines sets the tone of the poem. We do not expect a cheerful answer!)

3 How are natural phenomena used in the first few stanzas to suggest atmosphere or mood? What kind of atmosphere is created?

4 Would you agree that while the mood of the poem is melancholy, haunting, and even threatening, it cannot be described as harsh or ugly? Why not? What sensual or attractive elements are found in the poem?

5 The poem clearly deals with the supernatural. What does this contribute to tone and mood?

6 What warning signs does the mesmerized knight ignore? What does this suggest about enchantment or obsession?

7 What gender stereotypes are invoked in this poem?

Elizabeth Barrett Browning (1806–1861)

From A Curse for a Nation

Prologue

I heard an angel speak last night,
    And he said 'Write!
Write a Nation's curse for me,
And send it over the Western Sea.'

5 I faltered, taking up the word:
    'Not so, my lord!
If curses must be, choose another
To send thy curse against my brother.

'For I am bound by gratitude,
10   By love and blood,
To brothers of mine across the sea,
Who stretch out kindly hands to me.'

'Therefore,' the voice said, 'shalt thou write.
    My curse to-night.
15 From the summits of love a curse is driven,
As lightning is from the tops of heaven.'

'Not so,' I answered. 'Evermore
    My heart is sore
For my own land's sins: for little feet
20 Of children bleeding along the street:

'For parked-up honours that gainsay°   *deny, contradict*
    The right of way:
For almsgiving° through a door that is   *charity*
Not open enough for two friends to kiss:

Barrett was a brilliant child, who was educated by the best scholars and tutors. She studied Latin and Greek from an early age, although it was fairly unusual for a girl of that time to be allowed to do so. Her ill health meant that, unlike many Victorian women, she had plenty of time for writing and reading. A secret romantic relationship with Robert Browning began through their writing to each other. She eventually ran away to marry him, against the wishes of her tyrannical father. The couple moved to Italy, and were extremely happy together. Although her poetry was at first so popular that she was considered for the position of Poet Laureate, she was attacked for the political and social criticism she voiced in her later poems. The subjects she dealt with in these poems (child labour, slavery, rape, prostitution,

25 'For love of freedom which abates
        Beyond the Straits:[1]
    For patriot virtue starved to vice on
    Self-praise, self-interest, and suspicion:

    'For an oligarchic° parliament,   *government by a few*
30   And bribes well-meant.
    What curse to another land assign,
    When heavy-souled for the sins of mine?'

    'Therefore,' the voice said, 'shalt thou write
        My curse to-night.
35 Because thou hast strength to see and hate
    A foul thing done *within* thy gate.'

    'Not so,' I answered once again.
        'To curse, choose men.
    For I, a woman, have only known
40 How the heart melts and the tears run down.'

    'Therefore,' the voice said, 'shalt thou write
        My curse to-night.
    Some women weep and curse, I say
    (And no one marvels), night and day.

45 'And thou shalt take their part to-night,
        Weep and write.
    A curse from the depths of womanhood
    Is very salt, and bitter, and good.'

    So thus I wrote, and mourned indeed,
50   What all may read.
    And thus, as was enjoined on me,
    I send it over the Western Sea.

illegitimacy, politics, and nationalism) were considered to be shockingly inappropriate for a woman writer.

It is not certain precisely which country the speaker in 'A Curse for a Nation' is being urged to curse. Barrett Browning was a passionate supporter of Italian nationalism and its democratic movements, which were then being ruthlessly suppressed, and it is possible that Italy is her target; the reference to the 'Western Sea' also suggests the United States, at that stage bitterly divided and on the verge of a tragic and brutal civil war over the issue of slavery. However, it is ultimately the condemnation or indictment of Britain in stanzas five to eight that gives this piece its power.

Notes

[1] Either the Straits of Gibraltar, a headland controlled by Britain that guards the entrance to the Mediterranean Sea, or the Straits of Dover, another name for the English Channel, the narrow stretch of sea that separates Britain from France.

Henry Wadsworth Longfellow
(1807–1882)

Chaucer

An old man in a lodge within a park;
   The chamber walls depicted all around
      With portraitures° of huntsman, hawk, and hound,   *pictures*
   And the hurt deer. He listeneth to the lark,
5 Whose song comes with the sunshine through the dark
      Of painted glass in leaden lattice° bound;   *bars or strips of lead*
   He listeneth and he laugheth at the sound,
      Then writeth in a book like any clerk.°   *scholar*
He is the poet of the dawn, who wrote
10   The Canterbury Tales, and his old age
   Made beautiful with song; and as I read
I hear the crowing cock, I hear the note
      Of lark and linnet,° and from every page   *type of bird*
   Rise odours of ploughed field or flowery mead.°   *meadow*

An American, **Longfellow** studied in Europe before becoming a professor at Harvard University. His long narrative poems (such as 'The Song of Hiawatha') were hugely popular both at home and abroad, and he became the most famous American poet of his time. He was widowed twice, with his work becoming increasingly melancholy and nostalgic in his old age.

'Chaucer' is one of a series of sonnets that Longfellow wrote celebrating the great writers (see pp. 4–7 for details of Chaucer's life and extracts from *The Canterbury Tales*.) Try to identify what aspects of Chaucer's writing Longfellow imitates to add flavour to his poem.

Alfred, Lord Tennyson (1809–1892)

Ulysses[1]

It little profits that an idle king,
By this still hearth, among these barren crags,
Matched with an agéd wife, I mete° and dole°   *give out / distribute*
Unequal laws unto a savage race,
5   That hoard, and sleep, and feed, and know not me.
I cannot rest from travel: I will drink
Life to the lees:° all times I have enjoyed   *sediment of wine*
Greatly, have suffered greatly, both with those
That loved me, and alone; on shore, and when
10   Through scudding drifts the rainy Hyades[2]
Vext the dim sea: I am become a name;
For always roaming with a hungry heart
Much have I seen and known; cities of men
And manners, climates, councils, governments,
15   Myself not least, but honoured of them all;
And drunk delight of battle with my peers,
Far on the ringing plains of windy Troy.[3]
I am part of all that I have met;
Yet all experience is an arch wherethrough
20   Gleams that untravelled world, whose margin fades
For ever and for ever when I move.
How dull it is to pause, to make an end,
To rust unburnished,° not to shine in use!   *unpolished*
As though to breathe were life. Life piled on life
25   Were all too little, and of one to me
Little remains: but every hour is saved
From that eternal silence, something more,
A bringer of new things; and vile it were
For some three suns to store and hoard myself,

Tennyson studied at Cambridge University, where he became close friends with Arthur Hallam, a brilliant young man whose early death profoundly affected Tennyson. His attempts to come to terms with this loss led to his *In Memoriam* poems, which were to establish his fame. He became enormously popular during his lifetime, eventually holding the position of Poet Laureate for forty-two years. His public status was at odds with his melancholy nature; he delayed marriage to his fiancée for over a decade, fearing possible mental illness and experiencing religious doubts. Nevertheless, he became probably the most respected figure in Victorian literature, and was granted a title by Queen Victoria. He was particularly admired for his technically polished poetry, noteworthy for its mastery of sound (his poems must be read aloud) and often dreamlike, nostalgic quality.

Notes

1. Roman name for Odysseus, the Greek hero of Homer's *Odyssey*.
2. Group of stars; their rising was thought to herald rain.
3. Ancient city on the coast of what is now Turkey; scene of the Trojan War, a ten-year siege described in Homer's *Iliad*.

30 And this grey spirit yearning in desire
To follow knowledge like a sinking star,
Beyond the utmost bound of human thought.
   This is my son, mine own Telemachus,
To whom I leave the sceptre[4] and the isle –
35 Well-loved of me, discerning to fulfil
This labour, by slow prudence to make mild
A rugged people, and through soft degrees
Subdue them to the useful and the good.
Most blameless is he, centred in the sphere
40 Of common duties, decent not to fail
In offices of tenderness, and pay
Meet° adoration to my household gods,   *fitting*
When I am gone. He works his work, I mine.
   There lies the port; the vessel puffs her sail:
45 There gloom the dark broad seas. My mariners,
Souls that have toiled, and wrought, and thought with me –
That ever with a frolic welcome took
The thunder and the sunshine, and opposed
Free hearts, free foreheads – you and I are old;
50 Old age hath yet his honour and his toil;
Death closes all: but something ere the end,
Some work of noble note, may yet be done,
Not unbecoming men that strove with gods.
The lights begin to twinkle from the rocks:
55 The long day wanes: the slow moon climbs: the deep
Moans round with many voices. Come, my friends,
'Tis not too late to seek a newer world.
Push off, and sitting well in order smite
The sounding furrows;[5] for my purpose holds
60 To sail beyond the sunset, and the baths
Of all the western stars, until I die.
It may be that the gulfs will wash us down;
It may be we shall touch the Happy Isles,[6]
And see the great Achilles,[7] whom we knew.

'Ulysses' assumes some knowledge of the works of the classical Greek writer Homer. The *Iliad* tells the tale of the Trojan War, the subject of many Greek dramas. This was sparked off when the beautiful Helen left her husband, a Greek king, for Paris, the son of the king of Troy. The two kingdoms then fought an epic war, in which the gods actively took part, and deeds of great heroism were done. Odysseus (Ulysses in the poem) was a Greek warrior who fought bravely in this struggle. The *Odyssey* tells of his exciting adventures and explorations on the voyage home after the war.

Notes

[4] Staff; symbol of royalty and authority.
[5] This image refers to rowing through waves.
[6] The Greek Paradise, where the brave and the good lived after death.
[7] The most heroic of the Greeks killed in the Trojan war.

65 Though much is taken, much abides; and though
We are not now that strength which in old days
Moved earth and heaven; that which we are, we are;
One equal temper of heroic hearts,
Made weak by time and fate, but strong in will
70 To strive, to seek, to find, and not to yield.

From In Memoriam A.H.H.

LIV

Oh yet we trust that somehow good
   Will be the final goal of ill,
   To pangs of nature, sins of will,
Defects of doubt, and taints of blood;

5 That nothing walks with aimless feet;
   That not one life shall be destroyed,
   Or cast as rubbish to the void,°   *emptiness*
When God hath made the pile complete;

That not a worm is cloven° in vain;   *cut*
10   That not a moth with vain desire
   Is shrivelled in a fruitless fire,
Or but subserves another's gain.

Behold, we know not anything;
   I can but trust that good shall fall
15   At last – far off – at last, to all,
And every winter change to spring.

So runs my dream: but what am I?
   An infant crying in the night:
   An infant crying for the light:
20 And with no language but a cry.

'In Memoriam' is a series of poems that Tennyson wrote in memory of his closest friend, Arthur Henry Hallam, who died tragically young while on a trip to Europe. Tennyson's efforts to make sense of his loss coincided with the publication of Darwin's biological theories on evolution. These argued that the human species had a natural, rather than a divine origin, which at first caused shock and even scandal, before gaining some degree of acceptance.

LV

The wish, that of the living whole
    No life may fail beyond the grave,
    Derives it not from what we have
The likest God within the soul?

5 Are God and Nature then at strife,
    That Nature lends such evil dreams?
    So careful of the type° she seems,   *species*
So careless of the single life;

That I, considering everywhere
10   Her secret meaning in her deeds,
    And finding that of fifty seeds,
She often brings but one to bear,

I falter where I firmly trod,
    And falling with my weight of cares
15   Upon the great world's altar-stairs
That slope through darkness up to God,

I stretch lame hands of faith, and grope,
    And gather dust and chaff, and call
    To what I feel is Lord of all,
20 And faintly trust the larger hope.

LVI

'So careful of the type?' but no.
    From scarpèd° cliff and quarried stone   *steep*
    She cries, 'A thousand types are gone:
I care for nothing, all shall go.

5 'Thou makest thine appeal to me:
    I bring to life, I bring to death:
    The spirit does but mean the breath:
I know no more.' And he, shall he,

Man, her last work, who seemed so fair,
10   Such splendid purpose in his eyes,
    Who rolled the psalm to wintry skies,
Who built him fanes° of fruitless prayer,   *temples*

Who trusted God was love indeed
And love Creation's final law –
15   Though Nature, red in tooth and claw
With ravine,° shrieked against his creed –   *bloodshed*

Who loved, who suffered countless ills,
Who battled for the True, the Just,
Be blown about the desert dust,
20   Or sealed within the iron hills?

No more? A monster then, a dream,
A discord. Dragons of the prime,
That tare° each other in their slime,   *tear*
Were mellow music matched with him.

25   O life as futile, then, as frail!
O for thy voice to soothe and bless!
What hope of answer, or redress?
Behind the veil, behind the veil.

CVII

It is the day when he was born,
A bitter day that early sank
Behind a purple-frosty bank
Of vapour, leaving night forlorn.

5   The time admits not flowers or leaves
To deck the banquet. Fiercely flies
The blast of North and East, and ice
Makes daggers at the sharpened eaves,

And bristles all the brakes° and thorns   *thicket*
10   To yon hard crescent, as she hangs
Above the wood which grides° and clangs   *grinds*
Its leafless ribs and iron horns

Together, in the drifts that pass
To darken on the rolling brine
15   That breaks the coast. But fetch the wine,
Arrange the board and brim the glass;

Bring in great logs and let them lie,
To make a solid core of heat;
Be cheerful-minded, talk and treat
20   Of all things ev'n as he were by;

We keep the day. With festal° cheer,   *festive*
   With books and music, surely we
   Will drink to him, whate'er he be,
And sing the songs he loved to hear.

CXXX

Thy voice is on the rolling air;
   I hear thee where the waters run;
   Thou standest in the rising sun,
And in the setting thou art fair.

5   What art thou then? I cannot guess;
   But though I seem in star and flower
   To feel thee some diffusive power,
I do not therefore love thee less:

My love involves the love before;
10   My love is vaster passion now;
   Tho' mix'd with God and Nature thou,
I seem to love thee more and more.

Far off thou art, but ever nigh;
   I have thee still, and I rejoice;
15   I prosper, circled with thy voice;
I shall not lose thee though I die.

Talking points

1 The original series of *In Memoriam* poems (over 130 of them) shows a progression of emotions, which we have tried to reflect in this selection. What emotional shifts do you notice between the poems? What 'emotional journey' does the speaker make? (You may find it helpful to consider what emotional stages usually follow a loss or bereavement. Can you identify any of these here?)

2 The punctuation in all these poems is used simply but effectively to underscore the emotional progress of the speaker. How is this accomplished? Look at where the question marks, colons, and dashes occur, and what effect they have; also check where sentences end.

3 In the third poem (LVI), the first stanza refers to cliffs and quarries, then popular sites for the new craze of fossil-collecting. How does this allusion to fossilized and extinct species work in conjunction with the rest of this poem?

4 Still referring to poem LVI, who or what does the 'She' in line 3 refer to? What conclusions can you draw about the impact of evolutionary theories on the Romantic view of Nature?

5 There is a distinct shift in the way that Nature is used as a vehicle for the poet's feelings in the last three poems. What is the difference between poem LVI and poem CVII in this respect? And what has happened by the time we reach poem CXXX, which is one of the last poems in the series? Does anything in this poem remind you of Wordsworth's 'Three Years She Grew' (see pp. 54–5)? What does this suggest about how Tennyson finally resolves his grief?

6 Although the poems express very different feelings and use contrasting language and imagery, the series as a whole has a unified and cohesive feel to it. What structural features do all the poems share?

Robert Browning (1812–1889)

My Last Duchess

Ferrara

That's my last Duchess painted on the wall,
Looking as if she were alive. I call
That piece a wonder, now: Frà° Pandolf's hands   *friar, brother*
Worked busily a day, and there she stands.
5 Will't please you sit and look at her? I said
'Frà Pandolf' by design, for never read
Strangers like you that pictured countenance,
The depth and passion of its earnest glance,
But to myself they turned (since none puts by
10 The curtain I have drawn for you, but I)
And seemed as they would ask me, if they durst,°   *dared*
How such a glance came there; so, not the first
Are you to turn and ask thus. Sir, 't was not
Her husband's presence only, called that spot
15 Of joy into the Duchess' cheek: perhaps
Frà Pandolf chanced to say, 'Her mantle° laps   *cloak*
Over my lady's wrist too much,' or 'Paint
Must never hope to reproduce the faint
Half-flush that dies along her throat': such stuff
20 Was courtesy, she thought, and cause enough
For calling up that spot of joy. She had
A heart – how shall I say? – too soon made glad,
Too easily impressed; she liked whate'er
She looked on, and her looks went everywhere.
25 Sir, 'twas all one! My favour at her breast,
The dropping of the daylight in the West,
The bough of cherries some officious° fool   *busy*
Broke in the orchard for her, the white mule
She rode with round the terrace – all and each
30 Would draw from her alike the approving speech,

Browning received an unusual education based on the contents of his
father's huge library, and started to write poetry at an early age. On reading
Elizabeth Barrett's poems (see pp. 67–8), he began writing her admiring
letters that led to their secret romance and engagement. Eventually they ran
away together to be married. They lived happily in Italy until she died; after
this, Browning returned to London and became a well-known figure on the
English literary scene. His friends and colleagues sometimes considered his
poetry eccentric; others admired it for its ability to catch the flavour and
rhythm of everyday speech. He is best remembered for his dramatic
monologues,* of which 'My Last Duchess' is an excellent example.

Or blush, at least. She thanked men, – good! but thanked
Somehow – I know not how – as if she ranked
My gift of a nine-hundred-years-old name
With anybody's gift. Who'd stoop to blame
35 This sort of trifling? Even had you skill
In speech – (which I have not) – to make your will
Quite clear to such an one, and say, 'Just this
Or that in you disgusts me; here you miss,
Or there exceed the mark' – and if she let
40 Herself be lessoned so, nor plainly set
Her wits to yours, forsooth, and made excuse,
– E'en then would be some stooping; and I choose
Never to stoop. Oh sir, she smiled, no doubt,
Whene'er I passed her; but who passed without
45 Much the same smile? This grew; I gave commands;
Then all smiles stopped together. There she stands
As if alive. Will 't please you rise? We'll meet
The company below, then. I repeat,
The Count your master's known munificence°   *generosity*
50 Is ample warrant that no just pretence
Of mine for dowry will be disallowed;
Though his fair daughter's self, as I avowed
At starting, is my object. Nay, we'll go
Together down, sir. Notice Neptune,[1] though,
55 Taming a sea-horse, thought a rarity,
Which Claus of Innsbruck cast in bronze for me!

The speaker in 'My Last Duchess', the Duke of Ferrara, lived in the
sixteenth century. His first wife died very young in mysterious circumstances.
Browning here imagines a conversation that might have taken place during
the arrangements for his second marriage, to the Count of Tyrol's daughter.
Frà Pandolf is an imaginary name for an artist (his title makes it clear that he
is a monk or holy man). Claus of Innsbruck is also an invented name.

Notes

1 God of the sea.

Talking points

1 One of the more interesting features about this dramatic
   monologue is that there is a significant difference, or distance,
   between the poet and the first-person speaker in the poem. How
   do we know this, and why is this distance created?
2 Given that the only voice we hear is Ferrara's, do you agree that
   we 'hear' much more than he is telling us? How does he
   unintentionally or unwittingly reveal himself?
3 What kind of character sketch would you make of Ferrara? You
   might feel that he is more than simply a tyrant. Is there an
   element of fear in his refusal or inability to communicate with his
   first wife?
4 The form of the dramatic monologue makes for an immediate
   impact on the reader. Why is this so? In what way are we invited
   to become 'part' of the poem?

Emily Brontë (1818–1848)

No Coward Soul Is Mine

No coward soul is mine,
No trembler in the world's storm-troubled sphere:
I see Heaven's glories shine,
And faith shines equal, arming me from fear.

5   O God within my breast,
Almighty, ever-present Deity!
Life – that in me has rest,
As I – undying Life – have power in thee!

    Vain are the thousand creeds°   *beliefs, doctrines*
10 That move men's hearts: unutterably vain;
Worthless as withered weeds
Or idlest froth amid the boundless main,°   *sea*

To waken doubt in one
Holding so fast by thine infinity;
15 So surely anchored on
The steadfast rock of immortality.

With wide-embracing love
Thy spirit animates eternal years,
Pervades and broods above,
20 Changes, sustains, dissolves, creates and rears.

Though earth and man were gone,
And suns and universes ceased to be,
And thou were left alone,
Every existence would exist in thee.

Born into the gifted but tragically doomed **Brontë** family, Emily, together
with her siblings, wrote poetry and fantasy from an early age. Together with
her sisters Charlotte and Anne, she published a collection of poems under a
male pseudonym. These brought attention and interest that Emily despised
and shrank from. Both reclusive and fiercely independent, she worked briefly
as a governess to support her brother and father, but became sick with
longing for her native countryside and spent the rest of her short life at home.
She died of tuberculosis brought on by her own self-neglect. She is best
remembered for her extraordinary and shocking novel, *Wuthering Heights*.

25 There is not room for Death,
Nor atom that his might could render void:°   *vacant*
Thou – thou art Being and Breath,
And what thou art may never be destroyed.

EMILY BRONTË

Walt Whitman (1819–1892)

When I Heard at the Close of the Day[1]

When I heard at the close of the day how my name had been receiv'd with
      plaudits in the capitol, still it was not a happy night for me that follow'd,
And else when I carous'd,[2] or when my plans were accomplish'd, still I was
      not happy,
But the day when I rose at dawn from the bed of perfect health, refresh'd,
      singing, inhaling the ripe breath of autumn,
When I saw the full moon in the west grow pale and disappear in the morning
      light,
5   When I wander'd alone over the beach, and undressing bathed, laughing with
      the cool waters, and saw the sun rise,
And when I thought how my dear friend my lover was on his way coming, O
      then I was happy,
O then each breath tasted sweeter, and all that day my food nourish'd me
      more, and the beautiful day pass'd well,
And the next came with equal joy, and with the next at evening came my
      friend,
And that night while all was still I heard the waters roll slowly continually up
      the shores,
10 I heard the hissing rustle of the liquid and sands as directed to me whispering
      to congratulate me,
For the one I love most lay sleeping by me under the same cover in the cool
      night,
In the stillness in the autumn moonbeams his face was inclined toward me,
And his arm lay lightly around my breast – and that night I was happy.

Whitman broke new ground for American poetry, consciously identifying
himself with American culture. He was born on the north-eastern coast of the
USA, and spent much of his life wandering from job to job, working as a
printer, school-teacher, and journalist. During the American Civil War (the
subject of a collection of his poems), he volunteered to nurse the wounded.
His poetry was unusual (and considered shocking in his time) for its
courageous acknowledgement of his homosexuality, as well as its
fascination with the smaller details of daily life.

Notes

[1] This poem is part of a series that
Whitman wrote in celebration of
what he called 'manly love'.
[2] Enjoy a noisy drinking party.

Matthew Arnold (1822–1888)

Dover Beach

The sea is calm to-night.
The tide is full, the moon lies fair
Upon the straits;[1] – on the French coast the light
Gleams and is gone; the cliffs of England stand,
5 Glimmering and vast, out in the tranquil bay.
Come to the window, sweet is the night-air!
Only, from the long line of spray
Where the sea meets the moon-blanch'd° land,   *whitened*
Listen! you hear the grating roar
10 Of pebbles which the waves draw back, and fling,
At their return, up the high strand,
Begin, and cease, and then again begin,
With tremulous cadence slow, and bring
The eternal note of sadness in.

15 Sophocles[2] long ago
Heard it on the Aegean,[3] and it brought
Into his mind the turbid° ebb and flow   *muddy*
Of human misery; we
Find also in the sound a thought,
20 Hearing it by this distant northern sea.

The Sea of Faith
Was once, too, at the full, and round earth's shore
Lay like the folds of a bright girdle° furled.   *belt*
But now I only hear
25 Its melancholy, long, withdrawing roar,
Retreating, to the breath
Of the night-wind, down the vast edges drear
And naked shingles° of the world.   *pebble beaches*

The son of a respected teacher, **Arnold** himself became an inspector of schools after graduating from Oxford University. His career gave him considerable insight into the educational, social, and cultural problems of his age. His poetry is preoccupied with questions arising from these issues, including the loss of religious belief. However, he was best known in his time for his thoughtful prose, and became one of the most admired critics of his day. A happily married man, he was eventually made Professor of Poetry at Oxford.

Notes

1 Headlands on either side of a channel of water.
2 Classical Greek author of tragic dramas; much admired by Arnold.
3 Part of the Mediterranean Sea between Greece and Turkey.

     Ah, love, let us be true
30 To one another! for the world, which seems
     To lie before us like a land of dreams,
     So various, so beautiful, so new,
     Hath really neither joy, nor love, nor light,
     Nor certitude, nor peace, nor help for pain;
35 And we are here as on a darkling plain
     Swept with confused alarms of struggle and flight,
     Where ignorant armies clash by night.

Arnold wrote 'Dover Beach' while passing through Dover on honeymoon.
Dover is a port on the south-east coast of England facing France. It is famous
for its spectacular white chalk cliffs (their colour explains why Arnold
describes them as 'glimmering' in this poem.) These cliffs drop sharply to the
beach, which is made up of pebbles that have been washed and rubbed by
the sea. Waves breaking on these pebble or shingle beaches make a
distinctive roaring sound that is much louder than sea on sand.

Anonymous (*c.* 1850)

Translated by Perce Haslam

Kilaben Bay Song

Hail! Dawn is shining glory doing
The sun shining (blazing with warmth)
Night moving
Man stirring
5   Children restless
Women fire-wood thinking
Birds singing
Animals awakening (sleeping not)
Camp noise grows
10 Men bush towards moving
Women water gathering
Children they hungry, all shouting
Women water collected
Men spear fish, return
15 People all eating
Camp quiet again

Talking points

This is a traditional Australian aboriginal song or chant. You might
like to compare it with Watson's 'The Rain That Is Male' (p. 226).
Both are attempts by modern translators to salvage some fragments of
the lost or dying cultures of indigenous peoples subjected to genocide
or threatened with extinction through assimilation. This refers to the
process in which an indigenous culture is diluted by a foreign or
'outsider' culture (often a colonial, Western, industrialized, or urban
one) until little or none of the original traditions, languages, or social
structures remain.

You can also find a similar poem by the Zimbabwean poet Joseph
Kumbirai on p. 163. This is another example of how the everyday
rituals that accompany the dawn of a new day are celebrated in
traditional cultures.

Emily Dickinson (1830–1886)

I Taste a Liquor Never Brewed

I taste a liquor never brewed —
From Tankards scooped in Pearl —
Not all the Vats upon the Rhine[1]
Yield such an Alcohol!

5   Inebriate of Air — am I —
And Debauchee[2] of Dew —
Reeling — thro endless summer days —
From inns of Molten Blue —

When 'Landlords' turn the drunken Bee
10   Out of the Foxglove's door —
When Butterflies — renounce their 'drams'° —   *drinks, tots*
I shall but drink the more!

Till Seraphs° swing their snowy Hats —   *angels*
And Saints — to windows run —
15   To see the little Tippler
Leaning against the — Sun —

Dickinson was born and lived in the rural town of Amherst in the north-eastern USA. Well educated, she wrote startlingly modern poetry from an early age. Although she initially tried to publish her work, her friends and literary connections were puzzled or shocked by her poems, and almost none were published in her lifetime. As she grew older, she became increasingly reclusive, and eventually refused to meet people or leave her room, although she kept up close and often intimate correspondences with a number of close friends and scholars, including various women writers she admired. After her death, there was considerable argument about what should be done with her poems. They were eventually published in a heavily edited and censored form. The originals were only made available for publication in the 1950s; since then, Dickinson's distinctive voice has been greatly admired by critics. Her poetry has inspired several modern poets; see Adrienne Rich's 'I am in Danger – Sir –' (pp. 173–4).

Notes

[1] River in Germany, which runs through a region famous for its vineyards and wine.
[2] Person addicted to sensual indulgence.

Much Madness Is Divinest Sense

Much Madness is divinest Sense —
To a discerning Eye —
Much Sense — the starkest Madness —
'Tis the Majority
5 In this, as All, prevail —
Assent — and you are sane —
Demur° — you're straightway dangerous —   *disagree*
And handled with a Chain —

Wild Nights — Wild Nights

Wild Nights — Wild Nights!
Were I with thee
Wild Nights should be
Our luxury!

5 Futile — the Winds —
To a Heart in port —
Done with the Compass —
Done with the Chart!

Rowing in Eden —
10 Ah, the Sea!
Might I but moor — Tonight —
In Thee!

The Bustle in a House

The Bustle in a House
The Morning after Death
Is solemnest of industries
Enacted upon Earth —

5 The Sweeping up the Heart
And putting Love away
We shall not want to use again
Until Eternity.

Christina Rossetti (1830–1894)

Song

When I am dead, my dearest,
    Sing no sad songs for me;
Plant thou no roses at my head,
    Nor shady cypress tree:
5 Be the green grass above me
    With showers and dewdrops wet;
And if thou wilt, remember,
    And if thou wilt, forget.

I shall not see the shadows,
10   I shall not feel the rain;
I shall not hear the nightingale
    Sing on, as if in pain:
And dreaming through the twilight
    That doth not rise nor set,
15 Haply I may remember
    And haply may forget.

Born into a gifted family, **Rossetti** spent much of her life burying her passionate personality in religion, charity work, and the care of her family. She was the younger sister of the flamboyant artist and poet Dante Gabriel Rossetti, and their unspoken rivalry marked much of her life and work. She held an ambiguous position on the edges of the Pre-Raphaelite Brotherhood, an idealistic group of young artists and writers headed by her brother. They promoted a return to standards of beauty uncorrupted by bourgeois, middle-class standards, and a nostalgia for the idealized world seen in medieval and ancient myths, and these principles are reflected in Rossetti's work. She had a clear sense of her poetic vocation, and refused marriage twice (citing religious reasons) in order to focus on her writing. She was much admired by her contemporaries for the subtlety of her work and the originality of her religious poetry. Gerard Manley Hopkins and many other lesser poets were influenced by her. Rossetti died of breast cancer.

'In an Artist's Studio' refers to the relationship between the poet's brother, Dante Gabriel Rossetti, and his model and fiancée, Elizabeth Siddal. At first, he courted her obsessively, and she modelled for many of his paintings and drawings. She lived with him while they were engaged, compromising her reputation – such a step would have been strictly frowned upon in polite society of that time. Meanwhile he fell in love with another woman, and eventually only married Siddal (after nine years) because he believed she was dying. A year after their marriage, she committed suicide. Rossetti never publicly criticized her brother, but this poem stands as an indictment of his cruelty, as well as an unsentimental view of what it meant to be an artist's model. (She herself had posed for numerous pictures.)

In an Artist's Studio

One face looks out from all his canvases,
    One selfsame figure sits or walks or leans:
    We found her hidden just behind those screens,
That mirror gave back all her loveliness.
5 A queen in opal or in ruby dress,
    A nameless girl in freshest summer-greens,
    A saint, an angel – every canvas means
The same one meaning, neither more nor less.
He feeds upon her face by day and night,
10 And she with true kind eyes looks back on him,
Fair as the moon and joyful as the light:
    Not wan with waiting, not with sorrow dim;
Not as she is, but was when hope shone bright;
    Not as she is, but as she fills his dream.

Talking points

1 'Song' has been linked to 'The Unquiet Grave' (p. 11). If you have
not already done so, you might like to read the suggestions for
comparison and discussion on p. 12.
2 In what way does the speaker in 'In an Artist's Studio' reveal that
the woman in the pictures has been robbed of her own identity?
Where exactly is she 'found'? (Look at the nouns in lines 3 and 4.
Do you agree that these all suggest two-dimensional images?
What effect does this have?)
3 What stereotypes is the model turned into? (Read lines 5 to 7.)
4 What link is there between the paintings and the painter's view of
his model? What does this suggest about their relationship? Do
you think he actually 'sees' her? What does he see?
5 As can be seen from the notes on p. 88, this poem has a particular
history. Can it possibly succeed without this context? What could
its message be in a more general sense?

Thomas Hardy (1840–1928)

Drummer Hodge

They throw in drummer Hodge, to rest
    Uncoffined – just as found:
His landmark is a kopje°-crest   *hill*
    That breaks the veldt° around;   *grassy plain*
5 And foreign constellations west
    Each night above his mound.

Young Hodge the Drummer never knew –
    Fresh from his Wessex[1] home –
The meaning of the broad Karoo,[2]
10   The Bush, the dusty loam,°   *soil*
And why uprose to nightly view
    Strange stars amid the gloom.°   *gloom, dusk*

Yet portion of that unknown plain
    Will Hodge forever be;
15 His homely Northern breast and brain
    Grow to some Southern tree,
And strange-eyed constellations reign
    His stars eternally.

Hardy was born in Dorset, a beautiful rural part of south-western England, which was to be the setting of most of his works. He initially studied as an architect, but soon turned to writing novels. These were successful enough to allow him to become a full-time writer. Although many admired his works, most critics regarded his novels as gloomy and immoral. Disillusioned and unhappy in his marriage, he turned to writing poetry. His poems, which focus on the sufferings and ironies of life and love, brought him further recognition and praise.

'**Drummer Hodge**', written in 1902, refers to the Anglo-Boer War (now more correctly termed the South African War), fought after the establishment of the Orange Free State and the Transvaal as independent Boer (Afrikaner) republics. South Africa was at that stage a British colony, and although the Boers had moved ('trekked') beyond the reach of the established bounds of the colony, the discovery of gold in the Transvaal meant that Britain mounted two full-scale wars on South African territory to recover the 'republics'. After some initial defeats (mainly due to the guerrilla tactics of the heavily outnumbered Boers), the British crushed the rebels. In the process, they burnt down Boer farms and placed Afrikaner women and children in concentration camps, where thousands of them died. There was considerable international criticism of Britain's actions during this time.
    Hardy (unlike Olive Schreiner – see p. 94) expresses no strong views in this strangely peaceful poem, which was inspired by the death in the war of a young drummer from the poet's home town.

Notes

[1] Name given by Hardy to his home region of south-west England.
[2] Dry interior plateau of South Africa.

In Time of 'The Breaking of Nations'

Only a man harrowing° clods   *ploughing*
   In a slow silent walk
With an old horse that stumbles and nods
   Half asleep as they stalk.

5 Only thin smoke without flame
   From the heaps of couch-grass;
Yet this will go onward the same
   Though Dynasties pass.

Yonder a maid and her wight°   *man*
10   Come whispering by:
War's annals° will cloud into night   *records*
   Ere their story die.

'In Time of "The Breaking of Nations"'' was written during the First World War (1914–1918), sometimes called the Great War for its magnitude and impact on the social structure of Éurope. The loss of life alone was staggering. (See Yeats' 'An Irish Airman Foresees His Death' [p. 99], Owen's poems [pp. 122–3], and Brooke's 'The Soldier' [p. 110] for contrasting views of what it meant to fight in this war.) This poem is a response to the growing feeling that things would never be the same again after the war. In a strange way, the predictions in this poem were to be both right and wrong. See whether you agree after you have read the poem.

Gerard Manley Hopkins (1844–1889)

The Windhover:[1]

To Christ our Lord

I caught this morning morning's minion,° king-   *darling, king's favourite*
    dom of daylight's dauphin,[2] dapple-dawn-drawn Falcon, in his riding
    Of the rolling level underneath him steady air, and striding
High there, how he rung upon the rein of a wimpling° wing   *rippling*
5 In his ecstasy! then, off, off forth on swing,
    As a skate's heel sweeps smooth on a bow-bend: the hurl and gliding
    Rebuffed the big wind. My heart in hiding
Stirred for a bird, – the achieve of, the mastery of the thing!

Brute beauty and valour and act, oh, air, pride, plume, here
10   Buckle! AND the fire that breaks from thee then, a billion
Times told lovelier, more dangerous, O my chevalier![3]

    No wonder of it: shéer plód makes plough down sillion°   *furrow*
Shine, and blue-bleak embers, ah my dear,
    Fall, gall themselves, and gash gold-vermilion.°   *bright red*

Hopkins came from a cultured Anglican family and was an excellent student at Oxford University. Here he met the poet Robert Bridges (who was to preserve and eventually publish much of his friend's work). He was also caught up in a new intellectual and theological movement towards the Catholic faith. Hopkins converted to Catholicism and decided to become a priest, burning much of his poetry as a sign of commitment. While training for the priesthood, he developed unique poetic concepts that combined his delight in the beauty of the natural world with spiritual insight. Encouraged by his religious superiors, he began writing again. After his ordination, he served in a number of industrial parishes, work he found exhausting and discouraging. He was then sent to teach in Ireland, where he became severely depressed and later died. His poetry was first published, and his distinctive genius recognized, only thirty years after his death.

'The Windhover' is a good introduction to the verbal complexity of Hopkins' poems. This poem is particularly dense; words, associations, and images are crammed into a tight and demanding framework (in this case, the sonnet* form, with only three rhyming sounds – only one rhyme is used for the entire octave!) This is why Hopkins' poems sometimes have a sense of 'straining at the seams.' The richness of his writing makes critical analysis of his poetry

Notes

[1] Kestrel or falcon; bird of prey known for its ability to hover against the wind.
[2] Son of (and heir to) the king of France.
[3] French word for knight or nobleman.

No Worst, There Is None

No worst, there is none. Pitched past pitch of grief,
More pangs will, schooled at forepangs, wilder wring.
Comforter, where, where is your comforting?
Mary,[4] mother of us, where is your relief?
5 My cries heave, herds-long; huddle in a main, a chief-
woe, world-sorrow; on an age-old anvil[5] wince and sing –   *savage, fierce*
Then lull, then leave off. Fury had shrieked 'No ling–
ering! Let me be fell:° force[6] I must be brief.'
O the mind, mind has mountains; cliffs of fall
10 Frightful, sheer, no-man-fathomed. Hold them cheap
May who ne'er hung there. Nor does long our small
Durance° deal with that steep or deep. Here! creep,   *endurance*
Wretch, under a comfort serves in a whirlwind: all
Life death does end and each day dies with sleep.

Talking points

'No Worst, There Is None', one of a series known as the 'terrible'
sonnets, was written during a period of what would today be
recognized as severe clinical depression, which Hopkins suffered
towards the end of his life. We have already linked this poem to
Herbert's 'The Flower' (pp. 35–36), which also deals with spiritual
and emotional crisis. You might like to look at the suggestions for
comparison made there.

particularly rewarding. Interpreting his poetry is also an extremely personal
process; you and your classmates might like to work through one of his
poems individually, and then report your findings back to each other; you
could be surprised at the different interpretations that emerge.

   This poem is also often given as a good example of the practice of
Hopkins' theory of 'inscape', in which the uniqueness of a natural object at a
particular moment of beauty is captured, at the same time as the resulting
spiritual insight is celebrated.

Notes

4   Mary, mother of Jesus; a source
    of religious comfort to Catholic
    Christians.
5   Iron block on which metal is
    hammered into shape.
6   Perforce; necessarily.

Olive Schreiner (1855–1920)

The Cry of South Africa

Give back my dead!
They who by kop° and fountain   *hill*
First saw the light upon my rocky breast!
Give back my dead,
5   The sons who played upon me
When childhood's dews still rested on their heads.
Give back my dead
Whom thou hast riven° from me   *torn*
By arms of men loud called from earth's farthest bound
10   To wet my bosom with my children's blood!
Give back my dead,
The dead who grew up on me!

Talking points

This poem was written in 1900, during the South African War,
formerly called the Anglo-Boer War. You will find it helpful to check
the notes on p. 90, where you will find another Boer War poem,
written by Hardy. How do these two poems differ?

Olive Schreiner was born to missionary parents in what was then known as
the Cape Colony, and worked as a governess teaching the children of local
farmers. She travelled to England, where she published her novel *The Story
of an African Farm* under a male pseudonym. The success of her book gave
her access to progressive circles, and she continued to write passionately on
subjects such as women's rights, colonial imperialism, pacifism, and racism
throughout her life. She returned to South Africa to marry the politician
Samuel Cronwright, and although she spent the duration of the First World
War in England, she went back to South Africa to die. Unconventional and
often confrontational, she never lacked courage in either her writing or her
life.

Rudyard Kipling (1865–1936)

If –

If you can keep your head when all about you
Are losing theirs and blaming it on you;
If you can trust yourself when all men doubt you,
But make allowance for their doubting too;
5 If you can wait and not be tired by waiting,
Or being lied about, don't deal in lies,
Or being hated, don't give way to hating,
And yet don't look too good, not talk too wise:

If you can dream – and not make dreams your master;
10 If you can think – and not make thought your aim;
If you can meet with Triumph and Disaster
And treat those two imposters just the same;
If you can bear to hear the truth you've spoken
Twisted by knaves° to make a trap for fools,   *dishonest people*
15 Or watch the things you gave your life to, broken,
And stoop and build 'em up with worn-out tools:

If you can make one heap of all your winnings
And risk it on one turn of pitch-and-toss,[1]
And lose, and start again at your beginnings
20 And never breathe a word about your loss;
If you can force your heart and nerve and sinew°   *muscle*
To serve your turn long after they are gone,
And so hold on when there is nothing in you
Except the Will which says to them: 'Hold on!'

Kipling's novels, poems, and short stories epitomize to many the British Empire at its height. Born in India, he began his writing career as a journalist in Lahore (capital of present-day Pakistan, then part of India) in the 1880s. His vast body of work includes often satirical poems in lively rhythms that tell colourful tales of West meeting East. These made him instantly popular in his time. However, in the second half of the twentieth century, as nations around the globe began to count the cost of colonialism, there was a violent swing away from 'empire literature', and Kipling went rapidly from being one of the most widely read and admired writers in the world (and the first British writer to win the Nobel Prize for Literature) to almost pariah or outcast status. In recent years, however, as post-colonial* criticism has become increasingly widespread, many are beginning to recognize that along with the patronizing echoes of his time, his work contains many cynical glances at the hypocrisies of colonial rule, and real concern for the people and countries under British dominion.

Notes

[1] Game of combined skill and luck (involving tossing a coin repeatedly) that attracted bets.

25 If you can talk with crowds and keep your virtue,
   Or walk with Kings – nor lose the common touch,
   If neither foes nor loving friends can hurt you,
   If all men count with you, but none too much;
   If you can fill the unforgiving minute
30 With sixty seconds' worth of distance run,
   Yours is the Earth and everything that's in it,
   And – which is more – you'll be a Man, my son!

'If', once an extremely popular and well-known poem, fell out of favour several decades ago, as its sentiments became alien to an increasingly cynical age. However, it was recently revived in South Africa in interesting (and ironic) circumstances. The game of cricket (that great export of the British Empire) had suffered a terrible reverse when it was discovered that the South African team captain had been taking money and gifts from shady characters with an interest in manipulating games. In an attempt to clean up the now tarnished reputation of the sport, the United Cricket Board produced an advertising film in grainy, old-fashioned tints that showed South African cricketers nobly striving their best to the accompaniment of stirring music and a voice-over of the above poem. The clear implication was that there was a need for a return to a more innocent and morally gallant age – in life as much as in sport.

William Butler Yeats (1865–1939)

No Second Troy

Why should I blame her that she filled my days
With misery, or that she would of late
Have taught to ignorant men most violent ways,
Or hurled the little streets upon the great,
5   Had they but courage equal to desire?
What could have made her peaceful with a mind
That nobleness made simple as a fire,
With beauty like a tightened bow, a kind
That is not natural in an age like this,
10   Being high and solitary and most stern?
Why, what could she have done, being what she is?
Was there another Troy for her to burn?

Ireland's foremost poet, **Yeats** was born into a gifted family. His father and brother were well-known painters, and he initially followed in their footsteps before deciding on a literary career. Together with Lady Gregory, a writer and cultural nationalist, he began a campaign to revive Irish literature and drama, and founded a national theatre (see p. 101 for another poem from this movement, sometimes called the 'Celtic Twilight'). Yeats was fascinated by traditional Irish legends, as well as the supernatural. He was also an ardent Irish nationalist at a time when the colonial domination of Ireland by England had led to guerrilla warfare by Irish rebels. His passion for a beautiful revolutionary, Maud Gonne, who rejected him, inspired much of his love poetry. He eventually married Georgie Hyde-Lees, who was to influence the mysticism of his later writing. The doomed nationalist uprising of Easter 1916 rekindled Yeats' idealistic hopes for a free Ireland, and in 1922 he was appointed to the Senate of the new Irish Free State. A year later he won the Nobel Prize for Literature. His poetry is significant for encompassing the shift from late Romanticism to the new Modernist* principles.

'**No Second Troy**', one of many poems that Yeats wrote about Maud Gonne, likens her to Helen of Troy, who was reputed to be the most beautiful woman in the world. According to the tales of the Greek epic poet Homer, Helen's abduction led to the Trojan War and the ultimate destruction of the city and civilization of Troy. (For further details, see the notes to Tennyson's 'Ulysses' on p. 71.) For a less romantic perspective on Helen of Troy, see H.D's 'Helen' on p. 109.

The Second Coming

Turning and turning in the widening gyre°   *spiral*
The falcon cannot hear the falconer;
Things fall apart; the centre cannot hold;
Mere anarchy is loosed upon the world,
5   The blood-dimmed tide is loosed, and everywhere
The ceremony of innocence is drowned;
The best lack all conviction, while the worst
Are full of passionate intensity.

Surely some revelation is at hand;
10   Surely the Second Coming is at hand.
The Second Coming! Hardly are those words out
When a vast image out of *Spiritus Mundi*[1]
Troubles my sight: somewhere in sands of the desert
A shape with lion body and the head of a man,[2]
15   A gaze blank and pitiless as the sun,
Is moving its slow thighs, while all about it
Reel shadows of the indignant desert birds.
The darkness drops again; but now I know
That twenty centuries of stony sleep
20   Were vexed to nightmare by a rocking cradle,
And what rough beast, its hour come round at last,
Slouches towards Bethlehem[3] to be born?

The title 'The Second Coming' borrows from the biblical reference to the second coming of Jesus. This, it was prophesied, would take place after a period of increasing violence and turbulence, and would mark the end of time. However, in this poem, the speaker imagines the coming of a frightening and barbaric mythological being, rather than a Christian deity. Written shortly after the First World War, this poem seems to hint at the inevitability of another devastating war arising out of the brutal settlement of the first.

Notes

[1] Literally, 'universal spirit'.
[2] The Sphinx, a mythological monster worshipped and feared by the ancient Egyptians and Greeks.
[3] Birthplace of Jesus.

An Irish Airman Foresees His Death

I know that I shall meet my fate
Somewhere among the clouds above;
Those that I fight I do not hate,
Those that I guard I do not love;
5 My country is Kiltartan Cross,[4]
My countrymen Kiltartan's poor,
No likely end could bring them loss
Or leave them happier than before.
Nor law, nor duty bade me fight,
10 Nor public men, nor cheering crowds,
A lonely impulse of delight
Drove to this tumult in the clouds;
I balanced all, brought all to mind,
The years to come seemed waste of breath,
15 A waste of breath the years behind
In balance with this life, this death.

'An Irish Airman Foresees His Death' was written in memory of Major Robert Gregory (the son of Yeats' close friend and colleague, Lady Gregory), who was killed in action during the last year of the First World War. Does this poem sound like a traditional elegy*? In what ways is it unusual?

Notes

4 A village close to the airman's home in western Ireland.

Edwin Arlington Robinson (1869–1935)

Richard Cory

Whenever Richard Cory went down town,
We people on the pavement looked at him:
He was a gentleman from sole to crown,
Clean favoured, and imperially slim.

5   And he was always quietly arrayed,
And he was always human when he talked;
But still he fluttered pulses when he said,
'Good-morning', and he glittered when he walked.

And he was rich – yes, richer than a king –
10   And admirably schooled in every grace:
In fine, we thought that he was everything
To make us wish that we were in his place.

So on we worked, and waited for the light,
And went without the meat, and cursed the bread;
15   And Richard Cory, one calm summer night,
Went home and put a bullet through his head.

Robinson grew up in a small town in the north-eastern part of the USA known as New England, and much of his writing involves nostalgic reflection on the changing ways of life in this rural community. He studied at Harvard University, and through the influence of President Franklin D. Roosevelt, who was impressed by his poetry, he was given a customs post. This gave him financial security and the opportunity to concentrate on his writing. His popularity as a poet grew slowly but steadily during his lifetime.

Eva Gore-Booth (1870–1926)

The Land to a Landlord

You hug to your soul a handful of dust,
And you think the round world your sacred trust –
But the sun shines, and the wind blows,
And nobody cares and nobody knows.

5   O the bracken waves and the foxgloves flame,
And none of them ever has heard your name –
Near and dear is the curlew's cry,
You are merely a stranger passing by.

Sheer up through the shadows the mountain towers
10   And dreams wander free in this world of ours, –
Though you may turn the grass to gold,
The twilight has left you out in the cold.

Though you are king of the rose and the wheat,
Not for you, not for you is the bog-myrtle sweet,
15   Though you are lord of the long grass,
The hemlock bows not her head as you pass.

The poppies would flutter amongst the corn
Even if you had never been born,
With your will or without your will
20   The ragweed can wander over the hill.

Down there in the bog where the plovers call
You are but an outcast after all,
Over your head the sky gleams blue –
Not a cloud or star belongs to you.

Younger sister of the famous Irish activist and revolutionary, Countess
Markievicz, **Gore-Booth** was a poet associated with the 'Celtic Twilight', the
Irish literary revival led by Yeats and others (see p. 97). She was also a social
worker, socialist, and feminist activist. She left Ireland to live in Britain with
Esther Roper (known for her work in trying to secure the vote for women).
Theirs was most probably a lesbian relationship.

Talking points

The Celtic Twilight was as much a nationalist as a cultural movement. It drew on the stories and traditions of the oppressed and marginalized Irish community (see p. 97 for more details of this history). Although this poem is written in the romantic style associated with this literary movement, it is intensely political; the Irish had been tenants in their own land to the hated English for centuries, and few figures were resented as much as the arrogant absentee landlord.

Gore-Booth (making use of an argument similar to Rossetti's in her poem 'Song' – p. 88) underlines the ultimate powerlessness of the oppressor in the face of the land's indifference. You might like to compare her line of reasoning with that used by the very respectable and orthodox Samuel Johnson on a similar topic (see 'A Short Song of Congratulation', p. 46).

Taking a different view, this poem also presents a deliberately gendered* perspective of nature; see the discussion on pp. 54–5 for further details on the 'masculine' and 'feminine' presentations of nature, as well as examples of poems that represent or counter these traditions.

Robert Frost (1874–1963)

Mending Wall

Something there is that doesn't love a wall,
That sends the frozen-ground-swell under it
And spills the upper boulders in the sun,
And makes gaps even two can pass abreast.
5   The work of hunters is another thing:
I have come after them and made repair
Where they have left not one stone on a stone,
But they would have the rabbit out of hiding,
To please the yelping dogs. The gaps I mean,
10 No one has seen them made or heard them made,
But at spring mending-time we find them there.
I let my neighbour know beyond the hill;
And on a day we meet to walk the line
And set the wall between us once again.
15 We keep the wall between us as we go.
To each the boulders that have fallen to each.
And some are loaves and some so nearly balls
We have to use a spell to make them balance:
'Stay where you are until our backs are turned!'
20 We wear our fingers rough with handling them.
Oh, just another kind of outdoor game,
One on a side. It comes to little more:
There where it is we do not need the wall:
He is all pine and I am apple orchard.
25 My apple trees will never get across
And eat the cones under his pines, I tell him.
He only says, 'Good fences make good neighbours.'
Spring is the mischief in me, and I wonder
If I could put a notion in his head:

Frost grew up in New England, the beautiful rural north-eastern corner of the USA, which he was to become famous for describing in his poems. His education included two years at Harvard University, and he made a living teaching, farming, and doing odd jobs. Shortly before the First World War he and his family spent three years in England, where his poems were published for the first time. He returned home to growing recognition and admiration of his work. Once again he took up teaching, and became one of the best-known modern American poets. Although he is generally admired as a wise observer of rural life, some critics have suggested that a more troubled note underlies much of his work.

30   '*Why* do they make good neighbours? Isn't it
Where there are cows? But here there are no cows.
Before I built a wall I'd ask to know
What I was walling in or walling out,
And to whom I was like to give offense.
35   Something there is that doesn't love a wall,
That wants it down.' I could say 'Elves' to him,
But it's not elves exactly, and I'd rather
He said it for himself. I see him there,
Bringing a stone grasped firmly by the top
40   In each hand, like an old-stone savage armed.
He moves in darkness as it seems to me,
Not of woods only and the shade of trees.
He will not go behind his father's saying,
And he likes having thought of it so well
45   He says again, 'Good fences make good neighbours.'

The Road Not Taken

Two roads diverged in a yellow wood,
And sorry I could not travel both
And be one traveller, long I stood
And looked down one as far as I could
5   To where it bent in the undergrowth;

Then took the other, as just as fair,
And having perhaps the better claim,
Because it was grassy and wanted wear;
Though as for that, the passing there
10   Had worn them really about the same,

And both that morning equally lay
In leaves no step had trodden black.
Oh, I kept the first for another day!
Yet knowing how way leads on to way,
15   I doubted if I should ever come back.

I shall be telling this with a sigh
Somewhere ages and ages hence:
Two roads diverged in a wood, and I –
I took the one less travelled by,
20   And that has made all the difference.

Talking points

Both Frost's poems seem to describe simple, everyday events. Do you agree that both could also stand as extended metaphors* for something else? Pick one poem (or study each one in succession), and work out what else the description of mending a wall, or choosing a road, could be about. On what different levels does each poem operate? Compare your interpretations with those of your classmates. How many different readings emerge? Which do you find the most valid, and why?

William Carlos Williams (1883–1963)

This Is Just to Say

I have eaten
the plums
that were in
the icebox

5   and which
you were probably
saving
for breakfast

Forgive me
10 they were delicious
so sweet
and so cold

Talking points

You might enjoy comparing this poem with Pound's 'In a Station of the Metro' opposite. Questions about both poems can be found on page 108.

Williams studied medicine, and while he was at university he became friends with the important and controversial poet Ezra Pound (see opposite page). After qualifying as a doctor, Williams returned to his home town. Here he married and spent the rest of his life, working as a paediatrician (a doctor specializing in children's illnesses). His experiences with working-class families influenced much of his writing. Part of a new generation of modern American poets who were moving towards more natural use of language, Williams combines a conversational style with vivid observation of detail.

Ezra Pound (1885–1972)

In a Station of the Metro[1]

The apparition of these faces in the crowd;
Petals on a wet, black bough.

The River-Merchant's Wife: a Letter

While my hair was still cut straight across my forehead
I played about the front gate, pulling flowers.
You came by on bamboo stilts, playing horse,
You walked about my seat, playing with blue plums.
5 And we went on living in the village of Chokan:
Two small people, without dislike or suspicion.

At fourteen I married My Lord you.
I never laughed, being bashful.°   *shy*
Lowering my head, I looked at the wall.
10 Called to, a thousand times, I never looked back.

At fifteen I stopped scowling,
I desired my dust to be mingled with yours
Forever and forever and forever.
Why should I climb the look out?

Pound was born in the mid-western USA, and became friends with the poets William Carlos Williams and Hilda Doolittle (see pp. 106 and 109) at university. He was fired from his first teaching job for unconventional behaviour, and left for Europe, where he joined other important figures who were establishing new trends in literary circles. Together with T.S. Eliot and the Irish writer James Joyce, he led the movement towards Modernism* in literature. During four years in Paris, he was part of a group of American literary exiles that included the writers Ernest Hemingway and Gertrude Stein. Horrified by the aftermath of the First World War, he turned to fascism as the solution to Europe's troubles. During the Second World War, he was caught broadcasting enemy propaganda. He was judged to be insane, and sent to a mental institution instead of standing trial for treason. On his release, he returned to Italy, where he lived until his death.

'The River-Merchant's Wife: a Letter' is a free translation of a poem by Li Po (*c.* 700–762), a Chinese poet whose works were much admired by Pound. The place names in this poem all refer to various locations in eighth-century China. You might like to compare this poem with the English translations of works by Li Po's contemporaries (pp. 1–2).

Notes

[1] Underground railway system in Paris.

15 At sixteen you departed,
    You went into far Ku-to-yen, by the river of swirling eddies,
    And you have been gone five months.
    The monkeys make sorrowful noise overhead.

    You dragged your feet when you went out.
20 By the gate now, the moss is grown, the different mosses,
    Too deep to clear them away!
    The leaves fall early this autumn, in wind.
    The paired butterflies are already yellow with August
    Over the grass in the West garden;
25 They hurt me. I grow older.
    If you are coming through the narrows of the river Kiang,
    Please let me know beforehand,
    And I will come out to meet you
                    As far as Cho-fu-Sa.

Talking points

You might find it helpful to compare 'In a Station of the Metro' with
another very short poem, Williams' 'This Is Just to Say' (p. 106). Here
the similarity is not so much one of topic or style, but rather the
ability of the poets to evoke a great deal with very few words.

The following questions might help you come to grips with these
poems, as well as providing some guidelines for approaching very
short poems.

1   What function does the title serve in both poems? How does this
    differ from (or enlarge on) the usual role of the title in a poem?
2   Both poems concentrate on a very immediate, or fleeting, image
    or experience. How does the brevity (shortness) of the poems
    underline this fleeting quality? Do they succeed in 'preserving the
    moment'?
3   Both poems have a distinctive shape. What does Williams' poem
    resemble? For whom is it written, and where do you think it
    might be found? The shape of Pound's poem, meanwhile, reflects
    the influence of very short Chinese and Japanese poems in which
    an image or emotion is described in a set number of words or
    syllables.
4   In poems this short, every word counts. In Williams' poem, where
    the words suggest ordinary household communication, it is the
    way the words are laid out on the page that is significant. What
    effect does their structuring have? In Pound's poem, however,
    each word (and each punctuation mark) is carefully chosen for
    effect. Try critically analysing this poem, considering each word.
    Does it evoke an overall emotion as well as an image?

H. D. (Hilda Doolittle) (1886–1961)

Helen[1]

All Greece hates
the still eyes in the white face,
the lustre° as of olives[2]   *gloss, sheen*
where she stands,
5   And the white hands.

All Greece reviles
the wan° face when she smiles,   *pale*
hating it deeper still
when it grows wan and white,
10 remembering past enchantments
and past ills.

Greece sees unmoved,
God's daughter,[3] born of love,
the beauty of cool feet
15 and slenderest knees,
could love indeed the maid,
only if she were laid,
white ash amid funereal cypresses.°   *trees planted in graveyards*

Talking points

Here we find a completely different vision of Helen of Troy, and the
Trojan War, to that found in the poems 'Ulysses' by Tennyson (p. 70)
and 'No Second Troy' by Yeats (p. 97). (You will find information on
both Helen herself and the Trojan War in the notes to these poems.)
Tennyson and Yeats each glorify different aspects of the tragic saga;
what exactly enthrals each of them? What is H. D.'s response to the
legend, and how does her poem contrast with theirs? How do you
explain the differences? Do you think the gender of these poets might
be a factor?

H. D. was born in the USA, and became friends with Ezra Pound and William
Carlos Williams while studying (see pp. 106–8). She joined Pound in Europe,
and together they founded a new movement in modern poetry (called the
'Imagist movement') that focused on the significance of actual physical
images. She married the poet Robert Adlington, and worked with him
translating works in Greek and Latin and editing an important literary journal.
She also wrote novels, as well as an account of her psychoanalysis by
Sigmund Freud, considered by many to be the founder of modern psychology.
After her marriage ended, she moved to Switzerland.

Notes

1   Helen of Troy, whose abduction
    led to the Trojan War.
2   This could be a comparison
    either to olives themselves, or
    olive trees, which have silver-
    coloured leaves.
3   Helen was the result of the
    seduction of Leda (a human
    woman) by Zeus, ruler of the
    Greek gods.

Rupert Brooke (1887–1915)

The Soldier

If I should die, think only this of me:
    That there's some corner of a foreign field
That is for ever England. There shall be
    In that rich earth a richer dust concealed;
5 A dust whom England bore, shaped, made aware,
    Gave, once, her flowers to love, her ways to roam,
A body of England's, breathing English air,
    Washed by the rivers, blest by suns of home.

And think, this heart, all evil shed away,
10   A pulse in the eternal mind, no less
      Gives somewhere back the thoughts by England given;
Her sights and sounds; dreams happy as her day;
    And laughter, learnt of friends; and gentleness,
      In hearts at peace, under an English heaven.

An attractive and popular figure, **Brooke** was educated at Cambridge University, where he was a leader in literary circles. His early poetry was much admired and he was awarded a fellowship for further study, but he suffered a breakdown soon afterwards (possibly because of the pressure he felt in coming to terms with his homosexuality). While recovering, he travelled to the USA, Canada, and the Pacific islands. He volunteered to serve in the Navy as soon as the First World War broke out, and the poetry he sent home established him as the most celebrated (if unrealistic) war poet of his times. In 1915 he was posted to the Mediterranean, where he died of blood-poisoning.

'The Soldier' is an interesting remnant of a particularly rose-coloured tradition of patriotism, which glorified fighting and dying for one's country (today the notion of dying for a cause is more likely to be idealized). These sentiments were unable to survive the gruesome realities of the First World War; although Europe had a history of bloody wars going back centuries, nothing like the horrors of modern trench warfare had ever been experienced before. This war was also probably the first in which both working-class and aristocratic soldiers suffered equally devastating losses and injuries. Brooke's poem was prophetic; his body lies buried on a small Greek island. See Hardy's 'In Time of "The Breaking of Nations"' (p. 91), Yeats' 'An Irish Airman Foresees His Death' (p. 99) and Owen's 'Futility' and 'Dulce et Decorum est' (pp. 122–3), as well as the notes on these poems, for a variety of reflections on the First World War.

Talking points

Read this poem carefully, and then turn to Wilfred Owen's 'Dulce et Decorum Est' (p. 123). Consider the following questions after reading the notes on both poems.

1   Both speakers describe a soldier's response to dying in action. Yet the poems differ in their use of language, imagery, and tone, and draw different conclusions. Isolate these contrasting elements, establishing how these are communicated in each case. Your class might like to divide into two groups, one to study each poem, before reporting back to each other.

2   What impact would each poem have had on the audience of the time?

3   Why was Brooke's poem so much more popular? Does this suggest any thoughts on the role that poetry might play in a time of crisis?

4   What seems to be the primary intention underlying each poem? Do you think that both are valid, especially in times of war?

5   Are both poems sincere? How can this be so? Do you agree that Brooke is perhaps a poet of the past, and Owen a poet of the present?

Katherine Mansfield (1888–1923)

To God the Father

To the little, pitiful God I make my prayer,
The God with the long grey beard
And flowing robe fastened with a hempen° girdle   *rope*
Who sits nodding and muttering on the all-too-big throne of
    Heaven.
5 What a long, long time, dear God, since you set the stars in
    their places,
Girded° the earth with the sea, and invented the day and night.   *encircled*
And longer the time since you looked through the blue window
    of Heaven
To see your children at play in a garden . . .
Now we are all stronger than you and wiser and more
    arrogant,
10 In swift procession we pass you by.
'Who is that marionette° nodding and muttering   *puppet*
On the all-too-big throne of Heaven?
Come down from your place, Grey Beard,
We have had enough of your play-acting!'
15 It is centuries since I believed in you,
But to-day my need of you has come back.
I want no rose-coloured future,
No books of learning, no protestations and denials –
I am sick of this ugly scramble,
20 I am tired of being pulled about –
O God, I want to sit on your knees
On the all-too-big throne of Heaven,
And fall asleep with my hands tangled in your grey beard.

Mansfield was born in New Zealand, but went to London to study. Her first
marriage lasted only a few days, and she became involved with John
Middleton Murry, an influential editor and literary figure, whom she later
married. They shared a sometimes stormy friendship and various literary
projects with the novelist D. H. Lawrence and his unconventional wife,
Frieda. (Lawrence described their four-way relationship in his book *Women in
Love*.) Mansfield's writing was original and wide-ranging; she was best
known for her short stories. She travelled regularly to France and Switzerland
in the hopes of shaking off the tuberculosis that eventually killed her.

T. S. Eliot (1888–1965)

Preludes

I

The winter evening settles down
With smell of steaks in passageways.
Six o'clock.
The burnt-out ends of smoky days.
5   And now a gusty shower wraps
The grimy scraps
Of withered leaves about your feet
And newspapers from vacant lots;
The showers beat
10 On broken blinds and chimney-pots,
And at the corner of the street
A lonely cab-horse steams and stamps.
And then the lighting of the lamps.

II

The morning comes to consciousness
15 Of faint stale smells of beer
From the sawdust-trampled street
With all its muddy feet that press
To early coffee-stands.
With the other masquerades°   *pretences, play-acting*
20 That time resumes,
One thinks of all the hands
That are raising dingy shades
In a thousand furnished rooms.

Eliot was born in the USA and studied at Harvard University and Oxford. His friend Ezra Pound encouraged him to settle in England, where he married Vivien Haigh-Wood. Their relationship was an extremely troubled one, and eventually ended in separation. Eliot worked in a bank for several years while gathering a considerable reputation as an editor and critic. Meanwhile, his first collections of poetry were establishing him as the sophisticated new voice of a disillusioned post-war age. He became a director at the publishing house Faber and Faber, and guided their publications of poetry along the new lines of Modernism,* a movement that he and others such as Pound had established. By this time he was one of the most influential literary figures in England. In later life, he accepted the doctrines of the Anglican church, a step that marked a shift in his poetry from cynicism to mysticism. He also became increasingly traditional in his politics. He was awarded the Nobel Prize for Literature in 1948.

III

You tossed a blanket from the bed,
25 You lay upon your back, and waited;
You dozed, and watched the night revealing
The thousand sordid images
Of which your soul was constituted;
They flickered against the ceiling.
30 And when all the world came back
And the light crept up between the shutters
And you heard the sparrows in the gutters,
You had such a vision of the street
As the street hardly understands;
35 Sitting along the bed's edge, where
You curled the paper from your hair,
Or clasped the yellow soles of feet
In the palms of both soiled hands.

IV

His soul stretched tight across the skies
40 That fade behind a city block,
Or trampled by insistent feet
At four and five and six o'clock;
And short square fingers stuffing pipes,
And evening newspapers, and eyes
45 Assured of certain certainties,
The conscience of a blackened street
Impatient to assume the world.

I am moved by fancies that are curled
Around these images, and cling:
50 The notion of some infinitely gentle
Infinitely suffering thing.

Wipe your hand across your mouth, and laugh;
The worlds revolve like ancient women
Gathering fuel in vacant lots.

In his poems, Eliot's purpose is to evoke images and emotions by association, rather than description. This practice of using language rather like music – for emotional and aesthetic effect rather than to communicate meaning – was set out by Eliot as a new creative philosophy, and was to become a hallmark of Modernist* poetry. In 'Preludes', we are presented with four different evocative cameos or scenes, rather than any narrative progression or philosophical argument.

Journey of the Magi[1]

'A cold coming we had of it,
 Just the worst time of the year
For a journey, and such a long journey:
The ways deep and the weather sharp,
5   The very dead of winter.'
And the camels galled, sore-footed, refractory,°   *stubborn, obstinate*
Lying down in the melting snow.
There were times we regretted
The summer palaces on slopes, the terraces,
10 And the silken girls bringing sherbet.°   *sweet Oriental drink*
Then the camel men cursing and grumbling
And running away, and wanting their liquor and women,
And the night-fires going out, and the lack of shelters,
And the cities hostile and the towns unfriendly
15 And the villages dirty and charging high prices:
A hard time we had of it.
At the end we preferred to travel all night,
Sleeping in snatches,
With the voices singing in our ears, saying
20 That this was all folly.

Then at dawn we came down to a temperate valley,
Wet, below the snow line, smelling of vegetation;
With a running stream and a water-mill beating the darkness,
And three trees on the low sky,
25 And an old white horse galloped away in the meadow.
Then we came to a tavern with vine-leaves over the lintel,°   *door beam*
Six hands at an open door dicing for pieces of silver,
And feet kicking the empty wine-skins.
But there was no information, and so we continued
30 And arrived at evening, not a moment too soon
Finding the place; it was (you may say) satisfactory.

'Journey of the Magi' is about a life-changing experience. Eliot wrote it in
the same year he converted to the Anglican church and finally took on British
citizenship – both choices that meant permanent changes in his life. The first
five lines are adapted from a seventeenth-century sermon, and the second
stanza is packed with allusions to the New Testament. The 'three trees' in
line 24 refer to the three crosses described in the crucifixion story; the 'vine-
leaves' and the 'lintel' in line 26 suggest the parables Jesus told in which he

Notes

1   According to the Bible, the three
    wise men from the East who
    travelled to pay homage to the
    baby Jesus.

All this was a long time ago, I remember,
And I would do it again, but set down
This set down
35 This: were we led all that way for
Birth or Death? There was a Birth, certainly,
We had evidence and no doubt. I had seen birth and death,
But had thought they were different; this Birth was
Hard and bitter agony for us, like Death, our death.
40 We returned to our places, these Kingdoms,
But no longer at ease here, in the old dispensation,°   *order, system*
With an alien people clutching their gods.
I should be glad of another death.

Talking points

There are suggestions for comparison with David Wright's 'On the
Margin' on p. 155. Or you might like to turn to p. 144 for a South
African version of this story.

metaphorically described himself as a vine and a door; the 'dicing' in line 27
possibly alludes to the soldiers gambling for Jesus' clothes at the foot of the
cross; the 'pieces of silver' in the same line refer to the thirty pieces of silver
that Judas, one of Jesus' disciples, was paid as a reward for betraying his
master; and the 'wine-skins' in line 28 suggest another parable, which
features the image of new wine in old wine-skins.

Claude McKay (1890–1948)

If We Must Die

If we must die, let it not be like hogs
Hunted and penned in an inglorious spot,
While round us bark the mad and hungry dogs,
Making their mock at our accursèd lot.
5   If we must die, O let us nobly die,
So that our precious blood may not be shed
In vain; then even the monsters we defy
Shall be constrained° to honour us though dead!   *forced*
O kinsmen! we must meet the common foe!
10 Though far outnumbered let us show us brave,
And for their thousand blows deal one deathblow!
What though before us lies the open grave?
Like men we'll face the murderous, cowardly pack,
Pressed to the wall, dying, but fighting back!

Born in Jamaica in the Caribbean, **Claude McKay** moved to the USA as a
young man. A writer skilled in various fields, he wrote both poetry and
novels. His poems reflect his perceptions of life in Jamaica and New York,
and his novels deal honestly with the experiences of black communities in
the Caribbean, the USA, and Europe. He also produced a respected
sociological work on life in Harlem (a black residential area in New York
City).

'**If We Must Die**' was written as a response to race riots that took place in
Harlem in 1919. Later, it was to become a poem of encouragement in times
of war. In its use of the sonnet form, it borrows directly from the poetry of
previous ages. Do you agree that it sounds more like a nineteenth-century (or
earlier) poem than a twentieth-century poem? What features does it share
with the sonnets by Wordsworth (p. 57) or Milton (p. 37), for example? Why
do you think the writer chose to use this form?

Edna St. Vincent Millay (1892–1950)

I, Being Born a Woman and Distressed

I, being born a woman and distressed
By all the needs and notions of my kind,
Am urged by your propinquity° to find   *closeness*
Your person fair, and feel a certain zest°   *enthusiasm*
5 To bear your body's weight upon my breast:
So subtly is the fume° of life designed,   *essence*
To clarify the pulse and cloud the mind,
And leave me once again undone, possessed.
Think not for this, however, the poor treason
10 Of my stout° blood against my staggering brain,   *strong*
I shall remember you with love, or season
My scorn with pity, – let me make it plain:
I find this frenzy insufficient reason
For conversation when we meet again.

Millay was born in the USA and educated at Vassar College, a prestigious
university for women. She soon established a reputation as a bold and witty
poet, and was the leader of a new generation of writers who were
sophisticated and daring in both their writing and their lifestyles.

Talking points

1   At first glance, this poem looks like a formal sonnet. However, we soon discover that it is wickedly funny and mocking in its intention. What basic point is the speaker trying to make, and to whom? Why is the use of the sonnet form particularly humorous here?

2   If you agree that contrast forms the main ingredient of the humour, identify how this operates. What tone is used? And what kind of language? Given the subject of the poem, do you think this is appropriate, or deliberately inappropriate? How does the use of language and syntax compare with the topic (or argument) of the poem?

3   How does the poet use the formal structure of the sonnet to emphasize her argument?

4   Traditionally, the sonnet was often used as a form of love poetry (see, for example, the sonnets of Sidney [p. 18] and Shakespeare [pp. 23–5].) Do you agree that this sonnet, however, is almost an anti-love poem? In what ways does it subvert or undermine the tradition?

5   The sonnet form is sometimes used for subversive purposes; on p. 117, we see Claude McKay using this form for a far more serious, but still unusual purpose. There are other examples of sonnets being used to frame controversial or surprising views in this book; can you find them?

Archibald MacLeish (1892–1982)

Ars Poetica[1]

A poem should be palpable° and mute   *tangible, real*
As a globed fruit,

Dumb
As old medallions to the thumb,

5   Silent as the sleeve-worn stone
Of casement° ledges where the moss has grown –   *window*

A poem should be wordless
As the flight of birds.

      .

A poem should be motionless in time
10 As the moon climbs,

Leaving, as the moon releases
Twig by twig the night-entangled trees,

Leaving, as the moon behind the winter leaves,
Memory by memory the mind –

15 A poem should be motionless in time
As the moon climbs.

      .

A poem should be equal to:
Not true.

For all the history of grief
20 An empty doorway and a maple leaf.

Born in the mid-western USA, **MacLeish** was educated at Harvard
University. He joined the circle of American artists in Paris in the 1920s,
where he was greatly influenced by Ezra Pound. Another significant influence
was T. S. Eliot. A notable poet and playwright, MacLeish became increasingly
absorbed by politics. On his return to the USA, he held a series of important
governmental positions, including that of Assistant Secretary of State. He
was later appointed to a professor's post at Harvard.

Notes

[1] This title (which means 'the art
of poetry') is taken from a work
on the subject of poetry by the
classical Latin poet, Horace.

For love
The leaning grasses and two lights above the sea –

A poem should not mean
But be.

Wilfred Owen (1893–1918)

Futility

Move him into the sun —
Gently its touch awoke him once,
At home, whispering of fields unsown.
Always it woke him, even in France,
5   Until this morning and this snow.
If anything might rouse him now
The kind old sun will know.

Think how it wakes the seeds —
Woke, once, the clays of a cold star.
10   Are limbs, so dear-achieved, are sides,
Full-nerved — still warm — too hard to stir?
Was it for this the clay grew tall?
— O what made fatuous° sunbeams toil   *pointlessly foolish*
To break earth's sleep at all?

Owen came from a humble background and began writing poetry at an early age. Unable to afford university fees, he studied at a technical college, and did community work in an impoverished parish. Two years before the First World War broke out, he went to France to teach English. After the war began, he returned to England to join the army. His first-hand experience of the horrific conditions and casualties involved in the fighting in Europe were to have a dramatic influence on his poetry. He was injured and sent to hospital in Scotland to recover. Here he met the poet Siegfried Sassoon, who encouraged his writing. He returned to battle and was awarded the Military Cross for bravery, only to be killed a week before the war ended. At first his brutally realistic and bitter war poems were ignored by the public; however, he slowly came to be recognized as one of the finest poets of the First World War.

Dulce et Decorum Est

Bent double, like old beggars under sacks,
Knock-kneed, coughing like hags, we cursed through sludge,
Till on the haunting flares we turned our backs,
And towards our distant rest began to trudge.
5   Men marched asleep. Many had lost their boots,
But limped on, blood-shod. All went lame; all blind;
Drunk with fatigue; deaf even to the hoots
Of tired, outstripped Five-Nines[1] dropping softly behind.

Gas! GAS! Quick, boys! – An ecstasy of fumbling,
10   Fitting the clumsy helmets just in time;
But someone still was yelling out and stumbling
And flound'ring like a man in fire or lime[2] . . .
Dim through the misty panes and thick green light,
As under a green sea, I saw him drowning.

15   In all my dreams before my helpless sight,
He plunges at me, guttering, choking, drowning.

If in some smothering dreams you too could pace
Behind the wagon that we flung him in,
And watch the white eyes writhing in his face,
20   His hanging face, like a devil's sick of sin;
If you could hear at every jolt, the blood
Come gargling from the froth-corrupted lungs,
Obscene as cancer, bitter as the cud
Of vile, incurable sores on innocent tongues, –
25   My friend, you would not tell with such high zest
To children ardent for some desperate glory,
The old Lie: Dulce et decorum est
Pro patria mori.[3]

One of the most horrifying features of the First World War was the use of chemical weapons for the first time. The most feared and deadly of these was 'mustard' gas, which corroded the lungs, causing a horrible death in which victims effectively drowned in their own blood. Soldiers used gas-masks (the 'helmets' in line 10) to protect themselves. **Dulce et Decorum Est** graphically describes the effects of such a gas attack.

You might like to compare these two poems by Owen with Rupert Brooke's 'The Soldier'. Suggestions for discussion can be found on p. 110.

Notes

[1] Chemical gas bombs.
[2] Sticky chemical sometimes used to trap birds.
[3] Ironic quotation from the Latin poet Horace: 'Sweet and fitting it is to die for one's country'.

Elizabeth Cloete

The Spartan Woman

A spartan° woman is Africa,   *tough, austere*
Under the sun's relentless rays she lies,
With stern fingers pointing steadily upwards,
Her broad breast bare to the sky,
5   She watches with an immovable face,
Those who seek to nestle on her heart,
But it is hard, and the heat of her breath is scorching.
Vainly they strive to rest in her treacherous arms.
They cling to the hem of her garments praying for life,
10 Yet not a quiver betrays her thought.
Yet how they love her!
Once having seen her, once having known her,
They see, they love, they know no other.
Their last cry is always to be buried on her breast.
15 None but the bravest, none but the best
Shall earn her favour,
From them she will withhold nothing.
And maybe there shall arise a mighty race,
That maybe shall move with iron tread,
20 Towards the hills of God.

Talking points

This poem has certain features in common with Olive Schreiner's
'The Cry of South Africa' (see p. 94). Other poems in this book also
give Nature human and especially feminine qualities. You might like
to find these (start with Wordsworth) and compare them, especially if
you are interested in the way that writing is gendered (shaped by the
socially constructed understandings of masculinity and femininity).

No information is available about **Cloete**, other than that she was a South
African who wrote this poem in 1931.

Mao Tse-Tung (1893–1976)

Lou Mountain Pass

February 1935

West wind fierce,
immense sky, wild geese honking,
frosty morning moon.
Frosty morning moon.
5   Horse hooves clanging,
bugles sobbing.

Tough pass,
long trail, like iron.
Yet with strong steps
10   we climbed that peak.
Climbed that peak:
green mountains like oceans,
setting sun like blood.

Talking points

During the civil war, Mao led his followers on the gruelling 'Long
March', a 9 700 km trek across some of China's wildest terrain. It
took over a year, and bonded those who survived into a close and
determined military unit. Mao wrote 'Lou Mountain Pass' to
celebrate a battle during the Long March, the taking of a particularly
daunting mountain pass from the Nationalist forces. You might find
it interesting comparing this poem with the early Chinese poems
found on pp. 1–2. What differences and similarities can you find?

Mao Tse-Tung (also spelt Zedong) came from peasant stock, and was
attracted to communism as a young man. He helped form the Chinese
Communist Party, and was its leader for fifty years. They fought a prolonged
civil war for control of the country, eventually overcoming both the occupying
Japanese forces and the Chinese Nationalists. The Chinese People's Republic,
with Mao as its head, was established in 1949. He began a programme of
accelerated economic and industrial development that led to considerable
abuse of human rights. Two low points of his regime were the infamous
Cultural Revolution (in which millions were killed, unfairly punished, or
banished to remote areas) and the Chinese invasion and annexation of Tibet.
Mao controlled the country until his death in 1976, attaining almost mythical
status. In China, his sayings and poems were so extensively distributed as to
make him probably the most widely read poet of the twentieth century.

E. E. Cummings (1894–1962)

anyone lived in a pretty how town

anyone lived in a pretty how town
(with up so floating many bells down)
spring summer autumn winter
he sang his didn't he danced his did.

5   Women and men(both little and small)
cared for anyone not at all
they sowed their isn't they reaped their same
sun moon stars rain

children guessed(but only a few
10 and down they forgot as up they grew
autumn winter spring summer)
that noone loved him more by more

when by now and tree by leaf
she laughed his joy she cried his grief
15 bird by snow and stir by still
anyone's any was all to her

someones married their everyones
laughed their cryings and did their dance
(sleep wake hope and then)they
20 said their nevers they slept their dream

stars rain sun moon
(and only the snow can begin to explain
how children are apt to forget to remember
with up so floating many bells down)

The son of a clergyman, **Cummings** studied at Harvard University and joined
a volunteer ambulance unit in France during the First World War. He was
talented both as a painter and a writer, and his first book, an account of his
experiences in a French detention camp, generated much excitement. He
introduced striking visual and typographical innovations in his poetry; for
example, his unorthodox use of punctuation and lower-case letters has had a
lasting impact on the style of modern poetry. His work ranges from sharp
satire* to romantic and moving lyrics.*

25   one day anyone died i guess
    (and noone stooped to kiss his face)
    busy folk buried them side by side
    little by little and was by was

    all by all and deep by deep
30   and more by more they dream their sleep
    noone and anyone earth by april
    wish by spirit and if by yes.

    Women and men(both dong and ding)
    summer autumn winter spring
35   reaped their sowing and went their came
    sun moon stars rain

Bertolt Brecht (1898–1956)

Questions from a Worker who Reads

Translated by Michael Hamburger

Who built Thebes of the seven gates?
In the books you will find the names of kings.
Did the kings haul up the lumps of rock?
And Babylon, many times demolished,
5   Who raised it up so many times? In what houses
Of gold-glittering Lima did the builders live?
Where, the evening that the Wall of China was finished
Did the masons go? Great Rome
Is full of triumphal arches. Who erected them? Over whom
10   Did the Caesars triumph? Had Byzantium, much praised in song,
Only palaces for its inhabitants? Even in fabled Atlantis
The night the ocean engulfed it
The drowning still bawled° for their slaves.   *yelled, shouted*

The young Alexander conquered India.
15   Was he alone?
Caesar beat the Gauls.
Did he not have even a cook with him?

A German by nationality, **Brecht** was sympathetic to class and labour issues, and aligned himself with local communist groups. His radical and outspoken writings were banned by the Nazis, and after the establishment of Hitler's totalitarian regime in Germany during the 1930s, he emigrated to the USA. There he worked translating and producing his plays. After the Second World War, he returned to East Berlin, where he founded a company of actors, the Berliner Ensemble, as a vehicle for his work and theories of acting. He married the actress Helene Weigel, and she continued to direct the company after his death. Today he is recognized as a leading modern German poet and playwright.

Philip of Spain wept when his armada
Went down. Was he the only one to weep?
20   Frederick the Second won the Seven Years' War. Who
Else won it?

Every page a victory.
Who cooked the feast for the victors?

Every ten years a great man.
25   Who paid the bill?

So many reports.
So many questions.

Brief explanations of the events referred to in 'Questions from a Worker
who Reads' are given here. Thebes (lines 1–3) was the burial place of kings,
and a temple site in ancient Egypt. Babylon (lines 4–5) was a great capital of
the ancient Middle East; successive invaders destroyed and rebuilt it. Lima
(line 6) is the capital of the South American country Peru; it was once the
stronghold of the ancient and wealthy Inca civilization. The Great Wall of
China (line 7) was a long defensive barrier built to repel invaders (see also
footnote 2, p. 1). Rome (lines 8–10) was the centre of the Roman empire; its
rulers were known as Caesars. Many of them ordered monuments or arches
to be built to mark the conquest of other lands or peoples. Byzantium (lines
10–11) was the eastern capital of the Roman Empire, later named
Constantinople. Today it is the capital of Turkey, and is called Istanbul.
Atlantis (lines 11–13) was a mythical island civilization that was supposedly
engulfed by the sea. Alexander, also known as Alexander the Great (line 14),
was a brilliant young general of the ancient world; he conquered lands
stretching from Greece to India. The Gauls (line 16), the inhabitants of what
is now France, were defeated by Julius Caesar, probably the greatest of the
Roman rulers. Philip of Spain (line 18) was the king of Spain during the
sixteenth century; he sent a fleet of ships known as the Armada to attack
England, but it was defeated. Frederick the Second (line 20) was an
eighteenth-century German king, and a key figure in a major war in central
Europe that lasted seven years.

Hart Crane (1899–1932)

My Grandmother's Love Letters

There are no stars to-night
But those of memory.
Yet how much room for memory there is
In the loose girdle° of soft rain.   *belt*

5   There is even room enough
For the letters of my mother's mother,
Elizabeth,
That have been pressed so long
Into a corner of the roof
10 That they are brown and soft,
And liable to melt as snow.

Over the greatness of such space
Steps must be gentle.
It is all hung by an invisible white hair.
15 It trembles as birch limbs webbing the air.

And I ask myself:

'Are your fingers long enough to play
Old keys that are but echoes:
Is the silence strong enough
20 To carry back the music to its source
And back to you again
As though to her?'

Yet I would lead my grandmother by the hand
Through much of what she would not understand;
25 And so I stumble. And the rain continues on the roof
With such a sound of gently pitying laughter.

Crane's short life was not an easy one. He did not finish high school, but his two volumes of poetry nevertheless marked him as a talented and powerful writer, with a bleak vision of life. His work resembles Whitman's in its fascination with American experiences and values. An alcoholic, he had a succession of unhappy love affairs with both men and women. On a voyage home after a period of travel and study in Mexico, he committed suicide by jumping over the side of the ship.

Malvina Reynolds (1900–1978)

What Have They Done to the Rain?

Just a little rain falling all around,
The grass lifts its head to the heavenly sound,
Just a little rain, just a little rain,
What have they done to the rain?

5 Just a little breeze out of the sky,
The leaves nod their heads as the breeze blows by,
Just a little breeze with some smoke in its eye,
What have they done to the rain?

Just a little boy standing in the rain,
10 The gentle rain that falls for years,
And the grass is gone, the boy disappears,
And rain keeps falling like helpless tears,
And what have they done to the rain?

Talking points

'What Have They Done to the Rain?' was written at the height of the
Cold War between the USA and its allies and what was then the
communist Eastern bloc, headed by the USSR. It refers to the threat
of radioactive 'fallout' (minute particles of deadly waste matter from
either a nuclear explosion or a leaking nuclear power station, that
would be spread by wind and rain) that haunted most of the northern
hemisphere for decades after the Second World War. There was great
concern about the sickness, death, and long-term poisoning that such
nuclear fallout would cause for decades after an initial explosion or
leak.

The tragic events of 2001 have taught us that new weapons of war
and terrorism, like nuclear fallout, respect neither borders nor
innocent civilians. What kinds of global weapons and tactics are we
seeing now?

Reynolds was an American singer, guitarist, and song-writer who followed
in the protest folk tradition established by musicians such as Woodie Guthrie
and Pete Seeger. Their aim was to express political criticism in a way that
was both powerful and accessible, in the form of ballads, chants, and easily
remembered songs. Reynolds' songs are often apparently simple and
understated, but make telling points nevertheless.

Roy Campbell (1901–1957)

The Zulu Girl

When in the sun the hot red acres smoulder,
Down where the sweating gang its labour plies,
A girl flings down her hoe, and from her shoulder
Unslings her child tormented by the flies.

5 She takes him to a ring of shadow pooled
By thorn-trees: purpled with the blood of ticks,
While her sharp nails, in slow caresses ruled,
Prowl through his hair with sharp electric clicks.

His sleepy mouth plugged by the heavy nipple,
10 Tugs like a puppy, grunting as he feeds:
Through his frail nerves her own deep languors ripple
Like a broad river sighing through its reeds.

Yet in that drowsy stream his flesh imbibes°   *drinks*
An old unquenched unsmotherable heat –
15 The curbed ferocity of beaten tribes,
The sullen dignity of their defeat.

Her body looms above him like a hill
Within whose shade a village lies at rest,
Or the first cloud so terrible and still
20 That bears the coming harvest in its breast.

Born in Natal, **Campbell** studied at Oxford University for a year and lived briefly in Britain, where he successfully published his first volume of poetry, establishing himself as an energetic and inventive writer. On his return to South Africa, he founded a satirical literary journal (*Voorslag*, which means 'whiplash') together with the respected poet William Plomer. He left once again to wander through France and Spain before settling in Portugal. A prolific writer and translator, he regularly published poetry as well as two autobiographies. His personality was as colourful and flamboyant as his writing (his jobs included a brief stint as a bull-fighter), but his support of fascism earned him considerable criticism. However, he fought on the side of the British during the Second World War. He died in a car crash in Portugal.

Talking points

1 This poem is particularly interesting because it combines a far-sighted warning with stereotypical (and perhaps even patronizing) views of its topic. Do you agree, and if so, can you locate both these elements?

2 Look very closely at the presentation of both the Zulu mother and her baby. What positive and negative attributes are suggested by the language used to describe them?

3 This poem conveys an atmosphere that is both tranquil and threatening. What words are used to sustain both moods? Look especially closely at the last stanza. What final message is suggested?

4 In the presentation of the Zulu mother, we find a return to the Romantic tradition of likening the female body to natural phenomena. (Wordsworth's 'Three Years She Grew' [p. 54] is a good example of this practice.) How exactly does Campbell do this here, and what effect does it have?

Langston Hughes (1902–1967)

Mother to Son

Well, son, I'll tell you.
Life for me ain't been no crystal stair.
It's had tacks in it,
And splinters,
5   And boards torn up,
And bare places with no carpet on the floor . . .
Bare.
But all the time
I'se been a-climbin' on,
10   And reachin' landin's
And turnin' corners,
And sometimes goin' in the dark
Where there ain't been no light.
So, boy, don't you turn back.
15   Don't you set down on the steps
'Cause you'll find it kinda hard.
Don't you fall now . . .
For I'se still goin' honey,
I'se still climbin',
20   And life for me ain't been no crystal stair.

One of the first major black poets in the USA, **Hughes** was born in North
Caroline, in the southern part of America and travelled in Europe and Africa
before returning home to study and write. A leader of the Harlem
Renaissance (a flowering of talent and cultural creativity in Harlem, a black
residential area of New York City), he became known as the 'poet laureate of
Harlem'. Together with the poet Sterling Brown, he was an influential figure
in advancing 'Negritude', a cultural movement that promoted black
achievement. He was an innovator of 'jazz' poetry, which was drawn from the
speech and music of black Americans, and worked with musicians to perfect
this genre.* A meticulous writer who continually reworked his poems, he
also wrote novels, children's books, and newspaper articles.

Stevie Smith (1902–1971)

Not Waving but Drowning

Nobody heard him, the dead man,
But still he lay moaning:
I was much further out than you thought
And not waving but drowning.

5   Poor chap, he always loved larking°   *joking, teasing*
And now he's dead
It must have been too cold for him his heart gave way,
They said.

Oh, no no no, it was too cold always
10 (Still the dead one lay moaning)
I was much too far out all my life
And not waving but drowning.

Smith, born Florence Margaret, was nicknamed after a racing jockey
because she was so short. She lived in London throughout her life, and
published three novels and two volumes of poetry before her eccentric style
became popular. Her poetry, often illustrated with her own comic drawings,
was playful and witty, even when handling darker themes. She worked as a
radio broadcaster, and had a distinctive voice; many of her admirers
remember her reading her poems aloud over the air. She wrote this famous
poem shortly before making an unsuccessful attempt on her own life.

W. H. Auden (1907–1973)

Roman Wall Blues

Over the heather[1] the wet wind blows
I've lice in my tunic and a cold in my nose.

The rain comes pattering out of the sky,
I'm a Wall soldier, I don't know why.

5   The mist creeps over the hard grey stone,
My girl's in Tungria;[2] I sleep alone.

Aulus goes hanging around her place,
I don't like his manners, I don't like his face.

Piso's a Christian, he worships a fish;[3]
10   There'd be no kissing if he had his wish.

She gave me a ring but I diced it away;
I want my girl and I want my pay.

When I'm a veteran with only one eye
I shall do nothing but look at the sky.

The son of a doctor, **Auden** went to Oxford University to study science. However, he became part of a group of creative young writers, and recognition of his own poetic skills inspired him to change careers. After university he travelled widely, witnessing the civil wars in both China and Spain. A radical socialist as a young man, he was to become more conservative in later years. His first poems were accepted for publication by T. S. Eliot, and he was recognized as a brilliant new contributor to modern poetry. A homosexual, he married Erika Mann, daughter of the famous writer Thomas Mann, so that she could flee persecution in Nazi Germany. In 1939, he left for the USA, where he eventually took up American citizenship, a decision that cost him some popularity. Nevertheless, he was appointed Professor of Poetry at Oxford, where he spent the rest of his life. His poetry is known for its range and its ability to transform conventional forms.

'Roman Wall Blues' is set in early times, when Britain was one of the Roman Empire's occupied territories, and Roman soldiers were sent there to enforce the authority of the conqueror. However, the occupying militia had difficulty with fierce local tribes, who attacked from the north. Thus the Roman Wall (also known as Hadrian's Wall, named after the Emperor at the time) was built as a defensive structure across the northern part of England. (See Introductory notes, p. xiii; and compare with the Chinese peoms on pp. 1–2.)

Notes

1. Small grey-green bushes with purple flowers typically found in the north of England and Scotland.
2. Province in Italy.
3. A fish was one of the figures used by the early Christians to symbolize Jesus.

Stop all the Clocks

Stop all the clocks, cut off the telephone,
Prevent the dog from barking with a juicy bone,
Silence the pianos and with muffled drum
Bring out the coffin, let the mourners come.

5 Let aeroplanes circle moaning overhead
Scribbling on the sky the message He Is Dead,
Put crêpe⁴ bows round the necks of the public doves,
Let the traffic policemen wear black cotton gloves.

He was my North, my South, my East and West,
10 My working week and my Sunday rest,
My noon, my midnight, my talk, my song;
I thought love would last for ever: I was wrong.

The stars are not wanted now: put out every one;
Pack up the moon and dismantle the sun;
15 Pour away the ocean and sweep up the wood.
For nothing now can ever come to any good.

'Stop all the Clocks' is actually the first of a pair of poems, more accurately titled 'Two Songs for Hedli Anderson'. It became widely known (and informally renamed 'Stop all the Clocks') after the worldwide distribution of the hugely popular film *Four Weddings and a Funeral* in the mid-1990s. In this film, it was read aloud by one of the characters, and this led to a resurgence of interest in Auden's works by the general public. This is not only elegy* in its purest and most powerful form; it is also a particularly moving and poignant love poem. You may want to compare it with other elegies in this book (see those by Ben Jonson [p. 31], Wordsworth [p. 54], Tennyson [p. 72], Cope [p. 140], Jonker [p. 186], Bryer [p. 212], and de Kok [p. 221]), and look at how the relationship of the speaker to the deceased (lover, friend, parent, fellow poet) shapes these works.

Notes

⁴ Thin black fabric, worn to indicate mourning in Western cultures until about fifty years ago.

Modikwe Dikobe (1913–1970)

Khoikhoi-Son-of-Man

I thought I was soul and skin
Pedigree muntu[1]
Until yesterday I heard the truth
Grandfather was a Khoisan.[2]

5 A slave of a trekboer
Fleeing from the Cape laws
Freeing slaves.[3]

At night
He was tied to an oxwagon wheel
10 Groaning
Day by day leading sixteen span°   *pairs of oxen*
Fleeing from the Cape.

Night by night
Somewhere there was a cock-crow
15 A barking dog
A smell of damp fuel
Then he realized that beyond that ridge
Could be a village
Of people like him.

Dikobe was born in the Transvaal and raised in Sophiatown, a black township that was known for its cultural diversity and liveliness before it was rezoned as a 'white' residential area, and demolished by the apartheid government. He had limited access to schooling, and gained much of his education through correspondence. He held a variety of humble jobs, including selling newspapers. His first novel (*The Marabi Dance*), together with his poetry, identified him as a writer passionately concerned with black oppression under apartheid.

Notes

1. Slang term for a black African; now considered degrading.
2. Hunter-gatherer tribe (initially called Bushmen) indigenous to the Cape; now largely exterminated.
3. The 'trekboers' were farmers of Dutch descent who left the Cape and travelled ('trekked') with wagons drawn by oxen into the interior of the country. One of the reasons they left was to escape new laws that made slavery illegal, and that would have freed their slaves.

20   He unfastened himself,
Trotted out of the camp,
Vanished into the night.

At dawn he was at a village
Begging to be taken into the tribe
25   'A tribesman, hunter, chief's servant and messenger.'

Swift as an antelope° was he   *buck*
Outstripping runners
Chased by dogs.
    'Ka modimo',[4] they swore.
30   'He is a man of the cloud.
    Ompone ke tswa kae?'[5]
A legendary tale: where have you seen me?
    'I have seen you from the cloud.'
Khoikhoi-Son-of-Man.

35   I knew since yesterday
that he was my grandfather
Khoikhoi-Son-of-Man.

Notes

[4] By God' or 'I swear on oath' (Tswana).

[5] These words are translated in the next line.

Jack Cope (1913–1992)

The Flying Fish[1]

(For Ingrid)

The level ocean lies immeasurably blind
swept through green deeps to glutinous° weed. *sticky*

But the flying fish, how they leap away
in water-flashes to the enamelled° sun! *coated with glossy metal*
5 They break along the foam-lipped chorus
of sea swells. Mysterious
the sounds they loosen, arrows
singing on the air and lost:
mysterious the glass-winged birds
10 of the long blind sea.

On the storm-swung streams they ride
over free oceans over the locked ice
the groans of midnight fires
and moons returning on the tide.
15 Light as great winged travellers
of the endless South
urgent as birth
from gloomed fishweed and the dead underwave
the flying fish sing to light.

Cope grew up in KwaZulu-Natal, where he tried farming before turning to journalism as a career. He worked in London for several years before returning to South Africa to become a full-time writer. He wrote novels and short stories as well as poems, and edited the influential literary journal *Contrast*. One of his aims was to make South African writing accessible to a wider audience. He retired to England some time before his death.

'The Flying Fish' is an elegy* for the Afrikaans poet Ingrid Jonker, who committed suicide at a young age by drowning. (See p. 186 for notes on Jonker herself and an example of her poetry.)

Notes

1 Flying fish are small tropical fish with wing-like fins that they use to leap from the sea into the air.

Talking points

After reading this poem, turn to Sally Bryer's 'Ingrid Jonker' (p. 212).
Both poems are written to honour the same poet, and use similar
metaphors.* Yet they are also quite different.

1   What central images do both poets use, and why did they choose
    these images? (Jonker's method of suicide will give a clue.)
2   What are the chief differences in the way that the two poets
    approach their topics? Look, for example, at the use of pronouns
    in Bryer's poem, and the way the dead woman is physically
    conjured up. Apart from the sub-title, is Cope's poem specifically
    addressed to anyone? Does any human figure actually appear in
    it?
3   One of these poems, while written as an elegy,* also functions as
    a straightforward lyrical poem. Which one is it? How then do we
    know that the writer has Jonker's life and death in mind?
4   Which poem do you prefer? Which is more personal? Which
    one do you think offers the greater hope? (Remember that there
    are no 'right' or 'wrong' answers to these questions!)

Dylan Thomas (1914–1953)

In My Craft or Sullen Art

In my craft or sullen art
Exercised in the still night
When only the moon rages
And the lovers lie abed
5 With all their griefs in their arms,
I labour by singing light
Not for ambition or bread
Or the strut and trade of charms
On the ivory stages
10 But for the common wages
Of their most secret heart.

Not for the proud man apart
From the raging moon I write
On these spindrift° pages   *sea-spray*
15 Nor for the towering dead
With their nightingales and psalms
But for the lovers, their arms
Round the griefs of the ages,
Who pay no praise or wages
20 Nor heed my craft or art.

Born in Wales, **Thomas** was the son of a teacher, and began writing as a teenager. Initially a journalist, he became increasingly successful as a broadcaster and poet. He was a careful writer who laboured at his poems, which became famous for their vivid natural imagery and intensely lyrical style. A colourful and tragic figure, he was an alcoholic, a fact that was unfortunately glamorized as part of his larger-than-life public image. His readings of his own poetry were extremely popular, and led to a series of lecture tours to the USA. On his fourth trip, he died of alcoholic poisoning in New York, after a tremendous drinking binge.

Talking points

1   How does the speaker see his 'art', according to the first stanza?
    What words suggest that the business of creating poetry is hard
    work?
2   Thomas was famous for 'transferring' words that suggest a
    specific mood or emotion to ordinary nouns; see, for example,
    'the moon rages' (line 3) and 'singing light' (line 6). What could
    these constructions mean? Is the speaker describing the moon
    and the light, or something else? Can you find other examples of
    this kind of pairing in this poem?
3   Closely examine the structure of the poem. Look at the words
    that begin each line; with one exception, how many syllables does
    each of these words have? What word or words are repeated?
    What effect is created as a result? Also look at the rhyme scheme.
    How many rhyme-end sounds are there in the whole poem, and
    how are these laid out? How does the poet's careful use of rhyme
    underline the theme of the poem?
4   Why does the poet refer to his pages as 'spindrift' (line 14)?
    What does this suggest about the nature of poetry?
5   A central irony* is suggested throughout this poem. What is it?
    (See the last two lines.)

D. J. Opperman (1914–1985)

Christmas Carol

Translated from the Afrikaans by Anthony Delius

Three outas° from the High Karoo[1]   *men*
saw the star, believed the angel true,

took knob-sticks, and three bundles with
and set forth along a jackal path,

5   following that bright and moving thing
that shone on shanty, sack and spring,

on zinc and sacking of District Six –
in a broken bottle a candle flicks

where salt fish hangs and donkeys jib,°   *halt*
10 and lights them kneeling by the crib.

Biltong,° sheep fat and eggs they've piled   *spiced dried meat*
humbly before God's small brown child.

With hymn and prayer for thanks, they tell
That a child will save this folk as well ...

15 And on her nest, throughout the whole affair
a bantam clucks with a suspicious stare.

This South African poet is considered one of the foremost Afrikaans poets and literary scholars of the twentieth century. He taught at both Stellenbosch University and the University of Cape Town. He is perhaps best known as the editor of the standard and definitive anthology of Afrikaans poetry, *Die Groote Verseboek*.

Notes

[1] See footnote 2, p. 90.

Talking points

This translation from the Afrikaans recasts the story of the birth of
Jesus, setting it in a slum part of District Six, a racially mixed
residential area in Cape Town that was bulldozed in the 1960s under
apartheid legislation (see Essop Patel's 'In the Shadow of Signal Hill'
[p. 178] for further notes on District Six). The 'three wise men'
('outas' is a slang Afrikaans term that loosely translates as 'guys' or
'chaps') are obviously humble men (possibly shepherds, in keeping
with the biblical story) who bring as their gifts food traditionally
eaten in simple rural communities. The implication is also that both
they and the baby they visit are coloured – the somewhat contested
term used in South Africa to describe people of mixed-race descent.
(Given that this poem was written several decades ago, it is clear that
not just a religious, but a political point is being made.) You will find
it interesting to compare this poem with others on the same subject,
including Eliot's 'Journey of the Magi' (p. 115) and the poem by
Wright (p. 155). You will also find helpful notes and suggestions for
discussion on pp. 155–6.

Anthony Delius (1916–1989)

Deaf-and-Dumb School

On the black tarmac playground dark
Nuns, a white statue of the Virgin[1] watch
Bare feet of the muted children jerk
And scuffle over endless silence. Such

5   Is their element. Though I have heard
Them flute like evening swallows in the sky
The sounds were sad, irrelevant, absurd
And could not pierce the silences of play,

Nor break the glass that frames their world.
10 A soundless quality of painting grips
A small boy leaning from a bench enthralled
In thoughts that dance on other finger-tips.

One with the cry and stiffness of a crane
Dances before a dumb-struck clientele,
15 Beyond, some cheerless footballers bemoan
A speechless player's bungled goal.

And all around communication glimmers
From hand to eye, and each attentive face
Turns to a dream of mimicry and mummers,°   *play-actors*
20 Like songless planets signalling through space.

Sound there is, but silence underlies
The fire-flies of gesture. One cannot catch
Exactly what the muffled outcry says,
Or what it is the nuns and children watch.

Born in Cape Town, **Delius** was educated at Rhodes University. He was a
respected journalist (at one stage he was the leader writer for the liberal
newspaper *The Cape Times*), as well as a poet, satirist, and travel writer.
Later he moved to London and worked there in broadcasting. His poetry and
fiction won him a number of prizes.

Notes

[1] Mother of Jesus.

25   Silence like a window shows the room
Of minds that make their signs and mouth their cries,
But what leans out to touch you from the dream
Only the white statue and the darkness realise.

Talking points

This poem presents an unusually sensitive attempt to observe and
enter the world of hearing-impaired and mute children. Today,
however, we would not use the term 'deaf-and-dumb' to describe
people with these particular physical challenges. Although the use of
politically correct language can at times verge on the ridiculous, or
come across as patronising, it is worth noting that in the case of those
with physical and mental illnesses or impediments, advocacy groups
have made some very interesting and assertive recommendations
about the language they would prefer to be used to describe
themselves. These are beginning to be implemented in the media and
public discussion.

   The whole issue of language sensitivity is a topic that you and your
classmates might like to investigate more closely. Several poems in
this anthology that were written during earlier historical periods
contain language that today would be considered offensive or
inappropriate: look at Modikwe Dikobe's poem (p. 138), for example.
Also see how differently Mutiswayo Shandu and Gcina Mhlope use
the word 'tsotsi' (pp. 203 and 237). Can you find any other examples?
What does this suggest about language and its relation to society?

Gwendolyn Brooks (1917–2000)

We Real Cool

The Pool Players.
Seven at the Golden Shovel.[1]

We real cool. We
Left school. We

Lurk late. We
Strike straight. We

5   Sing sin. We
Thin gin. We

Jazz June. We
Die soon.

Brooks grew up in Chicago in the USA. Her distinctive poetic voice earned her a place as one of the first major black American women poets. She was appointed 'poet laureate' of Illinois, the American state in which she lived. She received fifty-one honorary degrees, as well as numerous fellowships and awards, including the Pulitzer Prize, probably the USA's most prestigious literary award.

Notes

1   A typical Chicago club.

Guy Butler (1918–2001)

Near Hout Bay

Stopping the car, our childhood friends, now hosts,
suggested we stroll to the fabulous view.
Blinding sun, and heat beating up from a path
gritty with pinkish granite crystals,
5   curtains of pines permitting
expected glimpses of throbbing cerulean° sky   *blue*
and steep striated° rockface plunging   *grooved*
through broken mirrors, torn lace, beautiful lawns of sea.

There had been much talk in the car, far less on the climb:
10   talk which, try as we would to make it heal or hide,
only exposed the gaps, unbandaged sentence by sentence
the gashes and wounds of time, great spaces and falls
between us all. Each thread of phrase drifted from lips
like a spider's web from a cave in a thousand-foot cliff,
15   out, out into distance, finding nothing to cling to –
the next land Buenos Aires.[1]

We gave up the effort. They tried a bit longer,
stopped in mid-sentence as we all stopped moving
in the space and the heat
20   before the sufficiently epic view.

Silence took charge, a blessed burial of words.
Each forgot his failure, longing, boredom, fury
in that subsidence of even a pretence at speech.
We stood a long time, still, just listening:
25   ten thousand sun-struck cicadas[2] ecstatically screaming;
near and far hundreds of doves in relays
imperturbably repeating themselves to each other;

Butler had a happy childhood on a farm in the Eastern Cape, an experience
described in the first volume of his well-known autobiography. During the
Second World War, he served in North Africa and Italy; afterwards, he
studied at Oxford. Eventually he became Professor of English at Rhodes
University, Grahamstown. A respected South African poet and educator, he
was always fascinated by the tension between the influence of Europe and
the experience of Africa that he saw in the works of many of his
contemporaries.

Notes

1 Port on the Atlantic coast of South America.
2 Insects that make a high, rhythmic chirping sound.

pine wood sighing into the wind from a thousand shimmering needles;
wind already burdened with the grumbling,
30   perpetual, unpitied,
crumbling of the surf.

Returning, the talk returned
but attempted nothing whatever.
What can be healed or hidden?
35   We accepted separation
as the ear those ignorant sounds
that filled that primitive silence
with sadness and with praise:
cicadas; doves; wind; surf.

Ruth Miller (1919–1969)

Blue-Mantled Mary

Blue-mantled Mary[1]
Bloody in the byre°   *cow-shed*
Brought forth. The hawthorn[2] was white
As milk, the berries all on fire.

5   Nine months waiting.
Nine months waiting.

Now I remember
The months ago annunciation –
First feathery thrust of the angel
10 Nine months ago, this December.
The tall touch of the stranger
On my breast, on my skin,
His insupportable maculate° breath   *defiled*
Breathing as I did, out and in,
15 Out and in
Waiting for the time of birth.

Untouched by man, blue-mantled Mary ran
Ran on her pencilled feet into the light
Of the cathedral window, serene as snow.
20 How was she then to know
What would be done? Whose Will it was she knew.

And I remember
Unhallowed, un-Mary'd, this seed must grow
Slowly toward its day – though each day is holy –
25 Toward the windowless
Breathless lusty breath
Of a full-term Death.

Miller was born in the Cape. She worked first as a typist, then as a teacher in Johannesburg. She wrote short stories and radio plays as well as poetry. Her first collection of poems displayed notable sensitivity to South African landscapes and wildlife, and won the Ingrid Jonker Memorial Prize. A complete edition of her writings was published by the poet Lionel Abrahams.

'**Blue-Mantled Mary**' is based on the New Testament story of the Annunciation. This was the occasion on which an angel appeared to Mary, and told her that regardless of her virginity, she was to conceive and give birth to the new 'Messiah', or saviour of humanity.

Notes

[1] Mother of Jesus.
[2] Thorny shrub with red berries.

Lawrence Ferlinghetti (1919–)

Constantly Risking Absurdity

    Constantly risking absurdity
          and death
       whenever he performs
         above the heads
5   of his audience
  the poet like an acrobat
        climbs on rhyme
           to a high wire of his own making
  and balancing on eyebeams
10   above a sea of faces
       paces his way
         to the other side of day
    performing entrechats°   *balletic leaps*
         and sleight-of-foot tricks
15   and other high theatrics
         and all without mistaking
       any thing
         for what it may not be

    For he's the super realist
20   who must perforce perceive
       taut truth
         before the taking of each stance or step
  in his supposed advance
         toward that still higher perch
25   where Beauty stands and waits
         with gravity
           to start her death-defying leap
  And he
    a little charleychaplin man
30   who may or may not catch
    her fair eternal form
         spreadeagled in the empty air
    of existence

The American poet **Ferlinghetti** was one of the first representatives of the
'Beat Generation', a style of poetry and song-writing that sprang up in the
1950s. The object was to escape from middle-class conventional values, and
to write poetry that reflected mysticism, youth culture, radical political and
social stances, and that had an improvized or informal style.

Es'kia (Ezekiel) Mphahlele (1919–2008)

A Poem

What is there that we can do or say
will sustain them
in those islands
where the sun was made for janitors?

5   What is there that we can say or do
will tear the years
from out the hands
of those who man the island galleys,

will bring them home and dry and mend them
10   bring them back
to celebrate
with us the song and dance and toil of living?

What is it that we must do or say
for children scattered
15   far from home
by hawks let loose to stay the judgement day?

The weeds run riot where our house is fallen
ourselves we roam
the wilderness.
20   'Go tell them there across the seas go tell him,'

so they say, 'his mother's dead six years,
he dare not come
he dare not write
the stars themselves have eyes and ears these days.'

Mphahlele was literary editor of *Drum*, the influential magazine of black culture in the 1950s. His writing was banned, and he spent twenty years in exile, first in Nigeria, and then teaching in France and the USA. His literary achievements as a novelist and a poet gained him international recognition. On his return to South Africa in the 1980s, he was at first placed under a banning order, but was nevertheless made Professor of African Literature at the University of the Witwatersrand. He held this position in an honorary capacity until his death.

25   You who fell before the cannon or
       the sabred° tooth   *sword-like*
       or lie on hallowed
       ground: oh tell us what to say or do.

       So many routes have led to exile since
30   your day our Elders
       we've been here
       and back in many cycles oh so many:

       no terrain different drummers borrowed
       dreams, and there
35   behind us now
       the hounds have diamond fangs and paws of steel.

       No time for dirge° or burial without corpses: *mourning song*
       teach us, Elders,
       how to wait
40   and feel the centre, tame the time like masters,
       sing the blues
       so pain will bleed and let the islands in,
       for exile is a ghetto° of the mind.   *slum, enclosed area*

Written when apartheid was at its height, 'A Poem' refers to the fate of
imprisonment or exile that faced most political activists. The first three
stanzas refer to Robben Island, a small island just off the coast of Cape
Town, for years a notorious maximum-security prison for those convicted of
political offences. It is now a museum and World Heritage Site, as well as a
lively research centre where the role of the past and its integration into the
future of South Africa is constantly debated. The remainder of this poem
refers to the experience of political exile; you might like to read these lines in
conjunction with Arthur Nortje and Stephen Watson's poems on the same
topic, both titled 'In Exile' (pp. 200 and 227–9).

David Wright (1920–1994)

From On the Margin

An anniversary approaches:[1] of the birth of god
In a stable, son of a virgin and a carpenter,
But really issued from loins of omnipotent° glory: *all–powerful*
A babe, ejected from the thighs, greased in mucus and blood,

5   Weeping with its first breath, suffering the cold air, high king
Of the galaxies, and powerless as a fieldmouse.
Over him breathe the oxen; shepherds who have seen a star
Honour the obscure event; and, they say, three travelling

Magi,[2] or charlatans.° This is the messenger of hope;   *imposters, cheats*
10   The military have been instructed to deal with him.
A wholesale killing, their invariable strategy,
While abolishing a generation, fails of effect.

We are asked to believe all this (it's only to start with).
What a jumble of the impossible and casual,
15   Of commonplace mixed with violence; ordinary muddle;
The props and characters scruffy; at best unheroic.

Yet accordant with the disposition of things holy
As we understand them; whose epiphanies° are banal,°   *revelations /*
Not very aesthetic; gnomic,[3] unremarkable;   *commonplace, boring*
20   And very much like what we have to put up with daily.

Deaf from childhood, **Wright** left South Africa for Britain as a teenager, and was educated first at a school for the hearing-impaired and then at Oxford University. He pursued a distinguished career as a writer and academic, which included writing poetry and literary criticism, and translating Old and Middle English. He repeatedly visited South Africa, and maintained a strong interest in South African literature.

'On the Margin' presents a version of the story of the birth of Jesus as told in the New Testament. This event took place in a stable, and shepherds were among those who came to give praise. Three wise men from the East (almost certainly astrologers) were alerted to a significant event by the appearance of a guiding star, and followed it to the stable, where they presented the baby with gifts. The ruler of the territory meanwhile heard of the birth of a powerful new king, and ordered the occupying Roman forces to murder all boys under the age of two years. The baby Jesus, however, escaped the massacre. (These are the events referred to in the third stanza.)

Notes

1. The festival of Christmas.
2. Wise men from the East.
3. Brief moralizing statement or generalization.

Talking points

You might find it interesting to compare this poem with Eliot's 'Journey of the Magi' (pp. 115–6), a very different work on the same topic.

1   What element do the poems share? Both contain notes of practical realism, even cynicism; can you identify these? Why do the speakers introduce these details?
2   What are the chief differences in tone between the two poems? It will help if you identify who is speaking in each poem. Which is the more detached voice?
3   How does the poet's own perspective emerge or operate in the Eliot poem? Judging from these poems, what perspectives would you say their authors have on the religious events they describe?
4   Towards the end of each poem, there is a shift in tone that results in a rather surprising conclusion. What is the final message of each poem, and how do these conclusions differ?
5   You might now like to read Opperman's South African treatment of this subject on p. 144 and apply the above questions to this far more context-specific and political poem.

Tatamkulu Afrika (1921–)

The Handshake

(For Nelson Mandela)

The day before,
I saw the low sun fell
my shadow inwards from the door.
Longer than the floor,
5   head, shoulders, kinked
up onto the opposite wall,
it could have been yours,
you suddenly such
a very tall man,
10   and I knew
I dared not sing your praises though
I am a spinner of words that readily strings
baubles° of glass and sounding brass,   *trinkets, cheap decorations*
and have a way
15   with the most of men.
So there were no pattings of drums,
clashings of calabash,[1]
rattlings of teeth or shells,
as you stood, garlanded, in the great hall.
20   But I thought you smiled a little
at the ordinariness of my poems:
or did you mock
the shaking of my hands?
I could not tell.
25   The light, bright
as an interrogation's, beat
down from the far,
imperial roof and I could have touched
you, had I stretched
30   an arm, but we were trapped,

A reclusive figure with a fascinating life history, **Afrika** writes under the above pseudonym to maintain his privacy. A passionate convert to Islam, he found a home in the Cape Muslim community after spending much of his life wandering around the world. Although he has written fiction since an early age, he began writing and publishing poetry only in the late 1980s, and is now recognized as one of South Africa's leading new poetic voices. His poetry is marked by a compassionate and acute observation of the shabbier side of urban life; he is also a strikingly original political poet.

Notes

[1] Container made from hollowed-out fruit or vegetable.

insectile, in the shared
yet isolating amber[2] of the air,
the white quiff of your hair
stilled as a flame
35 in a stopped cinema reel,
lean, aware
guards about you, poised,
patient, stepped
with you from a TV frame,
40 and I could not tell.
Kingliness clung
to you, less
in classic Roman folds[3]
than a tribal blanket's fall:
45 yet you were no tribal man,
skin's almost olive stayed
midway, your wide, encompassing smile
neither chief's nor tsar's.[4]
Only your immobility,
50 slow tongue, quiet tap
of your papers on the podium,
showed you knew
you were the icon,[5] must
take us with you in a dream
55 less cliché than a hunger of the soul.
At the end, you turned,
took my hand,
tricked me into thinking we were alone,
thanked me with the grave
60 courtesy of the old.
But I hardly heard:
as old ears opened now
to only the language of the eyes.

'The Handshake' describes a meeting with Nelson Rolihlahla Mandela. Born in 1918, he became the leader of the African National Congress, which organized and maintained opposition to apartheid for decades. Mandela was tried for 'treason' and sentenced to life imprisonment in 1964. He was sent to the maximum-security prison for political offenders on Robben Island, where he continued to serve as a symbol of courage and moral resistance. He was released early in 1990, and stepped back into his role as leader of the ANC. He was awarded a Nobel Peace Prize in 1993, and after South Africa's 1994 election he became the country's first democratically elected President. He stepped down from the Presidency in 1999, but remains probably South Africa's best-known and most loved public figure.

Although the speaker in this poem claims that his is not a formal 'praise poem' (see note on p. 164), this piece nevertheless acts both as a praise poem and a moving remembrance of a moment of personal contact.

Notes

[2] Gold-coloured fossilized plant sap; insects were sometimes trapped in it.
[3] Reference to the togas (garments) worn by rulers of the Roman Empire.
[4] Russian emperor.
[5] Holy image or symbol.

A little shy,
65   yours met mine,
like any other old man's, shared
the loneliness of the long road.
I did not have to ask you why
you sometimes walk
70   the silent places in the last of night,
remembering your dear dead,
refurbishing your dream.
We could have been friends:
but you have so many hands to shake,
75   how will you remember mine,
holding to yours like a drowning man's?
And though your feet stayed flesh,
you are the truer icon for that,
must fill so wide a space you would never hear
80   me bonga-ing[6] in my skins in the wind.

Notes

[6]   Sound made by African drums.

Philip Larkin (1922–1985)

Talking in Bed

Talking in bed ought to be easiest,
Lying together there goes back so far,
An emblem° of two people being honest.   *sign, symbol*

Yet more and more time passes silently.
5 Outside, the wind's incomplete unrest
Builds and disperses clouds about the sky,

And dark towns heap up on the horizon.
None of this cares for us. Nothing shows why
At this unique distance from isolation

10 It becomes still more difficult to find
Words at once true and kind,
Or not untrue and not unkind.

Born in England and educated at Oxford University, **Larkin** spent most of his life as a university librarian in the north of England, deliberately avoiding the literary scene of London. His writing is remarkable for its transformation of ordinary topics and practical language into thought-provoking poetry. A great fan of jazz music, he was a columnist on the subject for the newspaper *The Daily Telegraph*.

Agostinho Neto (1922–1979)

The Grieved Lands

The grieved lands of Africa
in the tearful woes of ancient and modern slave
in the degrading sweat of impure dance
of other seas
5   grieved

The grieved lands of Africa
in the infamous sensation of the stunning perfume of the
flower
crushed in the forest
10   by the wickedness of iron and fire
the grieved lands

The grieved lands of Africa
in the dream soon undone in jinglings of gaolers' keys
and in the stifled laughter and victorious voice of laments
15   and in the unconscious brilliance of hidden sensations
of the grieved lands of Africa

    Alive
    in themselves and with us alive

They bubble up in dreams
20   decked with dances by baobabs[1] over balances
by the antelope°   *buck*
in the perpetual alliance of everything that lives

They shout out the sound of life
shout it
25   even the corpses thrown up by the Atlantic
in putrid° offering of incoherence and death   *rotten*
and in the clearness of rivers.

An Angolan nationalist who fought for the liberation of his country, Neto
was also a poet who was deeply concerned with the issues facing colonial
and post-colonial Africa. During Portuguese rule over Angola, he was
repeatedly imprisoned for revolutionary activities. After independence in
1975, he held the position of President until his death. He is regarded as one
of Angola's foremost literary figures.

Notes

[1] African trees bearing edible fruit.

They live
the grieved lands of Africa
30   in the harmonious sound of consciences
contained in the honest blood of men
in the strong desire of men
in the sincerity of men
in the pure and simple rightness of the stars' existence

35   They live
the grieved lands of Africa
because we are living
and are imperishable particles
of the grieved lands of Africa.

Joseph Kumbirai (1922–1986)

Dawn

Translated from the Shona by Douglas Livingstone

Cock-crow and early-rise!
Venus, the morning star, appears
a first light, growing.

The sky is a blood-orange;
5   the first zestful breeze delights the heart
but shrivels up the morning star.

The roosters' voices fade
while the light gets brighter;
the elephants of dawn have finished washing.

10   The first dew steams
along with smoking hearths;
birds awaken, chirruping.

Brilliantly, pristine,
the great sun appears
15   like a large and glittering forehead.

Children warm their backs,
shouting: The sun,
the sun is King!

Their little polished heads
20   shimmer and glitter
like leaves turning from the west.

As the sun sets, so we set;
as the sun rises, so we rise:
the sun, the sun is King!

Kumbirai is considered one of the finest Shona-language poets Zimbabwe has produced. Some of his works have been translated into English, both by himself and others. Born on a mission station, he became a Catholic priest and teacher. He also lectured in African languages at the University of Zimbabwe.

Talking points

This poem clearly draws on the African tradition of praise poetry, in which an important person or phenomenon is described and celebrated in glowing and deliberately exaggerated terms. Repetition and natural imagery are typically used. This poem may remind you of the traditional Aboriginal chant found on p. 85, in which the new day is also described in almost ritual terms.

Denise Levertov (1923–1997)

What Were They Like?

(1) Did the people of Viet Nam
 use lanterns of stone?
(2) Did they hold ceremonies
 to reverence the opening of buds?
5 (3) Were they inclined to quiet laughter?
(4) Did they use bone and ivory,
 jade[1] and silver, for ornament?
(5) Had they an epic poem?
(6) Did they distinguish between speech and singing?

10 (1) Sir, their light hearts turned to stone.
 It is not remembered whether in gardens
 stone lanterns illumined pleasant ways.
(2) Perhaps they gathered once to delight in blossom,
 but after the children were killed
15 there were no more buds.
(3) Sir, laughter is bitter to the burned mouth.
(4) A dream ago, perhaps. Ornament is for joy.
 All the bones were charred.
(5) It is not remembered. Remember,
20 most were peasants; their life
 was in rice and bamboo.
 When peaceful clouds were reflected in the paddies
 and the water buffalo stepped surely along terraces,
 maybe fathers told their sons old tales.
25 When bombs smashed those mirrors
 there was time only to scream.
(6) There is an echo yet
 of their speech which was like a song.
 It was reported their singing resembled
30 the flight of moths in moonlight.
 Who can say? It is silent now.

Levertov was born in England to a Russian-Jewish family. Her father converted to Christianity and became a priest, but remained determined to draw the two religions together. During the 1930s, the Levertov home was a refuge for Jews escaping from Nazi Germany. Levertov was educated privately at home; during the Second World War she worked as a nurse, and afterwards married an American soldier, also a writer. She returned with him to the USA, and remained there, teaching at various universities and writing and editing poetry. She was a noted anti-war activist during the period of the American war in Vietnam. Her work is significant for the power of its imagery and close observation of daily human events.

Notes

[1] Green semi-precious stone, often used in Oriental carving, sculpture, and jewellery.

Talking points

'What Were They Like?' deals with the shattering effect of war on
the Vietnamese people. During the 1960s and 70s, the USA sent
conscripted troops to Vietnam to fight against guerrilla forces that
were striving to unite North and South Vietnam under socialist rule.
This intervention in what amounted to a civil war was enormously
costly (especially in terms of lives lost), caused acute suffering to the
Vietnamese people, and was eventually ineffective. Many US citizens
protested bitterly against their country's involvement in a foreign
nation's struggle.

You might like to consider the role of poetry and the arts in other
anti-war movements, both locally and globally.

Antonio Jacinto (1924– 1991)

Letter from a Contract Worker

I wanted to write you a letter
my love,
a letter that would tell
of this desire
5   to see you
of this fear
of losing you
of this more than benevolence that I feel
of this indefinable ill that pursues me
10   of this yearning to which I live in total surrender . . .

I wanted to write you a letter
my love,
a letter of intimate secrets,
a letter of memories of you,
15   of you
of your lips red as henna°   *reddish dye*
of your hair black as mud
of your eyes sweet as honey
of your breasts hard as wild orange
20   of your lynx° gait   *wild cat*
and of your caresses
such that I can find no better here . . .

I wanted to write you a letter
my love,
25   that would recall the days in our haunts
our nights lost in the long grass
that would recall the shade falling on us from the plum
trees
the moon filtering through the endless palm trees
30   that would recall the madness
of our passion
and the bitterness
of our separation . . .

This Angolan poet, like Neto p. 161, combined literary and cultural work with
revolutionary activities against Portuguese colonial rule of his land. He spent
many years in prison, but when independence came in 1975, he was
appointed Minister of Culture and Education.

I wanted to write you a letter
35   my love,
   that you would not read without sighing
   that you would hide from papa Bombo
   that you would withhold from mama Kieza
   that you would reread without the coldness
40   of forgetting
   a letter to which in all Kilombo
   no other would stand comparison . . .

I wanted to write you a letter
   my love
45   a letter that would be brought to you by the passing wind
   a letter that the cashews and coffee trees
   the hyenas and buffaloes
   the alligators and grayling°   *fish*
   could understand
50   so that if the wind should lose it on the way
   the beasts and plants
   with pity for our sharp suffering
   from song to song
   lament to lament
55   gabble to gabble
   would bring you pure and hot
   the burning words
   the sorrowful words of the letter
   I wanted to write to you my love . . .

60   I wanted to write you a letter . . .

But oh my love, I cannot understand
   why it is, why it is, why it is, my dear
   that you cannot read
   and I — Oh the hopelessness! — cannot write!

Maya Angelou (1928–)

Still I Rise

You may write me down in history
With your bitter, twisted lies,
You may trod me in the very dirt
But still, like dust, I'll rise.

5   Does my sassiness° upset you?   *cheekiness*
Why are you beset with gloom?
'Cause I walk like I've got oil wells
Pumping in my living room.

Just like moons and like suns,
10 With the certainty of tides,
Just like hopes springing high,
Still I'll rise.

Did you want to see me broken?
Bowed head and lowered eyes?
15 Shoulders falling down like teardrops,
Weakened by my soulful cries.

Does my haughtiness offend you?
Don't you take it awful hard
'Cause I laugh like I've got gold mines
20 Diggin' in my own back yard.

You may shoot me with your words,
You may cut me with your eyes,
You may kill me with your hatefulness,
But still, like air, I'll rise.

25 Does my sexiness upset you?
Does it come as a surprise
That I dance like I've got diamonds
At the meeting of my thighs?

Angelou was born and brought up in the southern USA, and the flavour of her black working-class roots marks her writing. She was sexually abused as a child by a family friend, an experience that left her mute (unable to speak) for years. One of the first black American writers to identify herself with feminist concerns, she is best known for her autobiographical books. She remains a popular speaker and university professor.

Out of the huts of history's shame
30 I rise
Up from a past that's rooted in pain
I rise
I'm a black ocean, leaping and wide,
Welling and swelling I bear in the tide.

35 Leaving behind nights of terror and fear
I rise
Into a daybreak that's wondrously clear
I rise
Bringing the gifts that my ancestors gave,
40 I am the dream and the hope of the slave.
I rise
I rise
I rise.

Helen Segal (1929–1988)

The Sea Is All Male

The sea is all male
that is why some women
walk in it
till they drown in ecstasy.
5 No earthly man
could hold them
handle
rule them;
the secret depths
10 salt-song
reckless order of the sea
tosses aside imagination
because it is.

They seek heroic consummation;
15 brains and bones
blood and brawn
have baffled.

On the floor of the sea
ploughing the heavy waters
20 they strain to the limit
beyond their limit
crash, are crushed,
jet to surface for a breath;
have found a land-locked lover
25 foaming blind words
in deafened ears;
whirled in cruel embrace
that peaks their world-wise shell
breaking brittle bonds
30 they are.

Segal was born in Johannesburg and educated at the universities of the Witwatersrand and South Africa. She worked both as a typist and a teacher. Her poetry is characterized by short, irregular lines.

On the surface
Spent and placid

weedy hair
combing waves

Talking points

Because we have included several poems that describe nature as
feminine, we also give this example of a poem (by a woman) that
describes a natural force (the sea) as masculine. How many poems
can you find in this anthology that ascribe gender (either female or
male) to natural phenomena?

The elegies for Ingrid Jonker by Jack Cope (p. 140) and Sally
Bryer (p. 212) also make powerful use of sea imagery. You may enjoy
comparing this poem with theirs.

Adrienne Rich (1929–)

'I am in Danger — Sir —'

'Half-cracked'° to Higginson, living,   *half-mad*
afterward famous in garbled versions,
your hoard of dazzling scraps a battlefield,
now your old snood°   *hairnet*

5   mothballed at Harvard
and you in your variorum monument
equivocal° to the end —   *having double meaning*
who are you?

Gardening the day-lily,
10 wiping the wine-glass stems,
your thought pulsed on behind
a forehead battered paper-thin,

you, woman, masculine
in single-mindedness,
15 for whom the word was more
than a symptom —

One of America's leading feminist poets and critics, **Rich** belongs to a generation that first married and had children, then moved on to more politically radical and women-centred lifestyles. While teaching at university, she became involved in protesting against the American war in Vietnam. In the 1970s, she was awarded a major prize for literature, which she personally rejected, but claimed on behalf of the black lesbian poet Audre Lorde (see p. 187) and 'in the name of all women'. Her poetry is sometimes angry, sometimes tender, and explores new ways of using language to tell women's stories.

'I am in Danger — Sir —,' refers to the nineteenth-century American poet Emily Dickinson. (For details of Dickinson's life and a selection of her poems, see pp. 86–7). Higginson (line 1) was a friend with literary contacts to whom Dickinson wrote for advice on her poems. His response was not encouraging, and she gave up trying to publish her work. Harvard University holds much Dickinson memorabilia (lines 4–5); the 'variorum monument' (line 6) refers to the full publication of Dickinson's poems (which finally took place during the 1950s), together with editorial comments. The last stanza refers to Dickinson's decision to withdraw from human contact and society during the last years of her life.

a condition of being.
Till the air buzzing with spoiled language
sang in your ears

20   of Perjury°   *lies told under oath*

and in your half-cracked way you chose
silence for entertainment,
chose to have it out at last
on your own premises.

Talking points

You might enjoy placing Rich's poem against those of Dickinson, to
see how Rich borrows from the earlier poet. What obvious feature of
Rich's poem immediately suggests Dickinson's poetry? How else does
Rich suggest her debt to Dickinson?

Ted Hughes (1930–1998)

The Thought-Fox

I imagine this midnight moment's forest:
Something else is alive
Beside the clock's loneliness
And this blank page where my fingers move.

5 Through the window I see no star:
Something more near
Though deeper within darkness
Is entering the loneliness:

Cold, delicately as the dark snow,
10 A fox's nose touches twig, leaf;
Two eyes serve a movement, that now
And again now, and now, and now

Sets neat prints into the snow
Between trees, and warily a lame
15 Shadow lags by stump and in hollow
Of a body that is bold to come

Across clearings, an eye,
A widening deepening greenness,
Brilliantly, concentratedly,
20 Coming about its own business

Till, with a sudden sharp hot stink of fox
It enters the dark hole of the head.
The window is starless still; the clock ticks,
The page is printed.

Much of **Hughes'** poetry reflects his encounters with nature while growing up in rural Yorkshire (in the north-east of England). He focuses not only on the beauty but also on the violence of the natural world, a distinctive and sometimes brutal approach, which can make reading his poetry an uncomfortable experience. While studying at Cambridge, he met the gifted young American poet Sylvia Plath (see p. 179). They married in 1956 and had two children, but the marriage was not a success. Hughes also wrote children's books and plays, and was appointed Poet Laureate in 1984.

Talking points

1 Identify the central metaphor* on which this poem is based, and
   trace its development. (The title will help you.) Why do you
   think the speaker chooses a fox returning to its lair to symbolize
   the dawning of an idea?
2 What does this metaphor suggest about the creative process, as
   viewed by this speaker? According to this poem, how does he
   experience composing or writing?
3 Although the fox in this poem is symbolic or metaphorical, it is
   described in vividly realistic terms. How does the close
   observation of the animal and its movements in stanzas three to
   six correspond with the coming of inspiration? In the last stanza,
   what role does the poet/speaker play?

Tractor

The tractor stands frozen – an agony
To think of. All night
Snow packed its open entrails. Now a head-pincering gale,
A spill of molten ice, smoking snow,
5 Pours into its steel.
At white heat of numbness it stands
In the aimed hosing of ground-level fieriness.

It defies flesh and won't start.
Hands are like wounds already
10 Inside armour gloves, and feet are unbelievable
As if the toe-nails were all just torn off.
I stare at it in hatred. Beyond it
The copse° hisses – capitulates miserably   *clump of trees*
In the fleeing, failing light. Starlings,
15 A dirtier sleetier snow, blow smokily, unendingly, over
Towards plantations Eastward.
All the time the tractor is sinking
Through the degrees, deepening
Into its hell of ice.

20 The starting lever
Cracks its action, like a snapping knuckle.
The battery is alive – but like a lamb
Trying to nudge its solid-frozen mother –
While the seat claims my buttock-bones, bites
25 With the space-cold of earth, which it has joined
In one solid lump.

I squirt commercial sure-fire
Down the black throat – it just coughs.
It ridicules me – a trap of iron stupidity
30 I've stepped into. I drive the battery
As if I were hammering and hammering
The frozen arrangement to pieces with a hammer
And it jabbers laughing pain-crying mockingly
Into happy life.

35 And stands
Shuddering itself full of heat, seeming to enlarge slowly
Like a demon demonstrating
A more-than-usually-complete materialisation –
Suddenly it jerks from its solidarity
40 With the concrete, and lurches towards a stanchion[1]
Bursting with superhuman well-being and abandon
Shouting Where Where?

Worse iron is waiting. Power-lift kneels
Levers awake imprisoned deadweight,
45 Shackle-pins bedded in cast-iron cow-shit.
The blind and vibrating condemned obedience
Of iron to the cruelty of iron,
Wheels screeched out of their night-locks –

Fingers
50 Among the tormented
Tonnage and burning of iron

Eyes
Weeping in the wind of chloroform[2]

And the tractor, streaming with sweat,
55 Raging and trembling and rejoicing.

Notes

1 An upright post or device used to shut cattle up in stalls.
2 Strong-smelling anaesthetic gas.

Essop Patel (1930–2007)

In the Shadow of Signal Hill

in the howling wind
by the murky waters
of the sea
children of colour
5   gather shells
and hold them to their ears
and listen to the lamentations of slaves
in the dungeon of death

in the howling wind
10   by the murky waters
of the sea
sons of langa
gather at the ruins of district six
and sharpen the spears of the night
15   and the heroes from the island urge
go towards the fiery dawn . . .

Patel is an attorney who lives in Johannesburg. His first volume of poetry established him as a compelling and committed political poet. Together with Tim Couzens he edited *The Return of the Amasi Bird: Black South African Poetry*, an anthology that first exposed to a wide audience the wealth of black poetry in South Africa.

'**Signal Hill**' is a strikingly shaped hill or small peak overlooking the harbour of Cape Town. It has been used as a lookout post since the early days of the Cape colony. From it, the viewer can see Robben Island (during the apartheid years, a notorious prison for those convicted of political crimes: see also the notes to Mphahlele's 'A Poem', p. 154); the bare scar where the suburb of District Six stood before its occupants were evicted and its buildings demolished under the Group Areas Act (apartheid legislation that restricted racial groups to certain residential areas) – see also the discussion of Opperman's 'Christmas Carol' (p. 145); and Langa, a black township on the outskirts of suburban Cape Town.

Sylvia Plath (1932–1963)

You're

Clownlike, happiest on your hands,
Feet to the stars, and moon-skulled,
Gilled like a fish. A common-sense
Thumbs-down on the dodo's[1] mode.
5 Wrapped up in yourself like a spool,
Trawling your dark as owls do.
Mute as a turnip from the Fourth
of July[2] to All Fools' Day,[3]
O high-riser, my little loaf.

10 Vague as fog and looked for like mail.
Farther off than Australia.
Bent-backed Atlas,[4] our travelled prawn.
Snug as a bud and at home
Like a sprat° in a pickle jug.
15 A creel° of eels, all ripples.
Jumpy as a Mexican bean.
Right, like a well-done sum.
A clean slate, with your own face on.

small fish
fishing basket

Plath was born in the north-eastern USA. Her father, a German immigrant and biology professor, died after a long and traumatic illness when she was eight, an experience she constantly referred to in her later writing. She met the poet Ted Hughes (see p. 175) while on a scholarship to Cambridge, married him and had two children. However, their marriage broke down. Plath had a history of clinical depression, and shortly after the publication of her first novel, she committed suicide. Although some of her poetry is extremely gloomy, it is always strikingly original, and capable of great tenderness and compassion.

Notes

1 Flightless bird, now extinct.
2 Day of Independence in the USA.
3 April Fool's Day, 1 April.
4 Mythical figure who, according to legend, carried the world on his back.

Pheasant[5]

You said you would kill it this morning.
Do not kill it. It startles me still,
The jut of that odd, dark head, pacing

Through the uncut grass on the elm's hill.
5   It is something to own a pheasant,
Or just to be visited at all.

I am not mystical: it isn't
As if I thought it had a spirit.
It is simply in its element.

10   That gives it a kingliness, a right.
The print of its big foot last winter
The tail-track, on the snow in our court –

The wonder of it, in that pallor
Through crosshatch of sparrow and starling.
15   Is it its rareness, then? It is rare.

But a dozen would be worth having,
A hundred, on that hill – green and red,
Crossing and recrossing: a fine thing!

It is such a good shape, so vivid.
20   It's a little cornucopia.[6]
It unclaps, brown as a leaf, and loud,

Settles in the elm, and is easy.
It was sunning in the narcissi.[7]
I trespass stupidly. Let be, let be.

Notes

5 Large bird (about the size of a
guinea fowl) with green and red
feathers; often hunted and
eaten.
6 Horn filled with natural produce;
a symbol of abundance.
7 White spring flowers.

Douglas Livingstone (1932–1996)

The Sleep of My Lions

O, *Mare Atlanticum,*
Mare Arabicum et Indicum,
Oceanus Orientalis,
Oceanus Aethiopicus
5   save me
           from civilization
       my pastory
           from further violation.

Leave me my magics
10 and tribes;
to the quagga, the dodo,
the sleep of my lions.

Rust me barbed fences.
Patrol what remains.
15 Accept bricks, hunting rifles
and realists, telephones
and diesels
to your antiseptic main.°   *sea*

Grant me a day of
20 moon-rites and rain-dances;
when rhinoceros
root in trained hibiscus borders;
when hippo flatten, with a smile,
deck-chairs at the beach resorts.

25 Accord me a time
of stick-insect gods, and impala
no longer crushed by concrete;
when love poems like this
can again be written in beads.

Livingstone was born in Malaysia, and came to southern Africa as a boy, living in both Zambia and Zimbabwe before settling in South Africa. He trained as a marine bacteriologist, and was in charge of research into sea pollution at the Centre for Scientific and Industrial Research in Durban until his death. His poetry vividly describes the characters, environment, and wildlife of southern Africa, and is often witty and satirical. He was also a critic and the author of several radio plays. A winner of many awards, he is still considered one of South Africa's foremost poets.

Talking points

If you work together with your classmates, you should be able to piece together the contextual information needed to appreciate this poem.

1   Who is speaking in this poem, and to whom? How do we know this? The first four lines are written in Latin, and the word 'Mare' means 'Sea'. Can you now work out what the other Latin words mean? Why do you think this ancient language is being used here?

2   What do you think the word 'pastory' (line 7) means? (The poet has coined it, or made it up – you will not find it in a dictionary.)

3   The quagga (a zebra-like wild animal) and the dodo (a large flightless bird) are both extinct. Why do you think they are mentioned here?

4   The 'stick-insect' god of line 26 refers to the original Khoisan belief that the praying-mantis was sacred. Why is this particular tradition invoked?

5   Rhinoceros, hippo, and impala are all wild animals indigenous to Africa. Hibiscus is a cultivated and imported flowering shrub. What does this information add to your interpretation of the last two stanzas?

Sipho Sepamla (1932–2007)

The Loneliness Beyond

Like raindrops pattering
They come singly and in pairs
Then as a torrent the rush of feet
Shuffles onto platforms
5   Dragging the last strains of energy.

I've seen hearts palpitating
Behind a single maskless face
Tired from the hurrying of the city
Spirits maimed by commands.

10   I've heard the clicks of tongues
Laughter rising above the grouse° of mouths   *grumbling*
That never rest
From grinding complaints.

Like sheep herded into a kraal°   *enclosure*
15   They crowd numbered coaches
Hopeful of a safe landing.

I've watched the multitudes rub shoulders
And I've wondered what they do
With the loneliness beyond;

20   I've seen throngs of people
Disappear into little holes of resting
And I've pondered what might be happening
With the loneliness beyond.

Born in the Transvaal, **Sepamla** trained as a teacher and worked in
Johannesburg as a personnel officer. He was instrumental in encouraging
and training black writers throughout his life, and was the director of the
Federated Union of Black Arts (FUBA). Together with Serote and Mtshali, he
was one of the giants of the black poetry movement of the 1970s, sometimes
called 'the new black poetry' or 'Soweto poetry'. This described the lives of
black South Africans with uncompromising realism, and was deeply critical
of apartheid. Sepamla's poetry is noted for the way it blends English with
township dialects and vernacular or indigenous languages.

Michael Gilkes (1933–)

From Prospero's Island

Miranda

There on the beach
all copper and cornsilk hair,
the eyes a blur of blue
she might have been the girl
5   on the brochure
of this green, paradisal island.
But mind, her mind has mountains
where deep forests grow,
liana°-hung: *rope–like creeper*
10 another Eden where, as yet,
no bird has sung.

It calls to her in dreams
She cannot go there yet.
There's too much needing
15 to be done
there, on the beach.
Each day, sand to be swept,
firewood to fetch:
The island's not the paradise
20 it seems.

Lately,
there have been storms
and hammering seas,
and she must run
25 to comfort Caliban[1]
when he screams.

Gilkes was born in Guyana in the West Indies. He studied in the UK, and is much in demand in the US as a gifted teacher of creative writing and West Indian literature. However, he retains a base in St Lucia in the Caribbean, where he is active in educational reform. He is also one of the most prominent figures in Caribbean film and theatre, and has written several award-winning plays.

Notes

[1] In Shakespeare's *The Tempest*, a sub-human monster who was lord of the island until Miranda and her father took over. In post-colonial criticism, often identified as a symbol of the demonized indigenous inhabitants of a colonized territory.

Talking points

'Miranda' is a deceptively simple poem that uses intertextuality* to make a number of interesting points about colonialism, gender, and more specifically, the clichés used to market the Caribbean as a tourist 'paradise'. It draws on a number of 'classic' Western texts, including Shakespeare's *The Tempest* (there is also possibly a masked reference to his sonnet 'My Mistress' Eyes Are Nothing Like the Sun') and Gerard Manley Hopkin's 'No Worst, There Is None' (see pp. 25 and 93). Post-colonial* writings often draw on Western culture for purposes of reinvention, questioning, and sometimes mockery. Why do you think these particular cross-references are used here?

Ingrid Jonker (1933–1965)

The Child Who Was Shot Dead by Soldiers at Nyanga

The child is not dead
the child lifts his fists against his mother
who shouts Afrika! shouts the breath
of freedom and the veld°   *grasslands*
5   in the locations² of the cordoned° heart   *fenced-in*

The child lifts his fists against his father
in the march of the generations
who shout Afrika! shout the breath
of righteousness and blood
10 in the streets of his embattled pride

The child is not dead
not at Langa nor at Nyanga
not at Orlando nor at Sharpeville
nor at the police station at Philippi
15 where he lies with a bullet through his brain.

The child is the dark shadow of the soldiers
on guard with rifles saracens¹ and batons
the child is present at all assemblies and law-givings
the child peers though the windows of houses and into the hearts of mothers
20 this child who just wanted to play in the sun at Nyanga is everywhere
the child grown to a man treks through all Africa
the child grown into a giant journeys through the whole world

Without a pass

One of South Africa's leading young Afrikaans poets, **Jonker** was born in the Cape and spent her short life in Cape Town. She was an outspoken critic of apartheid, and her writing was also unusual in its intimate portrayal of often painful emotions. Deeply disheartened by her private and political circumstances, she committed suicide by walking into the sea and drowning. Local scholars and poets continue to translate and be inspired by her poems.

'The Child Who Was Shot Dead' was written, originally in Afrikaans, in response to the notorious killings at Sharpeville in 1960. Police opened fire on an unarmed crowd of blacks who were protesting against the pass laws that restricted their movements and freedom. Riots and further deaths followed throughout the country, including the various townships listed in this poem.

Former President Nelson Mandela chose this poem to introduce his parliamentary address after the first non-racial and democratic election in South Africa in 1994.

Notes

[1] Name given to armoured cars.
[2] Term used under apartheid to describe the separate townships in which urban blacks were required to live.

Audre Lorde (1934–1993)

Coal

I
is the total black, being spoken
from the earth's inside.
There are many kinds of open
5   how a diamond comes into a knot of flame
how sound comes into a word, coloured
by who pays what for speaking.

Some words are open like a diamond
on glass windows
10   singing out within the passing crash of sun
Then there are words like stapled wagers
in a perforated book – buy and sign and tear apart –
and come whatever wills all chances
the stub remains
15   an ill-pulled tooth with a ragged edge.
Some words live in my throat
breeding like adders. Others know sun
seeking like gypsies over my tongue
to explode through my lips
20   like young sparrows bursting from shell.
Some words
bedevil me.

Love is a word, another kind of open.
As the diamond comes into a knot of flame
25   I am Black because I come from the earth's inside
now take my word for jewel in the open light.

Lorde was an outspoken black American poet who fearlessly used her
writing to proclaim her identity as a feminist and a lesbian. She was active in
the black power movements of the late 1960s, and taught at various
universities in the USA. In the last years of her life, she retired to the
Caribbean, where she died after a long and courageous battle against cancer.

Wole Soyinka (1934–)

Capital

It cannot be
That germ which earth has nurtured
Man tended – once I watched a waterfall
Of germ, a grain-spray plentitude
5   Belched from chutes of wide-mouthed
Glad satiation; I swear the grains
Were singing –

It cannot be
That policy, deliberation
10   Turns these embers of my life
To ashes, and in polluted seas
Lays sad beds of yeast to raise
Dough
On the world market.

Nigeria's foremost writer, **Soyinka** was educated both at home and in
England. A political prisoner during the 1960s, he has held a number of
prestigious teaching posts at universities in Nigeria, elsewhere in Africa,
Britain, and the USA. He also founded a number of Nigerian theatres. A
dramatist, poet, critic, and novelist of great stature, he has been awarded the
Nobel Prize for Literature.

Zulfikar Ghose (1935–)

The Attack on Sialkot

Grandfather, eighty now, his pilgrimage
to Mecca over, still lives there, at peace
with his Muslim conscience. At our last meeting
he sat in the courtyard of a mosque, still
5   as an idol, while I stood outside, garish
as a poster against the whitewashed wall
in my mohair suit and corduroy hat,
advertising my patent° secularism.   *obvious*

Gunfire made Sialkot a kiln¹ to fire
10   Pakistan's earthern-pot faith. I listened
to the news hour after hour the whole month
and saw maps in newspapers, an arrow
pointed at Sialkot. Grandfather's breastplate
of Islam had become fragile as china
15   in the intruding heresy of tanks.
I see that arrow still: aimed at grandfather.

It was a messy, a child's pudding plate
of a town during my first seven years.
I pulled at grandfather's beard and dragged down
20   his turban when he carried me to school.
He turned five times a day towards Mecca, bowed
low in prayer and at night swung me round
the bed so that my feet did not insult
the holy direction, the one truth he knew.

Ghose was born in Pakistan and received his higher education in the north of England. He worked as a cricket journalist for *The Observer* newspaper and as a teacher. He eventually took up a post in the English Department at the University of Texas, and is today recognized for an impressive list of novels and critical works. He is best known for a trilogy of novels that chart the history of Brazil. He occasionally writes poetry.

In order to appreciate 'The Attack on Sialkot', it is necessary to know some basic facts about the state of Pakistan and the Islamic faith. Sialkot is a city in northern Pakistan, very close to the disputed border of the state of Kashmir. At the time of India's independence in 1948, the country was controversially divided into East Pakistan, India, and West Pakistan (now Bangladesh) along primarily religious lines. The beautiful mountain kingdom of Kashmir was granted to India, and this has been a source of unrest ever since. In the early 1960s, India, Pakistan, and China were drawn into open war over the issue. This is the conflict referred to in the poem, and it is

Notes

¹ Oven used to bake clay pottery so that it is hardened and strengthened.

25 From the east and southeast the tanks, from the air
the jets converged all month on Sialkot
in a massive pilgrimage, bloodier than
the annual sacrifice of goats and sheep.
Grandfather, the landmarks are falling, which
30 way will you turn now? Islam, Islam, that's
all you cared for, stubborn as a child, while
I had gone westward, begun to eat pork.

Grandfather, if the old house falls, if you
die where you built and Sialkot collapses,
35 I shall have no Mecca to turn to, who
admire cathedrals for their architecture.
Religion is irrelevant to grief:
you will not agree, nor will Pakistan,
finding in this war the old Islamic
40 pride rise like a congregation in a mosque.

clearly a source of great anxiety to the speaker in the poem, who is
thousands of miles from his home.

The poem is also in some ways an elegy* for the speaker's loss of faith;
he shows his rejection of the religion of his ancestors by wearing Western
clothes (the 'mohair suit and corduroy hat' in line 7), as well as by eating
pork, which is forbidden to Muslims. Mecca, which occurs as a significant
reference point throughout the poem, is the holiest of all Islamic sites, and all
devout Muslims are expected to make a pilgrimage to it at least once in their
lifetime. It also serves as a literal and metaphorical compass point for the
direction of prayer. Towards the end of the poem, it becomes clear that the
speaker's own private Mecca is where his beloved grandfather is.

This is also very much a poem of the 'diaspora' – a word that describes
the geographical scattering of a specific community. Such movements can be
prompted by war, genocide, famine, unemployment, colonialism, political
exile or deportation, or simply restlessness. Members of such communities
often struggle with issues of identity and belonging. Can you think of
examples, both here and abroad?

Kofi Awoonor (1935–)

The Weaver Bird

The weaver bird built in our house
And laid its eggs on our only tree
We did not want to send it away
We watched the building of the nest
5   And supervised the egg-laying.
And the weaver returned in the guise of the owner
Preaching salvation to us that owned the house
They say it came from the west
Where the storms at sea had felled the gulls
10   And the fishers dried their nets by lantern light
Its sermon is the divination of ourselves
And our new horizons limit at its nest
But we cannot join the prayers and answers of the communicants.[1]
We look for new homes every day,
15   For new altars we strive to rebuild
The old shrines defiled by the weaver's excrement.

Awoonor was educated in his home country Ghana, as well as in London and the USA. He was imprisoned on suspicion of terrorism during the 1970s. Considered Ghana's leading poet, he has held a number of prestigious academic and diplomatic posts (including the post of ambassador to Cuba), and has edited various literary journals. His works include plays, critical writings, and a novel as well as poetry that specializes in 'lyric lament'.

'The Weaver Bird' is a metaphorical lament on the impact of Western missionaries on African traditional culture. It is an example of the growing body of post-colonial* writing that reflects on or analyses the impact of colonialism and empire-building by mostly European countries on what we would now call developing countries. A number of the poems in this anthology deal explicitly or implicitly with these issues; see Neto's 'The Grieved Lands' (pp. 161–2), Livingstone's 'The Sleep of My Lions' (p. 181), and Gilkes' 'Miranda' (p. 184). Can you find any others?

Notes

[1] Those who participate in the Christian ritual of holy communion.

Don Mattera (1935–)

Remember

Remember to call at my grave
When freedom finally
Walks the land
So that I may rise
5   To tread familiar paths
To see broken chains
Fallen prejudice
Forgotten injury
Pardoned pains.

10 And when my eyes have filled their sight
Do not run away for fright
If I crumble to dust again

It will only be the bliss
Of a long-awaited dream
15 That bids me rest
When freedom finally walks the land . . .

Mattera grew up in Sophiatown, and now lives in Johannesburg. His colourful and varied past has included spells as a footballer and gang leader. He founded a union for black journalists, and was banned for his part in the black consciousness movement of the 1970s. (Serote's poem 'For Don M. — Banned' was written for Mattera during this period; see p. 209.) Mattera is best known for his poetry, but has also written short stories, plays, and an autobiography. He has received both literary and human rights awards, and has been awarded an honorary Doctorate in Letters by the University of Natal.

'**Remember**' was written during the years of apartheid, and the speaker envisages freedom in South Africa only in the distant future, long after his death. Although Mattera's prophecy of freedom was fulfilled in his own lifetime, he dedicates this poem to the many who died before it came.

Geoffrey Haresnape (1939–)

In and Around the Yacht Basin – Simon's Town[1]

Beyond
the rigging[2] tangle
are

5   rhizomes°   *roots, stems*
of Club Mykonos[3]
    apartments

    Cape
Dutch[4] gable
    fungi

10   floral
    filigrees[5]
of English iron.

    The
scrubby hills
15   protest

that Europe's garden
wasn't always
planted here.

       * * *

Born in Natal, **Haresnape** currently teaches in the English Department at the University of Cape Town. His critical works include a collection of pioneering writings and a study of the novels of the South African writer Pauline Smith. He has always maintained a keen interest in South African poetry, and took over from Jack Cope as the editor of the literary magazine *Contrast*. He has published a novel and several prize-winning collections of poems.

Notes

1. Naval base and residential area on the Cape Peninsula.
2. Ropes that support masts.
3. Luxury resort with pseudo-Mediterranean architecture.
4. Eighteenth-century Cape farm architecture, famous for its beauty.
5. Ornamental patterning in wire and metal.

old   cling   strings   giant
20   tyres   like   of
          necklacing
mussels   the pier.

    * * *

          Masts   I
          (red   hard-
25   yell-   ly
         ow   dare
        blue)   to
        are   breathe
        pick   when
30   up   lift-
        sticks   ing
        criss-   each
       crossed   im-
       or   press-
35   slant-   ion:
       ed   one
      when   slip
       the   would
      o-   jar
40   cean   the
     breathes   whole.

    * * *

A brash South Easter[6]
barges in
upon the game,
45   displacing
all.

Talking points

1   This poem is a delightful experiment in form and shape. Why
    has the writer laid out the words on the page this way? How do
    the differing patterns contribute to meaning?
2   Read the second section carefully; you will need to do some
    reorganizing to make sense out of the word order. Why does the
    poet arrange the words like this? Can you visualize a 'picture' of
    the scene? Do you know of any other poems that present a visual
    image? (You might like to use a library or the Internet to track
    down George Herbert's poem 'Easter Wings'.)
3   In much of the poem, the writer seems to play with words and
    patterns simply to create different moods and pictures; yet there
    does seem to be a more serious point. Can you identify this?

Seamus Heaney (1939–)

Follower

My father worked with a horse-plough,
His shoulders globed like a full sail strung
Between the shafts and the furrow.
The horses strained at his clicking tongue.

5 An expert. He would set the wing
And fit the bright steel-pointed sock.
The sod rolled over without breaking.
At the headrig,° with a single pluck   *harness*

Of reins, the sweating team turned round
10 And back into the land. His eye
Narrowed and angled at the ground,
Mapping the furrow exactly.

I stumbled in his hob-nailed[1] wake,
Fell sometimes on the polished sod;
15 Sometimes he rode me on his back
Dipping and rising to his plod.

I wanted to grow up and plough,
To close one eye, stiffen my arm.
All I ever did was follow
20 In his broad shadow round the farm.

I was a nuisance, tripping, falling,
Yapping always. But today
It is my father who keeps stumbling
Behind me, and will not go away.

Born into a Catholic family in rural Northern Ireland, **Heaney** studied and later lectured at Queen's University in Belfast. He is almost certainly Ireland's greatest living poet. His work is deeply rooted in the history of his country, including the tragic violence of modern-day Northern Ireland. He was awarded the Nobel prize for Literature in 1995, partly in recognition for the compassion with which he regards his divided and troubled country.

Notes

[1] Reference to 'hob-nailed' boots (boots wth metal studs in the soles).

Wopko Jensma (1939–)

From Not Him

he forbids us to dance
he always leads the church service
he has a stable job
he is always on time for work
5   he never gets drunk
he has respect for most people
everybody respects him
we love our daddy
but sometimes I notice
10 when a kwela[1] blasts from the radio
he wiggles his toes

Raised in South Africa, **Jensma** is of Dutch descent. At the height of the apartheid regime, he insisted on being reclassified as black (at the time, every citizen was obliged to be racially identified and 'classified'). An artist as well as a poet, his collections of poetry feature his own woodcuts. His unorthodox and angry poetry, distinctive for its lack of punctuation, has always been identified with black protest poetry, and his second volume of poems was in fact banned. In recent years, he has repeatedly been admitted to psychiatric hospitals.

Notes

[1] Lively black township music, featuring the penny-whistle; made internationally famous through Mango Groove's song 'Special Star'.

Mbuyiseni Oswald Mtshali (1940–)

Men in Chains

The train stopped
at a country station.

Through sleep curtained eyes
I peered through the frosty window,
5   and saw six men:
men shorn
of all human honour
like sheep after shearing,
bleating at the blistering wind,
10   'Go away! Cold wind! Go away!
Can't you see we are naked?'

They hobbled into the train
on bare feet,
wrists handcuffed,
15   ankles manacled°   *chained*
with steel rings like cattle at the abbatoirs
shying away from the trapdoor.

One man with a head
shaven clean as a potato
20   whispered to the rising sun,
a red eye wiped by a tattered
handkerchief of clouds,
'Oh! Dear Sun!
Won't you warm my heart
25   with hope?'
The train went on its way to nowhere.

Mtshali was born in the Orange Free State but moved to Johannesburg, where the publication of his first volume of poetry, *Sounds of a Cowhide Drum*, was a huge success. Probably the first collection of poems to describe daily life in black townships under apartheid, it sold more copies than any other book of poetry in South Africa. Mtshali, who has studied in the USA and taught in Soweto, was one of the first exponents of the 'new black poetry' of the black consciousness movement of the 1970s. His work was banned for several years.

Talking points

1   A close examination of this poem will be useful in identifying different kinds of imagery. Remember that similes* are usually indicated by the use of the words 'as' and 'like', whereas metaphors* are more directly stated. What similes and metaphors can you identify here?

2   We find two central similes that are used to describe the men in chains. What do they have in common? Why does the speaker use this kind of imagery? Is his intention to patronize or degrade the prisoners, or is he using these images for a different reason? What is the accumulative impact?

3   How does the speaker describe the sun in the third stanza? (Think of the qualities we normally associate with the sun; does the imagery here seem surprising?) How does this add to the overall tone of the poem?

4   What effect does the last line have?

Arthur Nortje (1942–1970)

In Exile

Open skies flare wide enough
to make me vaguely anxious.
Nimbus° wisps   *storm-cloud*
trace patterns of the past.

5   Wind sweeps between the towers
through tunnels, old and new.
My heart is
hollowed with the boots passing through.

Garments gather and play about
10   my limbs: they tremble to a return
gust. Leaves and transient°   *passing*
streetscape conjure up that southern

blue sky and wind-beautiful
day, creating paradise.
15   Otherwise:
the soul decays in exile.

But wrong pigment has no scope,
so clot the blue channel of memory.
On a sand slope
20   I build a picture of the sea.

The grains that slide away
are wind-breathed, are stirred by finger.
Benign, a cloud
obscures the sun, this hunger.

Talking points

You might find it interesting to compare and contrast this poem with
Stephen Watson's poem of the same title on pp. 227–9. What
features do they have in common, and what differences can you find?

Nortje studied at the University of the Western Cape, and was a teacher for
a while before winning a scholarship to Oxford University. He then taught in
Canada before returning to Oxford. It would seem from his poetry, which
reflects an extreme sense of personal and cultural dislocation, that he
regarded his time overseas as a period of exile. He died tragically young as a
result of a drug overdose.

Jeni Couzyn (1942–)

The Red Hen's Last Will and Testament to The Last Cock on Earth

Mr Cockatoo I'm through.
You
can take your splendid
reasoning and quick
5   precision and elegant
vision somewhere
else.
    You can take your
fine red comb and fast
10 feathered sex and high
concepts somewhere
else.
    Your race can take its
good influence and careful
15 words and strong wings and
bright eyes some other
place.
    You may be the
last manifestation but
20 you're not worth it.
Now
that there's artificial
insemination[1] since the
evolution of the cock

25 as a different species
you may as well wither
too.
    Hens need something
else. You make us feel
30 abandoned. You make us
feel like a place cocks
Pop into. We stay in the
place alone.

Couzyn was born in Johannesburg and has lived in London since the mid-1960s. She was a founder member of the Poet's Conference and the Poet's Union, and has taught at the University of Victoria in Canada. Her poetry includes chants and spells for women.

Notes

1   Impregnation by medical means.

We await your
35 visitation. You pop in and
pop out. When we wake up
in the morning it is
silent.
All the hens in the
40 farmyard feel exactly as
I do about you. We have
decided to quit.
You all
can take off on your
45 massive Coxes High Powered
Jet Propelled
wings.
We hens will stay here
laying our eggs in the
50 warm straw, dreaming of
foxes.

Mutiswayo Shandu

Bye Bye, Overcoat

The day before yesterday Mr Straun
gives me this overcoat. Today I catch
this train to my Stepmother's, wearing it.
It is a splendid coat, fawn,° almost new   *pale brown*
5   – just this small gap in the seam of one sleeve.

It is past midday, the train not crowded
with mostly shoppers and halfday meisies.°   *girls*
Still, I am standing, straphanging, swaying
but I prefer it: such a cool garment
10 of such swaggering cut should not be creased.

Comes payday: a good hat – maybe a fine
snapbrim fedora, perhaps from PATEL'S[1]
is quite definitely indicated.
Stepmama has a Singer[2] at her place . . .
15 The air around me goes into deepfreeze.

Turning, I see at the far end: Main Ou[3]
has joined us, accompanied by a pair
of toughlooking tsotsis.[4] Over dozens
of heads his eyes meet mine. He is staring
20 at my new overcoat. Tixo![5] Such luck!

They start working the silent, sullen folks,
towards me: peering in wallets, purses,
emptying handbags; some men have to stand
to have their back-pockets patted. Main Ou
25 does not work or hang on. His legs are braced.

No dates are available for this South African poet. Efforts to track down information about him have been fruitless; anyone who remembers him or can tell us about him is encouraged to contact us via the publishers.

Notes

[1] Name of a shop selling men's clothing.
[2] Type of sewing machine.
[3] Slang term for the gang leader; literally 'most important man' or 'big guy'.
[4] Township slang for young men, usually criminals or gangsters.
[5] Xhosa oath meaning Lord or God.

He hardly moves with the train's rock and roll.
He taps a bicyclespoke with a stained
wood handle, coolly, on his left thumbnail.
His two thugs work quietly and quickly:
30 it is nearly all money and trinkets . . .

But one man has already lost his fine
leather jacket. Bruce Lee,[6] where are you now!
There are dozens of us, just three of them.
As usual, each of us is alone
35 against the predator, the oppressor . . .

For once, even the SAP[7] would do!
When I reach Stepmama's distinctive house
I am too sad to speak, and she sees it.
She serves me tea, strokes my defeated neck.
40 Her Singer stays, unused, under her bed.

Notes

[6] Star of series of martial arts films, in which he played a hero who defeated criminals with his superior fighting skills.

[7] The South African Police.

Michael Ondaatje (1943–)

The Cinnamon Peeler

If I were a cinnamon peeler
I would ride your bed
and leave the yellow bark dust
on your pillow.

5   Your breasts and shoulders would reek
you could never walk through markets
without the profession of my fingers
floating over you. The blind would
stumble certain of whom they approached
10   though you might bathe
under rain gutters, monsoon.

Here on the upper thigh
at this smooth pasture
neighbour to your hair
15   or the crease
that cuts your back. This ankle.
You will be known among strangers
as the cinnamon peeler's wife.

I could hardly glance at you
20   before marriage
never touch you
– your keen nosed mother, your rough brothers.
I buried my hands
in saffron,[1] disguised them
25   over smoking tar,
helped the honey gatherers . . .

Ondaatje was born in Sri Lanka and now lives in Canada. An extremely accomplished poet and novelist, he has also written a moving memoir of his childhood in Sri Lanka, *Running in the Family*. He became widely known when his novel *The English Patient* first won the prestigious Booker Prize, and was then made into a lavishly produced and popular film.

Cinnamon is an extremely fragrant spice, with a distinctive sweet smell. It is used in baking and some Asian cooking. It grows and is harvested in tropical countries such as Sri Lanka.

Notes

[1] A spice with a subtle flavour and scent, also used as a dye.

When we swam once
I touched you in water
and our bodies remained free,
30   you could hold me and be blind of smell.
You climbed the bank and said

         this is how you touch other women
the grass cutter's wife, the lime burner's daughter.
And you searched your arms
35   for the missing perfume

         and knew

         what good is it
to be the lime burner's daughter
left with no trace
40   as if not spoken to in the act of love
as if wounded without the pleasure of a scar.

You touched
your belly to my hands
in the dry air and said
45   I am the cinnamon
peeler's wife. Smell me.

Wally Mongane Serote (1944–)

Alexandra[1]

Were it possible to say,
Mother, I have seen more beautiful mothers,
A most loving mother,
And tell her there I will go,
5   Alexandra, I would have long gone from you.

But we have only one mother, none can replace,
Just as we have no choice to be born,
We can't choose mothers;
We fall out of them like we fall out of life to death.

10 And Alexandra,
My beginning was knotted to you,
Just like you knot my destiny.
You throb in my inside silences
You are silent in my heart-beat that's loud to me.
15 Alexandra often I've cried.
When I was thirsty my tongue tasted dust,
Dust burdening your nipples.
I cry Alexandra when I am thirsty.
Your breasts ooze the dirty waters of your dongas,[2]
20 Waters diluted with the blood of my brothers, your children,
Who once chose dongas for death-beds.
Do you love me Alexandra, or what are you doing to me?

You frighten me, Mama,
You wear expressions like you would be nasty to me,
25 You frighten me, Mama,
When I lie on your breast to rest, something tells me,
You are bloody cruel.

Serote was born in Sophiatown, and went to school in the townships of Alexandra and Soweto. His political activism led to a period of detention (imprisonment without trial), and after studying art at Columbia University in the USA, he lived in exile in Botswana. His return to his homeland as the apartheid regime began to unravel marked the beginning of a period in which a number of exiled South African artists and musicians came home. He is now an MP and serves as Chair of the Parliamentary Portfolio Committee on Arts and Culture. He has won a number of noteworthy awards, and is one of the most significant poets to have emerged from the politically radical 'new black poetry' movement of the 1970s.

Notes

[1] Black township outside Johannesburg.
[2] Ravines caused by soil erosion; associated with drought and degradation of the land by overcrowding and overgrazing.

Alexandra, hell
What have you done to me?
30 I have seen people but I feel like I'm not one,
Alexandra what are you doing to me?
I feel I have sunk to such meekness!
I lie flat while others walk on me to far places.
I have gone from you, many times,
35 I come back.
Alexandra, I love you;
I know
When all these worlds became funny to me,
I silently waded back to you
40 And amid the rubble I lay,
Simple and black.

City Johannesburg[3]

This way I salute you:
My hand pulses to my back trousers pocket
Or into my inner jacket pocket
For my pass, my life,
5 Jo'burg City.
My hand like a starved snake tears my pockets
For my thin, ever lean wallet,
While my stomach groans a friendly smile to hunger,
Jo'burg City.
10 My stomach also devours coppers and papers
Don't you know?
Jo'burg City, I salute you;
When I run out, or roar in a bus to you,
I leave behind me, my love,
15 My comic houses and people, my dongas[4] and my ever whirling dust,
My death,
That's so related to me as a wink to the eye.

Notes

[3] City at the heart of the urban
sprawl centred on the mining
industries in and around
Gauteng. Historically, it relied on
black labour while remaining a
white residential area.
[4] See footnote 2, p. 207.

Jo'burg City
I travel on your black and white and robotted roads,
20   Through your thick iron breath that you inhale,
At six in the morning and exhale from five noon.
Jo'burg City
That is the time when I come to you,
When your neon[5] flowers flaunt from your electrical wind,
25   That is the time when I leave you,
When your neon flowers flaunt their way through the falling darkness
On your cement trees.
And as I go back, to my love,
My dongas, my dust, my people, my death,
30   Where death lurks in the dark like a blade in the flesh,
I can feel your roots, anchoring your might, my feebleness
In my flesh, in my mind, in my blood,
And everything about you says it,
That, that is all you need of me.
35   Jo'burg City, Johannesburg,
Listen when I tell you,
There is no fun, nothing, in it.
When you leave the women and men with such frozen expressions,
Expressions that have tears like furrows of soil erosion,
40   Jo'burg City, you are dry like death,
Jo'burg City, Johannesburg, Jo'burg City.

For Don M. — Banned

it is a dry white season
dark leaves don't last, their brief lives dry out
and with a broken heart they dive down gently headed for the earth,
not even bleeding.
5   it is a dry white season brother,
only the trees know the pain as they still stand erect
dry like steel, their branches dry like wire
indeed, it is a dry white season
but seasons come to pass.

Under the apartheid government, a banning order meant exile to a remote rural location, restrictions on movement, no contact with colleagues or fellow activists, and an embargo on any speeches, publication, or political activity. Serote wrote the above brief but powerful poem for Don Mattera, a friend and fellow poet who was banned during the 1970s. (See p. 192 for further information on Mattera, and an example of his writing.)

Notes

5   Luminous gas used in lighting and coloured signs.

Talking points

1 'Alexandra' and 'City Johannesburg' have already been compared with Blake's 'London'. As a class exercise, you could turn to p. 52, and work through the questions set out there.

2 'For Don M. — Banned' is deceptively simple. Much of the language and imagery operates on two different levels. Work through the poem identifying these 'double' words and images. Do you agree that the poem is a mini-allegory*? If so, what 'lesson' does it teach?

3 What tone or mood is conveyed by this poem? Look closely at how this is evoked or suggested.

4 The first line is repeated three times in the poem, and slightly altered each time. What effect do these small changes have on the tone and development of the poem?

5 This poem also speaks to two very different audiences. It carries a very personal message of comfort for Don Mattera; but who else does it address?

Kumalau Tawali (1947–2006)

The Old Woman's Message

Stick these words in your hair
And take them to Polin and Manuai
my sons:
the ripe fruit falls and returns
5   to the trunk – its mother.
But my sons, forgetful of me,
are like fruit borne by birds.
I see the sons of other women
returning. What is in their minds?
10   Let them keep the price of their labour
but their eyes are mine.
I have little breath left
to wait for them.
I am returning to childhood.
15   My stomach goes to my back
my hands are like broom sticks,
my legs can fit in the sand crab's hole.
I am dry like a carved image
only my head is God's.
20   Already I sway like a dry falling leaf
I see with my hands –
oh tell Polin and Manuai to hurry
and come to my death feast.

Talking points

The tendency for young people to leave rural communities for cities in order to pursue jobs and education has become increasingly marked in the last several decades. One result is that throughout the globe, rural, isolated, and impoverished areas tend to be disproportionately populated by the very young and the elderly. Pleas by older folk for their children to return home are common. This is one example of such a request; Charles Mungoshi's 'A Letter to a Son' (pp. 213–4) is another. What do these poems have in common? What might be some of the social and cultural consequences of the movement of young and able-bodied people to urban areas, especially in developing countries?

Tawali was born on a tiny Pacific island off the north coast of New Guinea, and graduated from the University of Papua New Guinea. A poet, dramatist, and story-writer, his works have been regularly published in Pacific and Australian journals. In the 1970s, he worked for the campaign for Moral Rearmament in Europe.

Sally Bryer (1947–)

Ingrid Jonker

(Afrikaans poet, drowned herself aged 33)

You walked straight into the water
like a hungry bird, your curly head
intent as a heron.[1]
You walked into the waves
5   like Persephone[2] herself,
your eyes dried seeds, your body a husk of light.
Your punishment was finding yourself
in a foreign element. You spoke
through interpreters. Your lips and fingers
10   betrayed you, turned away
from the darkness behind your eyes,
tried to sell themselves.
Your child dies, and lives on.
Your screams become seasonal.

15   We travel in packs. Hunting and hunted
we carry nets and each of us captures
a relic of pain, stark as bone.
Those of us who never saw a likeness
learn to tell the seasons of madness
20   from the sea. In every fragment of glass and shell
I pass, your dark eyes encounter me.

Talking points

This poem has already been linked to Jack Cope's 'The Flying Fish',
also written in memory of Ingrid Jonker. You might like to turn to
pp. 140–1 and work through the suggestions for comparing the two
poems.

Bryer is the daughter of professional and artistic parents, and was brought
up and educated in Johannesburg. She went on to study art in Italy. She
published relatively few poems before producing her first collection. She now
lives in Canada.

Notes

[1] Bird that fishes in rivers or dams.
[2] Figure in Greek legend who was kidnapped by the king of the underworld (the realm of the dead). Her return to the earth heralded the coming of spring, but while underground, she ate six seeds of a pomegranate (type of fruit), thus condemning herself to spend winter there each year.

Charles Mungoshi (1947–)

A Letter to a Son

Now the pumpkin is ripe.
We are only a few days from
the year's first mealie cob.
The cows are giving us lots of milk.
5 Taken in the round it isn't a bad year at all –
if it weren't for your father.
Your father's back is back again
and all the work has fallen on my shoulders.
Your little brothers and sisters are doing
10 fine at the day-school. Only Rindai
is becoming a problem. You will remember
we wrote you – did you get our letter? –
you didn't answer – you see, since your
father's back started we haven't been able
15 to raise enough to send your sister Rindai
to secondary school. She spends most of the time
crying by the well. It's mainly because of her
that I am writing this letter.
I had thought you would be with us last Christmas
20 then I thought maybe you were too busy
and you would make it at Easter –
it was then your father nearly left us, son.
Then I thought I would come to you some time
before the cold season settled in – you know how
25 I simply hate that time of year –
but then your father went down again
and this time worse than any other time before.
We were beginning to think he would never see
another sowing season. I asked your sister Rindai
30 to write you but your father would have none of it

Mungoshi is part of a generation of Zimbabwean poets that consciously sought to express their sense of identity and nationalism during their country's struggle for liberation during the 1970s. He has worked as an editor, publisher, and academic. Internationally recognized as a writer, his work includes novels and short stories as well as poems.

– you know how stubborn he can get when
he has to lie in bed all day or gets
one of those queer notions of his that
everybody is deserting him!
35 Now, Tambu, don't think I am asking for money –
although we had to borrow a little from
those who have it to get your father to hospital
and you know how he hates having to borrow!
That is all I wanted to tell you.
40 I do hope that you will be with us this July.
It's so long ago since we last heard from you –
I hope this letter finds you still at the old address.
It is the only address we know.

YOUR MOTHER

Talking points

From an entirely different corner of the globe, Kumalau Tawali has
written a very similar poem, 'The Old Woman's Message' (p. 211).
You might enjoy comparing the two pieces.

Shabbir Banoobhai (1949–)

when the first slave was brought to the cape

when the first slave was brought to the cape
he looked at the awesome mountain
which roots us to an eternal beauty
hundreds of years later, and affirmed

5   i am as free and as tall as this mountain
this mountain is more chained than i am
i will climb to the top one day
and call the adhaan before dawn

my voice will carry across the seas
10   to my loved ones in a land
i may never see again
and they will know that i

and the treasures i carry within me
are safe and always will be
15   for as long as beauty
and this mountain survive

Talking points

When the Dutch first occupied the Cape in the seventeenth century, they brought Muslim slaves from Indonesia (as well as from elsewhere) to work the land. However, 'when the first slave was brought to the cape' gives the traumatic topic of slavery a very different treatment to that seen in Cowper's 'The Negro's Complaint' (p. 48) and Nichol's 'Taint' (p. 220). Here the natural beauty of the Cape (the famous landmark of Table Mountain in particular), as well as the religious faith that binds the slave to the community from which he has been wrenched, both offer a measure of comfort and hope. The 'adhaan' (Muslim call to prayer) referred to in line 8 suggests the resilience of the human spirit in even the most alien and inhumane circumstances.

Banoobhai lives in Cape Town and works as an accountant. His poems are striking for their lyrical simplicity and expression of political, personal, and spiritual passion. He is a devoted husband and father.

they call you mister steve biko now you're dead

they call you mister steve biko now you're dead
and though your death
may leave them cold, may leave them cold
they who tormented you when you were alive
5   call you mister steve biko now you're dead

so many garlands others have placed
around your neck, around your neck
and you've been given coverage
the size of a rugby field
10   now you're dead, but you're dead

the best advocate in the land
was your voice, was your voice
and what does it matter what was said
at an inquest the best advocates in the land
15   may speak for the dead, but they're dead

they call you mister steve biko now you're dead
and though your death
may leave them cold, may leave them cold
they who tormented you when you were alive
20   call you mister steve biko now you're dead

Steven Bantu Biko was not only one of South Africa's most dynamic and influential political activists, he was also one of our finest thinkers. He is credited with developing the ideology of 'black consciousness' into a sophisticated political and personal philosophy, perhaps best expressed in his ground-breaking book, *I Write What I Like*. In the late 1970s, he was banned, detained, and beaten unconscious while in custody. While he lay dying, doctors were called to see him, but failed to take action. His death, as a result of head injuries, was one of the worst and most wasteful tragedies of that particular chapter of apartheid. Jimmy Kruger, Minister of Justice at the time, became infamous for his response on hearing the news: 'Dit laat my koud'. These words, which translate as 'It leaves me cold (unmoved)', are used as a refrain throughout this poem. The 'best advocate' referred to in line 11 is Sydney Kentridge, who acted on behalf of the Biko family in forcing an inquest into Biko's death. Although his death was ruled an 'accident', the trial was valuable in making public many of the human rights abuses prevalent in the system of detention without trial. The transcripts were later used as the basis for an impressive stage play.

Jeremy Cronin (1949–)

Faraway city, there

Faraway city, there
with salt in its stones,
under its windswept doek,°   *head-scarf*

There in our Cape Town where
5   they're smashing down homes
of the hungry, labouring people
– will you wait for me, my love?

In that most beautiful,
desolate city of my heart
10 where if staying on were passive
life wouldn't be what it is.

Not least for those rebuilding
yet again their demolished homes
with bits of plastic, port jackson° saplings,   *species of tree*
15 anything to hand – unshakeably

Defiant, frightened, broken,
and unbreakable are the people of our city.

– Will you wait for me, my love?

Cronin was a philosophy student at the University of Cape Town when he was charged under the Terrorism Act during the apartheid regime. He spent the next seven years as a political prisoner. On his release, he returned to Cape Town and published a collection of poems about his prison experiences, which attracted immediate recognition.

While Cronin was in prison, his wife died unexpectedly. This is one of the poems he wrote as a response; it is partly a love poem, partly an elegy,* and partly a political statement.

John Agard (*c.* 1949–)

Poetry Jump-Up[1]

Tell me if ah seeing right
take a look down de street

Words dancin
words dancin
5   till dey sweat
words like fishes
jumpin out a net
words wild and free
joining de poetry revelry
10   words back to back
words belly to belly

Come on everybody
come an join de poetry band
dis is poetry carnival
15   dis is poetry bacchanal[2]
when inspiration call
take yu pen in yu hand
if you dont have a pen
take yu pencil in yu hand
20   if you dont have a pencil
what the hell
so long de feeling start to swell
just shout de poem out

Words jumpin off de page
25   tell me if ah seeing right
words like birds
jumpin out a cage
take a look down de street
words shakin dey waist
30   words shakin dey bum

Agard was born in Guyana in the West Indies, and emigrated to the UK in 1977. He is one of the most respected and admired Caribbean poets, and is in great demand as a performer of his own poems. He gives the words of the Catholic mass and the cricket commentaries he listened to as a boy as influences that led to his love of language. He is known for his fascination with the rhythms of Caribbean speech and the oral quality of poetry. He works as a freelance poet and writer, and recently served as the BBC's (British Broadcasting Corporation) poet-in-residence.

Notes

1 In Caribbean dialect, a party.
2 Drunken and joyous festival; named after Bacchus, the Greek god of wine.

words wit black skin
words wit white skin
words wit brown skin
words wit no skin at all
35   words huggin up words
an saying I want to be a poem today
rhyme or no rhyme
I is a poem today
I mean to have a good time

40   Words feelin hot hot hot
big words feelin hot hot hot
lil words feelin hot hot hot
even sad words cant help
tappin dey toe
45   to de riddum of de poetry band

Dis is poetry carnival
dis is poetry bacchanal
so come on everybody
join de celebration
50   all yu need is plenty perspiration
an a little inspiration
plenty perspiration
an a little inspiration

Talking points

Like Siers' poem on pp. 224–5, this is written in a particular dialect
or variation of English (you might enjoy comparing the two poems).
Here the influence is predominantly Caribbean, or West Indian. The
spelling is largely phonetic, so it is especially important to read this
poem aloud.

Grace Nichols (1950–)

Taint

But I was stolen by men
the colour of my own skin
borne away by men whose heels
had become hoofs
5   whose hands had turned talons
bearing me down
    to the trail
of darkness

But I was traded by men
10 the colour of my own skin
traded like a fowl   like a goat
like a sack of kernels I was
traded
    for beads   for pans
15 for trinkets?

No it isn't easy to forget
What we refuse to remember

Daily I rinse the taint
of treachery from my mouth

Talking points

The issue of slavery remains as current as ever, whether we are
dealing with the difficulties of coming to terms with its history, or
facing the appalling reality that it remains far from eradicated. You
might find it useful to turn to pp. 48–9 for a perspective from a
different era. The notes and questions there will help you to compare
the two poems.

A poet and novelist, **Nichols** was born in Guyana, and moved to Britain in
her twenties. She came to public attention when her book of poems dealing
with slavery, *I Is a Long Memoried Woman*, won the Commonwealth Poetry
Prize in 1983 (the poem here is from this collection). By turns energetic,
funny, and angry, her work is perhaps best appreciated when performed
orally, and public recitals by her and her partner John Agard (see p. 218) have
heightened the popularity of both poets.

Ingrid de Kok (1951–)

Small Passing

For a woman whose baby died stillborn, and who was told by a man to stop
mourning, 'because the trials and horrors suffered daily by black women in this
country are more significant than the loss of one white child.'

1

In this country you may not
suffer the death of your stillborn,
remember the last push into shadow and silence,
the useless wires and cords on your stomach,
5   the nurse's face, the walls, the afterbirth in a basin.
Do not touch your breasts
still full of purpose.
Do not circle the house,
pack, unpack the small clothes.
10 Do not lie awake at night hearing
the doctor say 'It was just as well'
and 'You can have another.'
In this country you may not
mourn small passings.

15 See: the newspaper boy in the rain
will sleep tonight in a doorway.
The woman in the busline
may next month be on a train
to a place not her own.
20 The baby in the backyard now
will be sent to a tired aunt,
grow chubby, then lean,
return a stranger.
Mandela's daughter tried to find her father
25 through the glass. She thought they'd let her touch him.[1]

De Kok was born and educated in South Africa. She has spent part of her life living and studying in Canada, and often grapples in her writing with the difficulties of shifting between the two cultures. At present, she works in the Centre for Extra-Mural Studies at the University of Cape Town and is a respected commentator on South African literature and culture. Her poems have earned her recognition both at home and abroad. She occasionally writes under the name of Fiske.

Notes

[1] During Nelson Mandela's years as a political prisoner, family members had to sit behind a glass panel while visiting him. No physical contact was allowed.

And this woman's hands are so heavy when she dusts
the photographs of other children
they fall to the floor and break.
Clumsy woman, she moves so slowly
30 as if in a funeral rite.

On the pavements the nannies meet.
These are legal gatherings.
They talk about everything, about home,
while the children play among them,
35 their skins like litmus,[2] their bonnets clean.

2

Small wrist in the grave.
Baby no one carried live
between houses, among trees.
Child shot running,
40 stones in his pocket,
boy's swollen stomach
full of hungry air.
Girls carrying babies
not much smaller than themselves.
45 Erosion. Soil washed down to the sea.

3

I think these mothers dream
headstones of the unborn.
Their mourning rises like a wall
no vine will cling to.
50 They will not tell you your suffering is white.
They will not say it is just as well.
They will not compete for the ashes of infants.
I think they may say to you:
Come with us to the place of mothers.
55 We will stroke your flat empty belly,
let you weep with us in the dark,
and arm you with one of our babies
to carry home on your back.

Notes

2 Chemical substance that
changes colour to pinkish-red
under acid conditions.

Talking points

'Small Passing' has already been compared with Jonson's 'On My First Son' and 'On My First Daughter' (see p. 31). You might like to turn to the suggestions for comparative discussion that appear on p. 32.

Rushdy Siers (1952–)

Sets of Two and Their Silence

Today children our lesson will be about sets . . .
Kanalla¹ cheacher nie vandagie   *Please teacher not today*

Does every body know what a set is?
Yaa, a snytjie brood en a snytjie brood maak a sanwich.   *Yes, a slice of bread and*
                                                                          a slice of bread make a sandwich

5   Good, please pay attention and don't look so sleepy!
Ek slaap tot ek dai klokkie hoor – kostyd!   *I'm sleeping until I hear the bell*
                                                                          – time to eat!

Many things and any number of things can make a set . . .
Ek wonne wat gan op 'ie brood wies?   *I wonder what will be on the bread?*

For example, a tea set and a cutlery set . . .
10 *Nou moet jy nogal van kosgoed praat.*   *Now must you talk about food utensils.*

Can anyone give me an example of a set? quickly . . .
Set and ready to go, as ek dai klokkie hoor   *Set and ready to go, when I hear that bell.*

Class what is wrong?
Niks verkeet 'ie net honger.   *Nothing's wrong, just hungry*

15 Can nobody give me an example of a set?
Cheacher lat ek net slaap tot netnou.   *Teacher let me sleep for a while.*

Siers was born in District Six in Cape Town, an area from which his family was evicted under apartheid legislation. He has a history of activism in political and cultural circles, and has worked at the Centre for Development Studies at the University of the Western Cape. His writing includes poetry and short stories.

'Sets of Two and Their Silence' combines conventional use of the English language with use of one of the dialects found within the Cape Muslim community. This particular dialect combines Afrikaans and English, and flavours both with distinctive borrowings from the local community. Notice how flat and tame the English translation on the right-hand side of the page seems when compared with the original. What does this suggest about the value of dialect? For another example of a poem written in dialect, see John Agard's 'Poetry Jump-Up' on pp. 218–9.

Notes

¹ 'Please', a colloquial greeting in the Cape Muslim community, which translates literally as 'please in the name of God'.

Children you must pay attention!
Ya a snytjie brood en a snytjie brood maak a sanwich.

Yes a slice of bread and a slice of
bread make a sandwich.

20 And why this silence?
Jy's fokken doef as jy nie my maag kan hoor nie!

You're fucking deaf if you can't
hear my stomach!

Stephen Watson (1954–)

The Rain That Is Male

The rain that is male is an angry rain.
It brings with it lightning loud like our fear.
It brings water storming, making smoke out of dust.

And we, we beat our navels with our rigid fists.
5   We, we press a hand, flat to the navel.
We snap our fingers at the angry, male rain.

And we stand outside in the force of the water,
we stand out in the open, close to its thunder,
we snap our fingers and chant while it falls:

10   'Rain, be gone quickly! Fall but be gone!
Rain, turn away! Turn back from this place!
Rain, take your anger, be gone from our place!'

For we want the other, the rain that is female,
the one that falls softly, soaking into the ground,
15   the one we can welcome, feeding the plains –

So bushes sprout green, springbok° come galloping.   *indigenous buck*

Watson has spent most of his life, apart from brief periods in Britain and Australia, in Cape Town. He lectures in the English Department at the University of Cape Town, and is the author of several volumes of poetry (including a translation of /Xam legends), as well as a collection of critical essays. He is recognized for his sensitivity and accuracy in conveying a sense of place.

'The Rain That Is Male' is drawn from the records of a nineteenth-century linguist from the Cape and his sister in-law, who together transcribed legends passed on to them by members of an almost extinct tribe of indigenous people, the /Xam. They have since been completely eradicated or assimilated, and their language has died out. Watson's poem is thus a translation of a translation, and is an example of the attempts some modern writers and anthropologists have made to recover the cultures of indigenous peoples who have been exterminated. (See also 'Kilaben Bay Song' on p. 85.)

In Exile

for Douglas Reid Skinner

To be rooted is perhaps the most important and least recognized
need of the human soul – Simone Weil

Waiting for a tram, his gaze incurious, vague, as jaded
as the fog long rising off the Main[1], as the cold gone brown,
polluted in whatever sky there is, in what's left of day,
even now, years later, years after he had to leave, to flee,
5   dusk comes like a coma, his stare still hangs, abandoned,
as useless as his hands. The cobbled streets stretch away,
numb and bloodless as shin-bones. The stunted light lies
still and dead, diluted, never mellowing. In the early dark,
cold with lights, under the factory sky of Frankfurt am Main,[2]
10   the waters of the river, muffled, frigid in this German wind,
the misted hulks of barges, hold no echo, are faceless still,
the flagstones, leaden, fouled, are nothing but tombstones.

Again, the ash-trees turn to charcoal before his eyes.
He hears the echoes that damp footsteps hollow out on stone,
15   he looks upon the dead wood, the wooden faces, at buildings
that have blurred, are vague, indefinite as some threat,
and still can't hear, can't see – he can't feel a thing.
Nine years later, nothing, hardly anything has changed:
even now, as that torpor in the evening cold takes hold,
20   as something wads his hands, and fogs his eyes, both ears,
he's still standing there – the tram has left without him –
he's straining, is like a man possessed, going blind
for what he still sees, for what he can remember seeing.

Notes

[1] River in Germany.
[2] Major manufacturing city built on
the Main River.

And it's always one place only, always that same place
25 where a road swings high, climbing around a mountain-side.
It's the highway of his childhood, of many years before
that he's travelling now in memory, once more looking out
at hills, far-off, linear, naked, miles north across a bay.
Again, there's sunlight in blonde grass, there's that scent
30 of pine in dust, a heat that carries him still further back
to those folded slopes, unfolding, peppery with rough scrub,
to that very bend where the road swings left to right
and through the slanted pine-trunks, from its final crest,
backed by a mountain-wall, opening out along an oval bay,
35 an entire city lies revealed, frozen in silence, far below –
Cape Town stands there, suddenly, revealed for what it is:
a city of the southern hemisphere, more full of sky than streets.

Even now, years later, when at night the longing comes
nothing matters any more – not his memory of the people,
40 the vile, pretentious rich, corrupted poor, those politics
that beggar all description, that all but beggared him –
nothing matters now but his desire, but this mad longing
to know that there is still a place, that it still exists,
that you can come on that same road round Devil's Peak[3]
45 and there will be, as there was before, almost any evening,
that softness in the summer dark, the same warmth rising,
breathing from an earth long out of reach of its sunset.
All the rest's irrelevant; nothing matters now, or ever,
but to know that he can come, return to that road's crest
50 when the harbour's lighting up, the lights are shining
thinly through the pine-tops, in wind that's amber-toned,
and there will be the same view, clear across the city:
from the trees thinned out against the mass of Signal Hill,[4]
against that day's after-glow, down to a mountainy skyline
55 going far down the south peninsula, where the early stars –
the first he ever saw – will be out along the mountains.

He has to know there is a place – if only just one place –
where the water is not flat with cold, the silted colour
of cement; where the stones are not just made of stone
60 but are full of stories, memories. There has to be
that place where with a hand upon a stone you can touch
the time that went before, the years that will outlast you.

Notes

3 Distinctive peak in the Table
  Mountain range that encircles
  central Cape Town.
4 See the notes on p. 178.

There has to be a place. He's tired of watching, waiting,
while years pass quickly, blankly, become ever more unreal.
65 Tonight he's tired of talking, smiling, and knowing he's not
really talking, not smiling – it's just his lips, his teeth.
These rush-hour people passing by, all with somewhere to go
the buses that come shuddering past, these trams squealing
to a halt, that always jolt him back to this same street –
70 here, he can't find peace – the calm – to rest his nerves.

And shivers . . . That tram of his left almost an hour ago.
It's left him in a nearly ended year, with one more view
of leaves, long dead already, drowning in a wayside gutter.
He's still standing there, still transfixed as night falls,
75 as that other, loved city fades away, floats ten years off,
and he comes back to these dead things, to the dead years,
to a smell of air pollution freezing, falling below zero.
He's still lost in it, in his estranging gape, one of many,
a man without a wife, a child, arms wrapped round himself,
80 a man who has been left behind. And now he's growing smaller
is no larger than his pipe's glow as the river fog moves in,
flows over the embankment, blanking out what he once saw,
blotting out a figure, thin and frosted, dwindling quickly,
an exile, solo, incognito°, in transit through another night.   *in disguise*

Talking points

You might want to turn back to Arthur Nortje's poem, also titled 'In
Exile' (p. 200) and compare it with Watson's piece.

Mzi Mahola

I'm a Man

We spent the night drumming and dancing
Singing songs of courage.
Was it not the last
We would be together?
5   When the ripening period comes
We catapult
Into the waiting world
Like the seed of dry pods.

The crunching frost
10   Under my unshod feet
The biting breeze
Of that winter's dawn
Skinning my naked body
Menacing sticks and threatening words
15   Before I was forced
To break the icy stream
Was it a sort of vendetta?
Numb in body and soul
I cursed through chattering teeth
20   Like a caged beast
And defied the cutman's stiletto
That left a crimson ring
Round my shrunken stick of manhood
Where the stigma was
25   And I declared the divine words
Of the ultimate stage
'I'm a man!'

Mahola was born and educated in the Eastern Cape, and has worked for the
Port Elizabeth Museum on educational projects. He has had a number of his
poems published in local journals. His writing is particularly concerned with
the tensions between the rural and urban spheres, and the past and the
present.

'**I'm a Man**' describes some aspects of a traditional initiation rite found in
many southern African tribes, in which youths are taken apart from the
community, subjected to certain physical rigours, taught their duties as men,
and finally circumcised. The 'cutman' (line 21) was usually someone senior
and respected in the community, such as a *sangoma* (healer or seer) or
especially revered elder.

Fhazel Johennesse (1956–)

A Young Man's Thoughts Before June the 16th

tomorrow i travel on a road
that winds to the top of the hill
i take with me only the sweet
memories of my youth
5   my heart aches for my mother
for friday nights with friends
around a table with a broad belch of beer
i ask only for a sad song
sung by a woman with downturned eyes
10 and strummed by an old man with
a broken brow
o sing my sad song sing for me
for my sunset is drenched with red

Johennesse was born and lives in Johannesburg. He has worked on various
creative projects with other South African poets, and has published a
respected collection of poetry.

June 16 marks the anniversary of the 1976 uprising begun by schoolchildren
in Soweto to protest against the compulsory use of Afrikaans, seen as the
language of the oppressor, in black classrooms. Over 1 000 people, many of
them young, lost their lives.

Karen Press (1956–)

Hope for Refugees

    you can go back
    you can go back
    run backwards
    call back the cattle
5   unstitch the hems
    pull the photos out of the fire

    you can go back
    you can go back
    pull down your dress
10   button your shirt
    wipe off the blood
    scrub off the blood

    you can go back
    you can go back
15   wash the walls
    fix the door
    remember the step down in the dark
    avoid the dark

    you can go back
20   you can go back
    dig up the box in the front garden
    dig up the box in the yard
    dig up the box in your heart
    dig up the box in the child's heart

Born in Cape Town, **Karen Press** has worked on alternative education and publishing projects for much of her adult life. She has written non-fiction, poetry, and stories, and is particularly respected for her simple yet subtle poems.

In the wake of the 1994 election, South Africa became attractive to many living in less economically and politically stable countries. This was a period in which civil wars and genocides convulsed the African continent and elsewhere; also, international drug cartels targeted South Africa as a new market to be exploited. For all these reasons, South Africa experienced an influx of both refugees and undocumented migrants. This in turn led to a growing xenophobia and hardening of attitudes towards foreigners on the part of many citizens, who saw the newcomers as a threat to jobs and security. (It should be noted that South Africa has accepted far fewer

25   you can go back
    you can go back
    lay out the skeletons in their beds
    hang out the years to air
    plant seeds, keep watch at the well
30   tear up your nightmares, your footprints
    lock the door
    work hard
    give thanks to god

refugees than most neighbouring SADC countries.) During the period in
which the Immigration Act was drawn up, even though South Africa had
signed the Geneva Convention endorsing the rights of refugees, the
Department of Home Affairs sometimes resorted to 'apartheid-style' dirty
tricks in their efforts to deport asylum-seekers. Their stance reflects a
growing international tendency to make it much harder for refugees to seek
asylum. This poem refers critically to a policy that is gaining ground in the
developed world – that refugees should be repatriated (returned home)
whenever possible.

Sujata Bhatt (1956–)

A Different History

1

Great Pan[1] is not dead;
he simply emigrated
to India.
Here the gods roam freely,
5   disguised as snakes and monkeys;
every tree is sacred
and it is a sin
to be rude to a book.
It is a sin to shove a book aside
10   with your foot,
a sin to slam books down
hard on a table,
a sin to toss one carelessly
across a room
15   You must learn how to turn the pages gently
without disturbing Sarasvati,[2]
without offending the tree
from whose wood the paper was made.

2

Which language
20   has not been the oppressor's tongue?
Which language
truly meant to murder someone?
And how does it happen
that after the torture,
25   after the soul has been cropped
with a long scythe swooping out
of the conqueror's face –
the unborn grandchildren
grow to love that strange language.

Bhatt was born in India, and spent much of her childhood there before her family moved to the United States. She is a respected and award-winning poet. Although she writes in English, Gujarati is her mother tongue, and her poetry reflects the images and forms of this language as well. She has also translated Gujarati poetry into English. She now lives in Germany with her husband and daughter.

Notes

[1] Greek God of flocks and shepherds; musical and mischievous.
[2] Hindu goddess of wisdom; watches over libraries.

Chris van Wyk (1957–)

Memory

Derek is dangling on the kitchen chair
while I'm shuffling about in a flutter of flour.
Mummy is making vetkoek[1] on the primus.[2]
Derek is too small to peer over the table,
5   that's why Mummy has perched him on the chair.
His dummy twitters so he's a bird.

I'm not that small; I was four in July.
I'm tall enough to see what's going on;
I'm a giraffe and the blotches of shadow
10   on the ceiling and the walls
from the flames of the primus and candle
are the patches on my back.

Daddy's coming home soon
from the factory where they're turning him into
15   a cupboard that creaks,
but the vetkoek are sizzling and growing
like bloated gold coins,
we're rich!

This is the first vivid memory of childhood.
20   Why have I never written it all down before?
Maybe because the pan falls with a clatter
and the oil swims towards the twittering bird.
Mummy flattens her forearm on the table
stopping the seething flood.

25   As she does so she pleads with the bird to fly away,
but quietly so as not to ruffle his feathers.
But my brother clambers off the chair
as if he has all the time in the world.

Van Wyk was born in Johannesburg, where he currently lives. He has worked for various South African publishers and is now a freelance writer, editor, and consultant. A skilled writer, his work includes children's literature, poems, short stories, and an acclaimed novel. His poetry combines elements of the personal and the political in fresh and often moving ways.

Notes

[1] Cakes made of dough and fried in oil.
[2] Portable gas stove.

Sensing danger, the twittering gives way to a wail
30 and the giraffe's patches flare on the restive walls.

Ma gives a savage scream that echoes across the decades
and cauterizes° my childhood like a long scar.

°burns

Gcina Mhlophe (1958–)

Say No

Say No, Black Woman
Say No
When they call your jobless son
a Tsotsi[1]
5   Say No

Say No, Black Woman
Say No
When they call
Your husband at the age of 60
10   a boy
Say No

Say No, Black Woman
Say No
When they rape your daughter
15   in detention and call her
a whore
Say No

Say No, Black Woman
Say No
20   When they call your white sister
a madam
Say No

Say No, Black Woman
Say No
25   When they call your white brother
a Baas
Say No

One of South Africa's most innovative and talented actresses and directors, **Mhlophe** also writes plays and poetry. She has worked to advance the art of story-telling, and tours the country to bring her performances to as many levels of society as possible.

Notes

[1] See footnote 4, p. 203.

Say No, Black Woman
Say No
30   When they call a trade unionist
a terrorist
Say No

Say No, Black Woman
Say No
35   When they give you a back seat
in the liberation wagon
Say No
Yes Black Woman
a Big NO

Talking points

This poem was written during the 1980s, when the struggle to end
apartheid was particularly bitter. Its concerns nevertheless remain
extremely relevant. Do you feel that black South African women have
been able to share in the gains of democracy?

Kaizer Mabhilidi Nyatsumba (1963–)

so let it be

written in harare, zimbabwe on september 24 1990

if it be in your will
my lord
to demolish
where once you built a palace
5   and bring utter ruin
where once was order
so let it be

if it be in your holy plans
my lord
10   to cut in half
that which you once united
and plant hate
where once love reigned
so let it be

[ends]

Talking points

'so let it be' quite possibly operates on two levels; the speaker seems
to be referring to a marital crisis. What else could the breakdown
described refer to? Note that the author shows his journalistic
background by using the word [ends] to mark where his poem
finishes.

Nyatsumba was born and educated in South Africa, and began his career in
journalism while still in high school. He studied at the University of Zululand
and Georgetown University in Washington, D.C. Today he is one of South
Africa's most highly regarded newspaper editors, and has been attached to
The Star, The Mercury, and KwaZulu-Natal's biggest daily newspaper, the
Daily News. Winner of a number of media awards and honours, he also
writes poetry, short stories, and political analysis. His poems range from
African history to intimate memoirs of his family.

Isabella Motadinyane (1963– 2003)

She walked a painful lane home

She walked a painful lane home
wiping tears of change
from her soiled body
but told no one about those fakes

5   Now her poison intake
that lays skin on her bones
perspires with naked truth

Reading her medical record
as three little words
10   holding back the years

Talking points

A close look at this poem, and some careful guessing at what the 'three little words' (line 9) might mean in the context of a medical diagnosis, suggest that this is quite possibly a poem about the emotional impact of discovering that one has Aids.

A class project you might like to consider is putting together resources on HIV/Aids, including local hotline numbers. Does your campus have any education or support services in place? Perhaps this is something you might like to look into, given the urgency and seriousness of the HIV/Aids epidemic, which affects us all.

This poet and artist was one of the Botsotso Jesters, a publishing collective that works together to 'stretch the boundaries of the written form of poetry and mirror a fractured world'. They co-write works that incorporate art and graphics, and position themselves in an urban, post-1994 South Africa.

Mxolisi Nyezwa (1967–)

quiet place

and it seems that i live in a quiet place
at the end of time
with a blowing universe behind me.

i remain aware of the long-suffering of things
i remain aware with a simple truth
of how the planet eventually crumbles.

to me there is always the spaza shop[1] at the end of the street,
the vague colour of the moon
and of the southern sky.

sea

the sea is so heavy inside us
and i won't sleep tonight.
i have buckets of memory in a jar
that i keep for days and nights like these.

Nyezwa was born in New Brighton, Port Elizabeth, where he still lives. He is one of the most brilliant and startling new poets on the South African scene. His intensely lyrical poetry is complex, yet rewarding.

Notes

1 'Spaza' shops are informal stores, often found in townships, offering basic foodstuffs and supplies to local communities.

Roshila Nair (1970–)

an unforgiving poem

truth and forgiveness
are political epics
bigger and lonelier than words,
today I watched an old woman
5   recoil from the contrite hands of
patriot men who murdered her son
many years ago,
some say he lived long after
his flesh melted and his bones
10   turned the flames to ash,
some say it is the undoing of old women
to barricade their ancient bodies with so much hate,
these days it is easy to forget
that women give birth to children
15   not nations or memories,
that anger holds the breaking soul
when there's nothing left but words.

Nair was born and educated in KwaZulu-Natal. She has worked as an
academic and editor, and currently lives in Cape Town. Her poems and short
stories have been published both locally and abroad.

'**an unforgiving poem**' refers to the recently concluded Truth and
Reconciliation hearings in South Africa. These were set up after the elections
of 1994 to deal formally with the atrocities committed (on all sides) during
the years of apartheid rule. The understanding was that people who
voluntarily came forward to tell the truth about their participation in
'politically motivated' crimes and serious human rights violations could apply
for amnesty. The role and value of the hearings in the reconciliation process
continues to be hotly debated. There is no doubt, however, that while there
were sometimes moving scenes of confession and forgiveness, the hearings
were extraordinarily traumatic for all concerned, but particularly for the
families of activists who had 'disappeared', who often heard details of the
torture and murder of their loved ones for the first time.

Glossary

Aesthetic Those qualities of beauty that give pleasure and inspiration.

Allegory Symbolic tale, often with a moral message, in which figures and objects described in the story represent certain qualities (such as evil, truth, etc.). In some spiritual allegories, the characters symbolize religious figures or doctrines. Other allegories create fantasy characters that represent actual historical figures and events.

Ballad Narrative poem (i.e., it tells a story) that deals with folklore or legend, often containing supernatural elements and featuring dialogue. Originally meant to be sung, ballads have a regular rhythm, usually with repeating lines or a chorus.

Comedy (as in drama) Not necessarily humorous; however, there is always a happy resolution in which misunderstandings and conflicts are cleared up, and the potential for evil and harm is avoided. This happy ending usually involves the uniting of one or more pairs of lovers and their marriage.

Devotional Poetry or other literature written in praise of God, or as a meditation on a spiritual topic or text.

Dramatic monologue Poem where only one voice (and viewpoint) is heard, but in which the author's own (often very different) opinion is implied.

Elegy Commemoration of someone who has died; poem or other form of writing that expresses grief and mourning and finally moves towards some kind of resolution or comfort.

Epic Heroic narrative that tells of unusual adventures, travel, or feats of bravery and war.

Gender The socially constructed notions of masculinity and femininity. While sex is biologically determined, gender is learnt through conditioning. This term has entered modern understanding through feminist criticism.

Genre Identifiable type or form of literature; for example, novel, drama, poetry. Within poetry itself, different genres can be found, such as epic, lyric, and so forth.

Intertextuality The use of deliberate references to, or borrowings from, other works of literature in a piece of writing.

Irony It is difficult to provide a concrete definition of irony, as it relies on tone to succeed. It is primarily a form of criticism or mockery in which the very opposite meaning or message to what is written or spoken is communicated. It is often used to create a 'double' sense of communication, in which a distance is deliberately created between a character's perspective and that of the author. (See, for example, Chaucer's 'The Pardoner's Prologue' [pp. 4–7] or Browning's 'My Last Duchess' [p. 77]).

Lyric Expressive and gentle poem or song praising a specific object or scene, or describing a mood or emotion; often concerned with beauty or love.

Metaphor An image in which an object or figure is described as something else as an implied form of comparison, which is not meant to be understood literally; for example, 'the sun was a gold coin on the horizon'.

Metaphysical School of poetry associated with the seventeenth-century writers Donne, Herbert, Marvell, and others. Particularly known for its clever wit and inventive and unusual ideas and images, it features comparisons known as 'conceits', which are striking or original rather than accurate.

Metre The rhythmic shape of a line of poetry, identified by the number of stressed (or emphasized) syllables.

Mock-heroic Often used for satiric or humorous purposes, this involves describing a trivial or ordinary subject or event in an inappropriately grand and lofty style.

Modernism Movement in literature and art that sprang up at the beginning of the twentieth century. It swept away many of the 'rules' of art and culture, and set out to create inner realities and visions, experimenting with new forms of representation in the process. Modernist poetry relied increasingly on association rather than explanation, with words being used for their evocative and emotional qualities, rather than as means of communication and explanation.

Narrative Form of writing that tells a story with a distinct plot; the focus is on events, not description or reflection.

Pastoral Literature or poetry that provides an often artificial and utopian view of rural or outdoors life. It involves a very stylized representation of nature, and always draws on imagery of spring or summer. The object is to create an atmosphere of beauty rather than realism.

Polemic Piece written with an explicit (and often strongly worded) political or ideological message.

Post-colonial Criticism and scholarship that uses the tools of post-modern literary theories to analyse the cultural, historical, and political consequences of colonialism in post-independence writing and philosophy.

Romance (as in drama) Possesses characteristics of both tragedy and comedy; suffering and loss force deluded or weak characters to recognize their faults. At this point, magical elements transform or reverse tragic events (those believed to be dead are restored, spells are broken, lost children are found, and so on). The ending usually involves marriage, symbolizing the restoration of family and society.

Satire Writing that mocks or criticizes something by means of exaggeration or exposure. The difference between satire and irony (see above) is that irony says the opposite of what is intended to be understood, whereas satire describes its object accurately, but unflatteringly, by highlighting its flaws. The effect is often humorous. (See also mock-heroic above.)

Secular (see spiritual) Broadly, this means anything that is not religious or sacred. As a literary term, it is used (especially with reference to medieval and Renaissance poetry) to describe works that are not religious in tone or topic, and deal with non-spiritual matters.

Simile Imagery that takes the form of an explicit comparison by using the words 'as' or 'like'; for example, 'She runs like the wind, but he is as slow as a tortoise'.

Sonnet Carefully crafted fourteen-line poem, with a strict rhyme scheme and metre. The lines are either divided into three sets of four lines each, plus a rhyming couplet, or into an eight-line section (the octave, which usually describes the topic or sets out the argument) followed by six lines (the sestet), which reflect or comment on the subject of the octave. The last two lines usually sum up the argument of the poem or state the speaker's final message.

Spiritual (see secular) In the broad sense, that which is religious or sacred. Used in literature (especially with reference to medieval and Renaissance poetry) to distinguish works written for religious purposes (also often called devotional poetry) from secular works, which deal with non-religious topics (such as human love).

Tragedy (as in drama) Tragic events and actions befall characters either through their own weakness or sin (their 'fatal flaw') or through the twists of 'fate'. The narrative moves inevitably towards the death of the hero and/or heroine (as well as many of the other characters), after which a new sense of resolution is found. The Greek philosopher Aristotle argued that the purpose of tragedy was to arouse emotions of pity and fear in the audience, and then to provide a catharsis (outlet) for these feelings.

Vernacular Local or indigenous language. Throughout the centuries, the revival or flowering of vernacular languages has been associated with national and cultural pride.

Acknowledgements

The editors and publishers gratefully acknowledge permission to reproduce copyright poems in this book. Every effort has been made to trace copyright holders, but where this has proved impossible, the publishers would be grateful for information that would enable them to amend any omissions in future editions.

Lionel Abrahams: 'Note in Prosy Verse'. Printed by permission of the author.

Tatamkulu Afrika: 'The Handshake'. Printed by permission of the author.

John Agard: 'Poetry Jump-up' from *You'll Love That Stuff*, Cambridge University Press. Reprinted by permission of the Caroline Sheldon Literary Agency.

Maya Angelou: 'Still I Rise'. Reprinted by permission of the author and Little Brown and Company.

W.H. Auden: 'Roman Wall Blues' and 'Stop All the Clocks' from *Collected Poems* by W.H. Auden. Reprinted by permission of Faber and Faber Ltd.

Kofi Awoonor: 'The Weaver Bird' from *The Penguin Book of Modern African Poetry* edited by Gerald Moore and Uli Beier. Reprinted by permission of the author.

Shabbir Banoobhai: 'when the first slave was brought to the cape' and 'they call you mister steve biko now you're dead'. Reprinted by permission of the author.

Sujata Bhatt: 'A Different History' from *Brunizem*. Reprinted by permission of Carcanet Press Limited.

Bertolt Brecht: 'Questions From a Worker Who Reads' (translated by Michael Hamburger) from *Bertolt Brecht Poems 1913–1956*. Reprinted by permission of Methuen Publishing Limited.

Gwendolyn Brooks: 'We Real Cool'.

Sally Bryer: 'Ingrid Jonker' from *Breaking the Silence: A Century of South African Women's Poetry* edited by Cecily Lockett and published by Ad. Donker.

Guy Butler: 'Near Hout Bay'. Reprinted by permission of the author.

Roy Campbell: 'The Zulu Girl' from *Selected Poems* by Roy Campbell. Reprinted by permission of Francisco Campbell Custadio and Ad. Donker (Pty) Ltd.

Jeni Couzyn: 'The Red Hen's Last Will and Testament to the Last Cock on Earth' from *Life by Drowning, Selected Poems*, Bloodaxe Books, 1983.

Jack Cope. 'The Flying Fish'. Reprinted by permission of David Philip Publishers (Pty) Ltd.

Jeremy Cronin: 'Faraway city, there' from *Inside* by Jeremy Cronin published by Ravan Press, 1983.

E. E. Cummings: 'anyone lived in a pretty how town' from *The Collected Poems 1913–1962* by E. E. Cummings. Reprinted by permission of W. W. Norton & Company, Ltd.

Jennifer Davids: 'For Albert Luthuli (21.7.67)' from *Searching for Words* by Jennifer Davids. Reprinted by permission of Jennifer Davids and David Philip Publishers (Pty) Ltd.

Ingrid de Kok: 'Small Passing' from *Familiar Ground* © Ingrid de Kok. Reprinted by permission of the author.

Anthony Delius: 'Deaf-and-Dumb School'.

Modikwe Dikobe: 'Khoikhoi-Son-of-Man' from *Dispossessed* by Modikwe Dikobe published by Ravan Press, Johannesburg, 1983. Reprinted by permission of the author and Ravan Press.

H.D. (Hilda Doolittle): 'Helen' from *The Collected Poems of H.D.* Reprinted by permission of Carcanet Press, Ltd.

T.S. Eliot: 'The Journey of the Magi' and 'Preludes' from *Collected Poems 1909–1962* by T.S. Eliot. Reprinted by permission of Faber and Faber Ltd.

L. Ferlinghetti: 'Constantly Risking Absurdity' by Lawrence Ferlinghetti, from *A Coney Island of the Mind*, copyright © 1958 by Lawrence Ferlinghetti. Reprinted by permission of New Directions Publishing Corp.

Robert Frost: 'Mending Wall' and 'The Road Not Taken' from *The Poetry of Robert Frost* edited by Edward Connery Lathem, © 1944, 1958 by Robert Frost. Copyright 1967 by Lesley Frost Ballantine. Copyright 1916, 1930, 1939, 1969 by Henry Holt and Company, LLC. Reprinted by permission of Henry Holt and Company, LLC.

Zulfikar Ghose: 'The Attack on Sialot' © 1967 by Zulfikar Ghose. Reprinted by permission of the author.

Michael Gilkes: 'Miranda' from 'Prospero's Island' from *The Arnold Anthology of Post-Colonial Literatures in English* (1996).

Geoffrey Haresnape: 'In and around the Yacht-Basin Simon's Town'. Reprinted by permission of the author.

Seamus Heaney: 'Follower' from *Death of a Naturalist*. Reprinted by permission of Faber and Faber Ltd.

Li Ho: 'On the Frontier' from *Poems of the Late T'ang* (translated by A.C. Graham), Penguin Classics. © 1965. A. C. Graham. Reprinted by permission of Penguin Books Ltd.

Langston Hughes: 'Mother to Son' from *Collected Poems*. Reprinted by permission of David Higham Associates Ltd.

Ted Hughes: 'The Thought-Fox' and 'Tractor'. Reprinted by permission of Faber and Faber Ltd.

Antonio Jacinto: 'Letter From a Contract Worker' from *The Penguin Book of Modern African Poetry* edited by Geoffrey Moore and Uli Beier (Penguin Books, 1984). This collection copyright © Geoffrey Moore and Uli Beier, 1984. Reproduced by permission of Penguin Books Ltd.

Wopko Jensma: Poem 3 from 'Not Him' from *Sing for our Execution* published by Ravan Press, 1973.

Fhazel Johennesse: 'A Young Man's Thoughts Before June 16th' from *The Rainmaker*. Reprinted by permission of the author.

Ingrid Jonker: 'The Child Who Was Shot Dead by Soldiers at Nyanga'.

'Kilaben Bay Song' (translated by Perce Haslan) from *The Oxford Book of Australian Verse*. Reprinted by permission of Oxford University Press Australia.

Joseph Kumbirai: 'Dawn' (translated by Douglas Livingstone). Reprinted by permission of Monica Fairall, executor.

Philip Larkin: 'Talking in Bed' from *Collected Poems*. Reprinted by permission of Faber and Faber Ltd.

Denise Levertov: 'What Were They Like?' from *To Stay Alive* by Denise Levertov. Reprinted by permission of Laurence Pollinger Limited.

Douglas Livingstone: 'The Sleep of My Lions'. Reprinted by permission of Monica Fairall, executor.

Audre Lorde: 'Coal'.

Claude Mackay: 'If We Must Die' from *Selected Poems of Claude Mackay*.

Archibald MacLeish: 'Ars Poetica' from *Collected Poems 1917–1982*. © 1985 The Estate of Archibald MacLeish. Reprinted by permission of Houghton Mifflin Company.

Mzi Mahola: 'I'm a Man' from *Strange Things*. Reprinted by permission of the author and Snailpress.

Don Mattera: 'Remember'. Reprinted by permission of the author.

Gcina Mhlope: 'Say No'.

Ruth Miller: 'Blue-mantled Mary'. Reprinted by permission of Lionel Abrahams on behalf of Mrs Pat Campbell and the estate of Ruth Miller.

Isabella Motadinyane: 'She walked a painful lane home'. Reprinted by permission of Botsotso Publishing.

Mbuyiseni Oswald Mtshali: 'Men in Chains'. Reprinted by permission of the author and Ad. Donker (Pty) Ltd.

Es'kia Mphahlele: 'A Poem'. Reprinted by permission of the author.

Tu Mu: 'The Gate Tower of Ch'i-an City' and 'To Judge Han Ch'o at Yang-chou' from *Poems of the Late T'ang* (translated by A.C. Graham), Penguin Classics. © 1965 A.C. Graham. Reprinted by permission of Penguin Books Ltd.

ACKNOWLEDGEMENTS

Charles Mungoshi: 'A Letter to a Son' from *Zimbabwean Poetry in English*.

Roshila Nair: 'an unforgiving poem' © Roshila Nair. Reprinted by permission of the author.

Agostinho Neto: 'The Grieved Lands' from *The Penguin Book of Modern African Poetry* edited by Gerald Moore and Uli Beier.

Grace Nichols: 'Taint'.

Arthur Nortje: 'In Exile'.

Kaizer Mabhilidi Nyatsumba: 'so let it be'. Reprinted by permission of the author.

Mxolisi Nyezwa: 'quiet place' and 'sea'. Reprinted by permission of the University of Natal Press.

Michael Ondaatje: 'The Cinnamon Peeler'.

D. J. Opperman: 'Christmas Carol'.

Essop Patel: 'In the Shadow of Signal Hill'. Reprinted by permission of the author.

Sylvia Plath: 'You're' and 'Pheasant'. Reprinted by permission of Faber and Faber Ltd.

Ezra Pound: 'In a Station of the Metro' and 'The River Merchant's Wife' from *Collected Shorter Poems* by Ezra Pound. Reprinted by permission of Faber and Faber Ltd.

Karen Press: 'Hope for Refugees'.

Malvina Reynolds: 'What Have They Done to the Rain?'

Adrienne Rich: 'I Am in Danger — Sir —'. Copyright © 1993 by Adrienne Rich. Copyright © 1966 by W. W. Norton & Company, Inc, from *Collected Early Poems: 1950–1970* by Adrienne Rich. Used by permission of the author and W. W. Norton & Company, Inc.

Helen Segal: 'The Sea is all Male' from *Breaking the Silence: A Century of South African Women's Poetry* edited by Cecily Lockett and published by Ad. Donker.

Sipho Sepamla: 'The Loneliness Beyond'.

Wally Mongane Serote: 'Alexandra', 'City Johannesburg', 'For Don M. — Banned'. Reprinted by permission of the author and Ad. Donker (Pty) Ltd.

Mutiswayo Shandu: 'Bye Bye, Overcoat' from *Quarry 80–82*.

Rushdy Siers: 'Sets of Two and Their Silence' from *Essential Things: an Anthology of New South African Poetry* edited by Andries Oliphant. Reprinted by permission of the author.

Stevie Smith: 'Not Waving but Drowning' from *The Collected Poems of Stevie Smith*, Penguin Twentieth Century Classics. Reprinted by permission of James MacGibbon, executor.

Wole Soyinka: 'Capital' from *Poems of Black Africa* edited by Wole Soyinka.

Kumalau Tawali: 'The Old Woman's Message' from *Black Writing from New Guinea*, ed. Ulli Beier, 1972. Reprinted by permission of the University of Queensland Press.

Dylan Thomas: 'In My Craft or Sullen Art' from *Selected Poems* by Dylan Thomas. Reprinted by permission of David Higham Associates.

Mao Tse-Tung: 'Lou Mountain Pass' from *Poems of Mao Tse-Tung* (translated by Hua-ling Nieh Engle and Paul Engle).

Chris van Wyk: 'Memory'. Reprinted by permission of the author.

Stephen Watson: 'In Exile' from *In This City* and 'The Rain That Is Male' from *Return of the Moon*, both by Stephen Watson. Reprinted by permission of the author.

William Carlos Williams: 'This Is Just to Say' from *Collected Poems*. Reprinted by permission of Carcanet Press, Ltd.

David Wright: 'On the Margin'.

Index